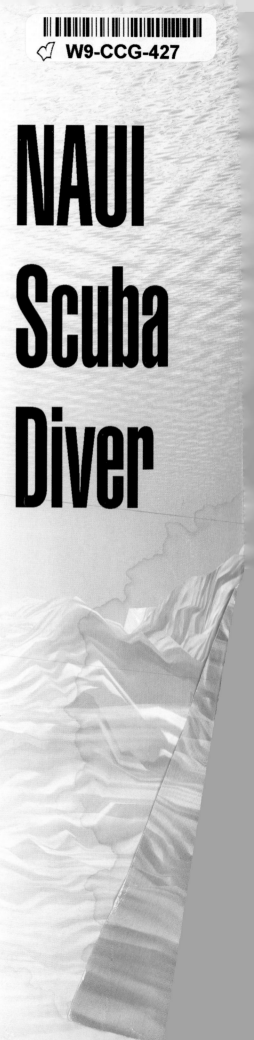

NAUI
Scuba
Diver

NAUI
Scuba
Diver

PREFACE

NAUI Scuba Diver describes the gear, skills, and basic concepts of scuba diving. Scuba diving is a wonderful adventure sport. However, like any adventure sport, there is a small but real risk that you can be injured any time you enter the water to dive. Even if you do everything right, even if your equipment functions perfectly, there are always some risks in scuba diving. When you decide to become a scuba diver, you must do it of your own personal desire and be willing to accept the risks of the sport.

This book is written as a reference for all students taking the NAUI Scuba Diver certification course. If you have any questions about the contents of this book, ask your NAUI instructor. Your instructor will let you know in which order they would like you to read the information contained in this book.

HOW THIS BOOK IS ORGANIZED

This book is organized into the following chapters and appendixes:

- **Chapter One, "Introduction,"** gives an overview of scuba diving, certification, NAUI, your obligations, and rewards from this exciting sport.
- **Chapter Two, "Diving Equipment,"** describes the items of gear you will use in scuba diving.
- **Chapter Three, "Diving Skills,"** describes the skills you need to master to be a safe scuba diver.
- **Chapter Four, "Diving Science,"** describes the concept of pressure and the ways it affects your body under water. The chapter also describes the immediate and cumulative indirect effects of pressure.
- **Chapter Five, "Decompression, Dive Tables, and Dive Computers,"** describes the concept of ingassing and offgassing, dive tables and their use, the NAUI Dive Time Calculator, and dive computers.
- **Chapter Six, "Dive Planning and Recording,"** describes long term and short term dive planning, preparing to dive, conducting your dive, and recording your dive.
- **Chapter Seven, "Problem Solving,"** describes problem solving and explains why it is so important in scuba diving. The chapter also describes how to assist other divers as well as how to rescue another diver.
- **Chapter Eight, "Diving Environments,"** describes factors that affect the diving environment, such as water conditions, physical characteristics of a site, waves and surf, and tides and currents. The chapter also describes some popular diving areas throughout the world, marine life, and conservation.
- **Chapter Nine, "Diving Activities,"** describes some of the different continuing education courses you can take once you are a certified diver, and special diving interests you can pursue.
- **Appendix A, "Answers to Review Questions,"** includes the answers to the review questions found throughout the book.
- **Appendix B, "Being a Responsible Diver,"** includes guidelines to follow to be a responsible and considerate diver.
- **Appendix C, "Checklists,"** includes checklists for dive planning, diving equipment, and a first aid kit.
- **Glossary** defines the terms, acronyms, and concepts used in this book.

CONVERSIONS USED IN THIS BOOK

Unless exact equivelents are absolutely necessary table 1 shows a list of the conversions used in this book. The first column shows the unit being converted. The second column shows the exact conversion. The third column shows the unit to which the conversion was rounded for ease of reading throughout this book.

Table 1: Conversions

Unit	Equivalent	Rounded Unit
1 bar	0.9869 atmosphere	1 atmosphere
1 bar	14.51 pounds per square inch (psi)	14.7 psi
1 atmosphere	1.013 bar	1 bar
200 bar	2902 psi	3000 psi
2 centimeters	0.79 inches	3/4 inch
10 meters	32.81 feet	33 feet
20 meters	65.62 feet	66 feet
1 inch	2.54 centimeters	2.5 centimeters
2 inches	5.08 centimeters	5 centimeters
10 feet	3.05 meters	3 meters
100 feet	30.48 meters	30 meters
1 kilogram	2.20 pounds	2 pounds
6.5 kilograms	14.33 pounds	14 pounds
1 pound	0.45 kilograms	0.5 kilograms
4 pounds	1.81 kilograms	2 kilograms
21°Celsius	69.8°Fahrenheit	70°Fahrenheit
80°Fahrenheit	26.67°Celsius	27°Celsius

Table of Contents

TABLE OF CONTENTS

4 CHAPTER — Diving Science 92

5 CHAPTER — Decompression, Dive Tables, and Dive Computers 122

Table of Contents

7 CHAPTER **Problem Solving 158**

6 CHAPTER **Dive Planning and Recording 148**

Table of Contents

GETTING THE MOST OUT OF THIS BOOK

Throughout this study book there will be sections that require your special attention. The following icons are used to mark these sections.

Indicates that you should take note of the information, because it forms the basis for the final exam.

Indicates information that will help you complete the workbook.

Indicates a warning or safety information.

Indicates responsible diving practice.

NAUI
Scuba
Diver

CHAPTER

1

Introduction

LEARNING GOALS

In this chapter you will:
- Learn the meaning of the acronym SCUBA.
- Learn about scuba certification.
- Be introduced to NAUI Worldwide.
- Learn about other NAUI courses.
- Be introduced to some of the risks of scuba diving.
- Understand your obligations for attendance, health, and fitness.
- Understand why drugs, alcohol, and diving do not mix.

Scuba diving is the most unique adventure sport on earth. In the underwater world, you can watch the delicate beauty of tiny fish as they dart around a colorful tropical reef. You can experience the thrill of swimming eye to eye with sea turtles, whales, or manta rays (figure 1-1). With very little training, you can shoot underwater video footage that will dazzle your family and friends. As a scuba diver, you can see history as you discover fabulous underwater treasures and lost sunken cities.

Scuba diving is an adventure sport you can pursue almost anywhere in the world. From the shipwrecks of the Great Lakes to the tropical reefs of Australia, from the kelp forests of California to the rocky coast of the Mediterranean, where there is water, there is usually diving. As long as you are in good health and have the proper equipment and training, you can enjoy diving.

FIGURE 1-2. WRECK EXPLORING MIGHT BE ONE OF THE ACTIVITIES YOU WILL ENJOY.

FIGURE 1-3. DIVING IN COLD WATER CAN BE JUST AS ENJOYABLE AS DIVING IN WARM WATER.

Although it might seem that there is a great deal of information you must learn about diving, you do not need to be an expert to enjoy it. You can experience all the excitement of scuba diving by completing your NAUI Scuba Diver certification course. There are dives that are more advanced and challenges you can choose to experience later, but the basics of diving will enable you to begin your underwater adventures.

FIGURE 1-1. IMAGINE THE THRILL OF SWIMMING WITH LARGE ANIMALS UNDER WATER!

To enjoy diving where you live, you will need to learn how to use the scuba equipment commonly used in your area. The equipment might appear intimidating at first, but it is very simple to use. Just like driving a car, you don't need to understand every aspect of the equipment to be able to use it. Just remember that if you dive in other areas or pursue certain specialized types of diving, you will need additional training and equipment.

WHAT IS SCUBA DIVING?

You might already know that the word scuba stands for Self Contained Underwater Breathing Apparatus. You scuba dive with a compressed air cylinder or tank that you wear on your back (figure 1-4). The air is supplied to your mouth through a regulator that reduces the high pressure inside the tank to the same pressure as the water surrounding you.

You will hear divers referring to scuba diving as recreational diving or sport diving. These terms are used interchangeably to refer to scuba diving for fun, as opposed to commercial diving work, which professionals perform for pay.

You might also hear the term technical diving. This term refers to highly specialized diving that

FIGURE 1-5. SKIN DIVING IS DONE WITHOUT ANY UNDERWATER BREATHING APPARATUS.

requires additional equipment and training to explore the more demanding areas of the underwater world.

You will also hear the term skin diving. Skin diving involves diving without any underwater breathing apparatus. In skin diving, you hold your breath and dive below the surface. Skin diving is also known as free diving or breath-hold diving (figure 1-5).

Your NAUI Scuba Diver certification course will teach you to become a beginning scuba diver. Your instructor will also teach you the fundamentals of skin diving. Mastering the skills of skin diving will make you a much better scuba diver.

WHAT IS SCUBA CERTIFICATION?

Because there are no laws governing recreational scuba diving in most countries, the professional instructors who work in the scuba industry have agreed on certain minimum standards of training for sport divers. You must meet these standards to receive a certification card. Your NAUI instructor will also add special training specific to the area in which you are learning to dive. Your certification card will enable you to receive scuba diving services, such as renting a cylinder or enjoying a day of diving on a charter dive boat.

FIGURE 1-4. YOU WEAR A COMPRESSED AIR CYLINDER ON YOUR BACK WHEN YOU SCUBA DIVE.

Your NAUI Scuba Diver certification course will teach you the fundamentals of diving. You will learn the principles of selecting and operating your equipment, the effects of diving on your body, and basic information about your local diving environment. Once you have completed the course and your open water certification dives, you will be qualified to dive in conditions similar to those in which you did your open water certification dives.

Different levels of diving certification signify special knowledge in diving. After you complete the NAUI Scuba Diver certification course, you will be eligible to take specialty courses to learn about the different special interest areas in diving. For example, you might want to take a course in rescue diving or underwater photography (figure 1-6). There are also courses in underwater hunting and collecting, night diving, and many other topics.

Your instructor probably learned to dive in a course similar to the one you are taking now. In addition, your instructor completed additional leadership courses in running organized dives and diver rescue techniques. Before being granted an instructor certification, your instructor also completed a demanding course in instructional techniques and was required to demonstrate the required knowledge and skills to a panel of experienced diving instructors.

Your NAUI Scuba Diver Certification card is just the beginning of your adventures in diving. It is your license to learn more about the underwater world. There is no one who knows everything there is to know about diving, but in diving, you'll find much of the fun is in the learning.

WHAT IS NAUI?

Your NAUI Scuba Diver certification course is being taught by an instructor certified through the National Association of Underwater Instructors, more commonly referred to as **NAUI** or **NAUI Worldwide** (figure 1-7). NAUI was founded in 1959 and is one of the oldest and most respected diver certifying agencies in the world. You can take pride in your NAUI certification because NAUI courses are among the most thorough, routinely exceeding minimum industry standards.

NAUI Courses

In addition to teaching the NAUI Scuba Diver certification course you are currently taking, NAUI instructors also teach courses to further your diving education. Two of the NAUI courses you can take to continue your education are:
- Advanced Scuba Diver
- Master Scuba Diver

FIGURE 1-6. ONE OF THE SPECIALTY CLASSES YOU MIGHT WANT TO TAKE IS UNDERWATER PHOTOGRAPHY.

FIGURE 1-7. YOUR INSTRUCTOR IS CERTIFIED THROUGH THE NATIONAL ASSOCIATION OF UNDERWATER INSTRUCTORS (NAUI).

The NAUI Advanced Scuba Diver certification course improves your overall knowledge and skills in the water. It is designed for newly certified divers and introduces you to the many different types of activities available to certified divers.

The NAUI Master Scuba Diver certification course helps you acquire leadership-level academic knowledge and enables you to participate in exciting advanced diving activities in a challenging course.

Many people find that diving changes their careers and even their lives. By gaining diving experience and taking the progressive courses your NAUI facility or instructor offers, you can gain knowledge, skills, and experience that will prepare you to earn your own certification as a NAUI instructor.

NAUI Specialty Courses

NAUI instructors also teach many kinds of specialty courses. Some of the NAUI specialty courses you can take cover:

- Rescue diving
- Wreck diving
- Deep diving
- Underwater photography and video

FIGURE 1-8. SOMETIMES CONDITIONS ARE SO BAD THAT IT IS ADVISABLE NOT TO DIVE.

- Ice diving
- Cavern and cave diving
- Underwater hunting and collecting
- Night diving
- Technical diving

These courses are fun and emphasize the practical application of the knowledge you will gain in your NAUI Scuba Diver certification course. Specialty courses give you the opportunity to learn these exciting activities safely and faster than if you tried to accumulate the same knowledge and experience on your own. The more experience you can gain under the supervision of a NAUI instructor, the more comfortable and confident you will be in the water.

WHAT ARE THE RISKS OF SCUBA?

In any sport, there are risks. Scuba diving, as any sport, has some risk and you must understand this before you become a diver.

Most dives are very easy. However, on every dive there is always a chance that you will need to exert yourself greatly. At times, diving can be very strenuous. This is particularly true if you dive in cold water, dive in strong currents, or make beach entries through surf (figure 1-8).

As in any activity, the ultimate risk in diving is of being injured or killed. Serious injuries and deaths caused by diving are extremely rare though, and most divers never suffer any type of mishap. However, you need to recognize that risk exists. As a diver, you must be willing to accept this risk and take responsibility for your own actions. You will be asked to sign an *Express Assumption of Risk Associated with Diving and Related Activities* which explains the risks of diving. Also, this textbook clearly explains each type of risk associated with diving. In addition, your instructor will explain the risks in diving in general and any risks that are unique to your local dive sites.

If you are a minor, your parents will also have to understand the risks you face in diving. They will be asked to sign your waiver and *medical history* form.

A Little Apprehension is Normal

Most people who have not spent much time swimming in the ocean or other open bodies of water have a little apprehension about learning to dive. You might have concerns about the strange equipment, the marine life, and the environment. This is normal and to be expected.

Diving is seldom like it is portrayed in popular films or television shows. Once you become a diver, you will quickly begin to spot the flaws in most of the movies that feature diving. When you go under water, you will find that most fish swim away from divers and that humans are almost always the most dangerous creatures there.

There are ways to minimize the risks in diving. By knowing the risks, you can deal with them and make the probability of problems occurring extremely small. This is one major objective of your NAUI Scuba Diver certification course.

Misconceptions About Diving

One of the most popular misconceptions about diving is that you can easily run out of air under water.

FIGURE 1-9. YOU MONITOR A SUBMERSIBLE PRESSURE GAUGE THROUGHOUT YOUR DIVE TO SEE HOW MUCH AIR YOU HAVE LEFT.

The amount of air you have in your cylinder limits the amount of time you spend under water on any given dive. Divers use a submersible pressure gauge (SPG) connected to their cylinder to monitor their air supply and help them determine when it is time to surface (figure 1-9). Just as a person driving a car monitors their fuel gauge, you will monitor your pressure gauge under water. However, you must monitor your pressure gauge more frequently than you would a fuel gauge. As an extra precaution, most divers carry either an additional regulator, which allows their dive buddy to share air during an emergency, or a totally independent backup air supply. If you are a responsible and reasonably cautious diver, the risk of running out of air under water is very slight.

Another common misconception is that diving equipment is unreliable. Few divers ever experience an equipment failure in diving gear that has been properly maintained. A poorly maintained regulator is more likely to freeflow and deliver more air than you need than to deliver no air at all. As part of your NAUI Scuba Diver certification course, you will learn how to properly care for your equipment and inspect it before each dive. Occasionally, a piece of gear might become loose or go out of adjustment under water, but you will learn how to deal with these minor nuisances as part of the course.

Another common concern is that when you are diving in the ocean, you will always be under the threat of a shark attack. Few divers ever have the opportunity to even see a shark during normal scuba dives. There are special trips for experienced divers that have the sole purpose of seeing and photographing sharks. The opportunity to dive with these unique creatures is something rare and special.

In most cases when sharks do encounter divers, they show little or no interest in the divers unless they have been baited with food. Divers who remain calm, swim slowly, and stay under water usually receive little or no attention from a passing shark. They, like most creatures under water, will leave you alone if you do not harass them.

WHAT ARE YOUR OBLIGATIONS?

As a student enrolled in the NAUI Scuba Diver certification course, you have certain obligations.

Attendance

You have an obligation to attend, participate in, and satisfactorily complete every classroom and water session. Diving is not complicated, but the knowledge and skills you learn build throughout the course. You must understand the simple concepts in diving to be able to apply them to the diving you will do in open water. If you do not attend every training session, your knowledge and skills will be incomplete. If you do miss any sessions, it is **your responsibility** to arrange with your instructor to complete them satisfactorily.

Be sure to take notes during all classroom sessions. Your instructor will provide you with supplemental information that might not be in this textbook. In particular, you will learn about local diving techniques during the lectures and open water dives.

You will learn the skills of diving in a confined-water setting. These sessions might take place in a swimming pool or a calm, clear body of water. Once you have learned the skills of diving and can demonstrate them comfortably, your instructor will take you on a series of open water dives where you will practice these skills under actual diving conditions.

You will need to complete knowledge examinations, plus confined and open water evaluations of your diving skills before your instructor will issue you a NAUI Scuba Diver certification card. Even if you pass all the knowledge and skill tests, but your instructor does not believe that you have the judgment needed to dive properly or responsibly, it is your instructor's obligation to withhold your certification. You instructor will explain what you need to do to complete your certification and will help you to achieve that goal.

Health

Health is the state of being sound in body and mind and is a prerequisite for diving. To engage in diving, you must:

- Have a sound heart and healthy lungs.
- Have clear ears and sinuses.
- Be free of any limiting disease or serious ailment.
- Be free of any condition that can cause unconsciousness.

Your instructor will ask you to complete a *medical history* form before you can participate in the water sessions for this course. If you indicate any problems that might affect your ability to dive, you will be asked to have a medical examination and obtain written medical approval before starting your training.

Your age and overall physical condition might also cause your instructor to require that you see a physician for a physical examination before diving. This is for your own well being. However, regardless of a physician's opinion, a NAUI instructor may well decline to train you if you have an absolute *contraindication* (a medical condition, such as asthma, diabetes, or epilepsy) to diving.

Women have special health considerations, especially during pregnancy. No definitive studies have been done on the effects of increased air pressure on an unborn child. Therefore, if a woman is pregnant, she should not dive.

If a woman can engage in physical activities on land during menstruation, it is usually all right to participate in diving. If cramps or other effects of menstruation limit a woman's activity on land, it is best to not dive when these symptoms exist.

Fitness

Fitness is the ability to meet the physical demands of a particular activity. You must be fit to dive. Initially, this means that you need good aquatic ability, such as being able to swim at novice level non-stop without fins or other aids. This demonstrates the aquatic skill needed to be comfortable in the water. Later, you will need to develop abilities for using fins and performing other waterskills.

Just because you are in shape for some sports does not mean that you are in shape for diving, because different muscles are used in different ways. Playing sports such as baseball does not necessarily keep you fit for diving. To be in shape for a particular activity requires regular participation in that activity.

The best way to stay fit for diving is to dive regularly, or swim with mask, snorkel, and fins. Remember that your ability to dive safely is decreased by inactivity. Before resuming diving after a layoff of one month or longer, you should re-establish your skills and fitness by pool workouts before any open water dives. Refresher courses offered by NAUI facilities and NAUI instructors also afford opportunities to polish skills, add new knowledge to the basics, and help restore fitness and skill proficiency. Refresher courses are highly recommended if you haven't been diving in a while.

Divers take pride in their health and fitness. It is essential to maintain your health and fitness if you want to enjoy the sport and reduce its risks.

Use of Drugs and Alcohol

Good health and fitness are important for diving safety, but use of drugs can lead to problems under water. Substances such as alcohol, marijuana, and cocaine, which alter your physiology and affect your ability to think clearly, **should never be used before diving.**

FIGURE 1-10 DIVING IS ONE OF THE MOST EXCITING AND FUN ACTIVITIES YOU WILL EVER ENJOY.

Any such substance would be particularly dangerous if taken before diving. Avoid taking any over-the-counter or even prescription drugs that recommend you not operate machinery . Even if you are on medication prescribed by a physician, its effects under pressure are probably unpredictable, especially side effects. Complete your treatment before diving. Do not drink alcohol before diving.

If you are ill and do not feel well enough to dive without taking a drug, you should not dive, even if you feel fine with medication. The effects of drugs can be changed by pressure in unpredictable ways. Medication can mask the symptoms of your illness, but that illness still exists.

Verify What You Have Learned

Review the following questions about health and fitness:

1. Good health is a requirement for diving because
   _____.

2. A person should refrain from diving when
   _____.

3. True or False: Only people with problems in their medical history should have a physical examination for diving.

4. The best way to maintain fitness for diving is to
   _____.

5. If you are not feeling well but medication helps you feel better, you should refrain from diving because _____
   _____.

WHAT'S NEXT

You will find that scuba diving is one of the best activities that you will ever enjoy (figure 1-10). By completing this Scuba Diver certification course, you will be prepared to participate in diving adventures unlike anything you have experienced before. Read this book completely, complete the workbook, and follow your instructor's directions and you will be ready to learn how to dive.

Notes

CHAPTER

2

Diving Equipment

LEARNING GOALS

In this chapter you will:
- Learn about the basic equipment you need to go skin diving.
- Learn about scuba cylinders, including types and sizes, valves, maintenance, and inspections.
- Be introduced to regulators and the equipment usually attached to the regulator.
- Learn about different types of diving instruments.
- Understand the types of buoyancy control devices and how to select one that meets your needs.
- Learn about weighting systems.
- Be introduced to the many different types of diving suits for warmth and protection and learn how to choose the right suit for your diving conditions.
- Learn about some the accessory equipment that makes diving more enjoyable.

You must use some specialized equipment to go skin diving or scuba diving. When you first put on the equipment needed, you will probably feel awkward before you enter the water. Keep in mind that each item serves a purpose in the underwater environment. The gear is designed to be comfortable in the water, rather than on land. The sooner you get in the water, the better the equipment will feel to you.

BUYING EQUIPMENT FOR DIVING

You can buy diving equipment from a variety of outlets. However, your best choice for purchasing equipment is your local dive shop or sporting goods store, if it has a dedicated diving section (figure 2-1).

There are several reasons why you should buy your gear from a specialized retailer, such as a NAUI affiliated dive store. These include:
- You can see and wear the equipment in the store before you buy it and possibly even try out similar rental items in the store pool.
- Your local retailer is able to help you adjust items such as buoyancy compensators (BCs) and to

FIGURE 2-1. A DIVE RETAILER IS THE BEST CHOICE FOR PURCHASING EQUIPMENT.

measure you properly for custom-tailored wetsuits.
- Local retailers can provide you with the instruction needed when you purchase a specialized piece of gear, such as a dive computer, video housing, or dry suit.
- Your local retailer is usually able to service any gear that you buy at their shop.
- Local retailers might rent or loan you equipment while yours is in the shop for repair.
- Your local retailer is your only source for scuba cylinder fills and last minute required items.

Develop a good relationship with your local diving retailer. The salespeople there will be able to help you select the right type of gear for local diving conditions and for your personal diving interests.

Most new divers wait until they have finished their course to buy all of their scuba equipment. This is a good idea because you will usually have the opportunity to try several different types of gear during your course. However, most instructors will require that you have certain personal items of gear when you start your NAUI Scuba Diver certification course. These items can include:
- Mask
- Snorkel
- Booties
- Fins
- Gloves

BASIC PERSONAL EQUIPMENT

You can go skin diving under optimal conditions with four pieces of gear:

- Mask
- Fins
- Snorkel
- Flotation device

 Because you wear most pieces of dive gear directly on your body, the comfort and fit of each item is extremely important.

Masks

If you have ever opened your eyes under water without a mask, you know that it is impossible to see clearly there. Our eyes are designed to focus in air. A scuba mask places a layer of air between your eyes and the water, enabling you to see underwater objects clearly.

A scuba mask differs from swimming goggles in that it covers your nose. Having your nose covered enables you to equalize the pressure inside the mask, which increases as you dive deeper in the water. The air pressure inside the mask is equalized with the water pressure outside the mask when you exhale air from your nose into the mask.

 The most important consideration when you select a mask is whether the mask fits your face. To check for fit:

1. Place the mask gently against your face without putting the strap over your head.
2. Inhale briefly through your nose and hold your breath.

If the mask sticks against your face and does not fall off when you look down, it is a good fit. If you must push the mask against your face or continue to inhale to get the mask to stay on, it is not a well-fitting mask. (However, this is not true for men with moustaches.) Keep looking for a mask that fits. Be sure to try several different masks, even if the first one you try fits well. You might find another style that fits better.

You can choose from many different styles of masks. Some of the features of masks are essential and others are optional (figure 2-2). Essential features include:

- A tempered glass lens to help resist breaking and avoid injury if the lens breaks.
- A solid frame to hold the lens in position.
- An adjustable, split or wide headstrap that fits over the wide portion of your head.

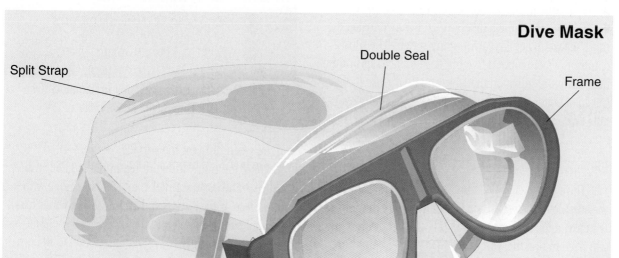

Dive Mask

Split Strap

Double Seal

Frame

Nose Pocket

FIGURE 2-2. SOME FEATURES OF YOUR MASK ARE ESSENTIAL.

• The ability to block off your nose to help equalize the pressure in your ears.

• A double featheredge seal to help the mask fit to your face.

There are many optional features you might want to consider when you select your mask. Some popular optional features include:

• Side windows to provide a wider field of vision.

• A purge valve to help clear water from the mask.

• A low-volume mask that fits closely to your face to give you a wider angle of vision. It is also easier to clear of water.

• Prescription lenses.

New mask lenses are covered with a thin film of lubricant. You can use toothpaste to remove this lubricant by using the following procedure:

1. Put a little toothpaste on the inside of each lens of the mask.

2. Rub the toothpaste over the entire lens with your fingers or a soft, wet cloth.

3. Rinse well with fresh water.

Washing the lens with toothpaste helps keep the lens from fogging, which occurs when condensation forms on the inside of the lens. Each time you don your mask for diving, you will need to prepare it so that it will not fog because of the temperature difference inside the mask compared to the surrounding water. The most common way to prevent fogging used to be to spit in the mask, rub the saliva on the lens, and then rinse the mask. A better alternative is to use commercially available anti-fog sprays, drops, or creams.

Snorkels

Have you ever noticed that you can lie face down on the surface of the water and float completely motionless? It's easy, and most people can do it. However, every time you need to breathe, you must lift your head out of the water and that takes exertion and gets tiring. A snorkel is the answer to this problem. (figure 2-3).

A snorkel enables you to breathe normally while you watch the beauty beneath you. Even little kids can easily enjoy the activity. The snorkel helps you conserve energy – and the air in your scuba cylinder – any time

FIGURE 2-3. DIFFERENT TYPES OF SNORKELS.

FIGURE 2-4. A SNORKEL ENABLES YOU TO BREATHE AS YOU ENJOY THE BEAUTY BENEATH YOU.

you are swimming on the surface (figure 2-4).

There are many different features available with snorkels. The basic snorkel is a "J" shaped tube with a mouthpiece at the curved end (figure 2-5). Other features that can be added to the basic snorkel include:

• Flexible hosing to enable the snorkel to fit comfortably in your mouth.

• A purge valve to allow water to drain out of the bottom of the tube.

• A swivel mouthpiece so you can adjust the mouthpiece in your mouth and swivel it out of the way when you switch to a regulator.

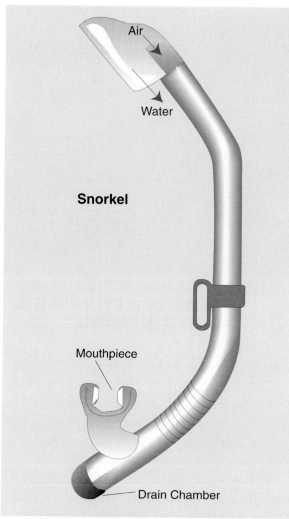

FIGURE 2-5. SNORKELS HAVE BOTH ESSENTIAL AND OPTIONAL FEATURES.

FIGURE 2-6. BOOTIES PROVIDE WARMTH AND PROTECTION FOR YOUR FEET WHEN WALKING OVER ROUGH SURFACES.

The inside diameter of the snorkel should be no less than 2 centimeters (3/4 inch). If the diameter is too small, it is like breathing through a straw. If the diameter is too large (over 2.5 centimeters or 1 inch), the snorkel is awkward to clear. Also, avoid a snorkel that has any sharp bends or angles.

Booties

Booties provide protection and warmth for your feet. They also serve as shoes when you are walking around a dive boat or dive site. Booties are made from neoprene, which is synthetic rubber injected with a gas, usually nitrogen, to make it spongy. The tiny gas cells in the rubber provide insulation for your feet. The neoprene is usually covered with nylon to make the bootie comfortable against your skin and easy to put on and take off. The neoprene can be thin or thick for warm-water or cold-water diving, respectively. The bootie should also have a sole to protect the bottom of your foot from rocks and rough surfaces (figure 2-6).

You wear booties with heel-strap fins and sometimes with full-foot fins. Some of the different types of booties you can find are:

• Slip-on 3 millimeter (1/8 inch) booties that come up to your ankle for warm-water diving.

• Baffles at the top of the "J" tube to keep water from getting into the snorkel at the surface.
• A molded or soft mouthpiece for added comfort.

The two most important things to consider when selecting your snorkel are comfort and breathing ease. The mouthpiece must fit comfortably in your mouth and should not be twisted when you place the tube or barrel of the snorkel over your left ear.

The snorkel itself should be between 30 and 35 centimeters (12 and 14 inches) tall. If your snorkel is too short, it will constantly fill with water. If your snorkel is too long, it will be harder to get a good breath of fresh air.

FIGURE 2-8. IF YOU ARE WEARING BOOTIES WITH YOUR FINS, BE SURE TO TRY THEM ON AT THE SAME TIME SO YOU CHOOSE A FIN THAT IS THE RIGHT SIZE.

FIGURE 2-7. FINS COME IN BOTH FULL-FOOT AND HEEL-STRAP STYLES.

- Booties with zippers that come up over your ankle. The zipper should have a backing to prevent water from entering directly through the zipper and to keep the zipper from rubbing your skin.

The bootie should fit snugly but comfortably on your foot. If it is too large for your foot, you will have a lot of water transfer in and out of your bootie during a dive and your foot will get cold. The excess room might also prevent your fin from fitting properly or make it loose enough to come off.

Fins

Fins provide your means of propulsion or way to move yourself through the water. Once you have all your scuba gear on, it is difficult and awkward to use your hands and arms to move through the water. With fins, you can use the larger muscles in your legs for swimming and have your hands free for other uses.

There are two basic types of fins: *full-foot fins* and *heel-strap fins* (figure 2-7). Full-foot fins are typically used for snorkeling and in warm water. Your entire foot

is enclosed in the *foot pocket* of the fin.

Heel-strap fins also have a foot pocket, but the back of the pocket is open and an adjustable strap goes across the opening. You must wear booties with heel-strap fins to protect your feet from blisters. You can use heel-strap fins for diving in any temperature water.

Fins come in a range of sizes from small to extra-large. The size of the fin determines the size of the foot-pocket and the blade length and width. The blade of the fin is the flat portion that extends away from the foot pocket. You must choose a fin that fits snugly to your foot without cramping your toes or pinching your feet (figure 2-8). If your fin is too large, it will be too hard to kick, can cause cramps, and can easily be lost.

You must pick the fin that is right for you and your level of physical conditioning. You must be able to kick comfortably with your fins for long periods. Fins that are too large and stiff for your leg muscles can cause your legs to cramp and will not be comfortable. You might be more comfortable with a shorter, more flexible fin.

Fins come in many different materials and styles depending on the manufacturer. The fin must withstand exposure to sun, salt, and sand, so you should purchase a good quality fin that can withstand hard use.

Some fins come with a plastic insert in each foot

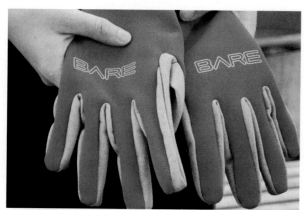

FIGURE 2-9. GLOVES PROTECT YOUR HANDS FROM CUTS AND ABRA-
SIONS AND KEEP YOUR HANDS WARM IN COLD WATER.

pocket. The insert helps maintain the shape of the foot
pocket when your foot is not in the pocket. You should
keep the inserts in the foot pockets whenever you store
your fins.

Gloves

Gloves are considered basic gear in many parts of
the world. Gloves protect your hands from cuts and
scrapes and provide warmth in cold water (figure 2-9).

You wear gloves in warm water to protect your
hands from injury. They can be made out of cotton, a
thin nylon material, or thin neoprene, some with a
leather or simulated-leather palm.

You wear gloves or mitts in cold water to keep your
hands warm and to protect your hands from the environment. Cold-water gloves are made from neoprene.

Your gloves should fit snugly and allow you to
move your fingers easily. You must be able to handle
your equipment while wearing gloves. Your instructor
might have you wear gloves during your confined water
training so you learn how to work while wearing gloves.

You should not touch or handle the creatures you
find under water just because your gloves are protecting
you from the environment. In many cases, you can
hurt or kill plants or animals just by touching them.
Coral reefs are particularly sensitive to touch and many
corals are easily broken. Many fish are covered with a
protective slime, and removing the slime makes the fish
subject to infection or parasites.

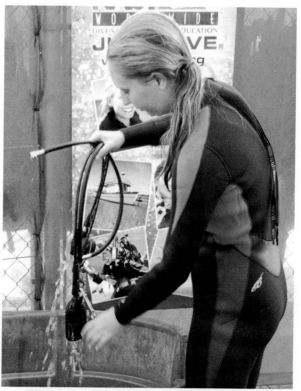

FIGURE 2-10. YOU SHOULD RINSE YOUR EQUIPMENT WITH FRESH
WATER AFTER EVERY DIVING DAY.

Note

In some areas of the world, you are no longer
allowed to wear gloves when diving (for example:
Cozumel, Mexico). This is to ensure that you will not
touch the reef and harm delicate corals or other aquatic life.

Flotation Device

Divers should wear some type of personal flotation
device for snorkeling and skin diving. The most commonly used piece of flotation equipment is an inflatable
vest that is worn on the chest and is usually referred to
as a skin diving or snorkeling vest . The vest is designed
to slip over your head and fasten at your waist with a
strap. Most vests of this design also have some type of
oral inflation tube.

Maintenance

Maintaining your basic skin diving gear, as well as

Diving Equipment

your scuba gear, is simple. You should rinse your gear with fresh water after every diving day (figure 2-10). Be sure that you do not leave your gear in the sun any more than necessary because sunlight and heat are extremely damaging to scuba gear and neoprene.

At the end of a diving trip, soak your gear overnight in fresh water and then rinse it thoroughly with fresh water. Make sure the gear is dry before you store it in a cool, dry area, like a closet. For extra protection, you can store your dry gear in a sealed, plastic bag.

No matter how well you maintain your gear, you will need to replace some parts periodically. Fin straps, mask straps, and snorkel keepers wear out. You must inspect your gear regularly, and especially before a dive trip, to give you a chance to replace worn parts before they break.

Verify What You Have Learned

Review the following questions on basic equipment:
1. The two most important features for the selection of your mask, snorkel, booties, and fins are:

❑ Comfort ❑ Style

❑ Fit ❑ Color

❑ Price ❑ Material

2. One feature that is not essential in a dive mask is:
   a. Purge valve
   b. Tempered glass
   c. Nose-blocking device
   d. Rigid frame
3. List two factors that can reduce the ease or efficiency of breathing through a snorkel:

_____,

_____.

CYLINDERS

When most people think of scuba diving, they immediately think of the cylinders that divers wear on their backs. Scuba cylinders allow you to store large amounts of air in a small space. Scuba cylinders are also known as *bottles* or *tanks*.

Every country can be expected to have standards regulating scuba cylinders. In the United States, cylinders are regulated by the Department of Transportation (DOT) and must be pressure tested according to government standards. In Canada, cylinders are regulated by the Canadian Transport Commission (CTC), which has standards similar to the United States Department of Transportation.

Characteristics

The air in a scuba cylinder is highly compressed, so a cylinder must have strong walls to withstand the pressure. The pressure rating of cylinders ranges from 120 bar (1800 pounds per square inch [psi]) to 310 bar (4500 psi). One bar is equal to approximately 14.7 psi or 1 atmosphere (atm). Most cylinders are made of aluminum or steel.

Aluminum

Aluminum cylinders do not rust, which is an advantage over steel cylinders. However, aluminum cylinders are more easily damaged than steel cylinders on the outside and the thread area where the cylinder valve screws in must be inspected regularly for cracks and other problems.

If water enters an aluminum cylinder, the cylinder corrodes and forms aluminum oxide. Once a layer of aluminum oxide has formed, it slows further corrosion of the cylinder.

Steel

Steel cylinders are more resistant to exterior damage. However, if water enters a steel cylinder, the cylinder corrodes and forms rust that can quickly ruin a steel cylinder. If you suspect that water has entered

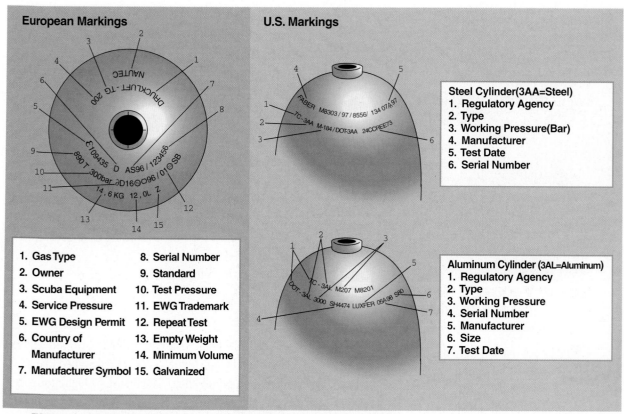

European Markings

U.S. Markings

Steel Cylinder(3AA=Steel)
1. Regulatory Agency
2. Type
3. Working Pressure(Bar)
4. Manufacturer
5. Test Date
6. Serial Number

Aluminum Cylinder (3AL=Aluminum)
1. Regulatory Agency
2. Type
3. Working Pressure
4. Serial Number
5. Manufacturer
6. Size
7. Test Date

1. Gas Type
2. Owner
3. Scuba Equipment
4. Service Pressure
5. EWG Design Permit
6. Country of Manufacturer
7. Manufacturer Symbol

8. Serial Number
9. Standard
10. Test Pressure
11. EWG Trademark
12. Repeat Test
13. Empty Weight
14. Minimum Volume
15. Galvanized

FIGURE 2-11. CYLINDER MARKINGS PROVIDE IMPORTANT INFORMATION ABOUT THE CYLINDER.

the cylinder, an internal inspection should be made at a qualified facility.

Sizes

Scuba cylinders come in many different sizes. In the metric system, the size of the cylinder is expressed as the volume the cylinder actually holds. In the United States, the size of the cylinder is expressed as the volume of compressed air the cylinder will hold.

Some metric sizes you may see when diving include:

- A 12-liter cylinder made out of aluminum rated for a pressure of 200 bar.
- A 10-liter cylinder made out of aluminum rated for a pressure of 200 bar.
- A 10-liter cylinder made out of steel rated for a pressure of 150 bar.
- An 18-liter cylinder made out of steel rated for a pressure of 160 bar.

Some United States sizes you may see when diving include:

- An 80 cubic foot cylinder made out of aluminum rated for a pressure of 3000 psi.
- A 63 cubic foot cylinder made out of aluminum rated for a pressure of 3000 psi.
- A 72 cubic foot cylinder made out of steel rated for a pressure of 2475 psi.
- A 95 cubic foot cylinder made out of steel rated for a pressure of 2640 psi.

Markings

Markings are placed on the shoulder of each cylinder to provide important pieces of information about the cylinder (figure 2-11). The markings include:

- The serial number of the cylinder, which is unique for each cylinder made by a single manufacturer.
- The name of the manufacturer or their symbol.
- Government-required marks to signify that the

Diving Equipment

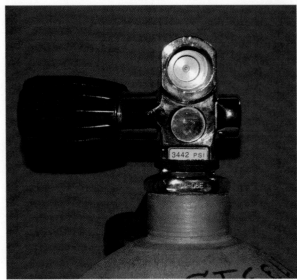

FIGURE 2-12. "K" VALVES ARE THE MOST COMMON TYPE OF VALVE FOUND IN THE UNITED STATES.

cylinder was manufactured according to its standards.

- The service pressure of the cylinder, which is the pressure to which the cylinder can be filled (for example, 200 bar or 3000 psi).
- A "+" mark on steel tanks, authorizing a 10 percent pressure overfill beyond the stamped service pressure.
- The material of which the cylinder is composed (for example, 3AL stands for a particular aluminum alloy).
- The hydrostatic testing date of the cylinder (for example, 8/07 signifies that the cylinder was tested in August of 2007). In the United States, hydrostatic testing must be performed every five years. In Japan, hydrostatic testing must be performed every three years. In Australia, hydrostatic testing must be done every year.

Accessories

Cylinders sometimes have boots on the bottom to protect the bottom of the cylinder and its environment. Some steel cylinders have a rounded bottom and need a boot to be able to temporarily stand upright. You must remove the boot on a cylinder periodically to properly rinse the bottom of the cylinder.

Cylinders can also be covered with a rubber or plastic net. The net protects the exterior of the cylinder and its paint.

You might also see divers with two cylinders hooked together with a manifold sharing a common valve.

Valves

Every cylinder must have a valve to hold the air in the cylinder when it is not in use, to control the flow of air out of the cylinder, and to provide an attachment point for the scuba regulator. A valve acts like a water faucet. You open the valve by turning its knob counter-clockwise and close the valve by turning the knob clock-wise, as seen from the top of the valve.

"K" Valves

The United States "K" valve is one valve you will see often when diving (figure 2-12). It is designed like a post with an on/off knob. The first stage regulator yoke fits over the post and the regulator is tightened against the post with a screw. These valves are not usually used at pressures higher than 200 bar (3000 psi).

An O-ring or gasket found on the cylinder valve makes a seal between the regulator and valve. If the O-ring is damaged or missing, the regulator will not seal to the cylinder and air will escape. You should replace O-rings frequently because of wear.

"J" Valves

A "J" valve looks like the "K" valve with a lever opposite the on/off knob. This lever is known as a *reserve mechanism*. The mechanism is designed to begin to restrict airflow at about 20 bar (300 psi) to 33 bar (500 psi) of pressure in the cylinder. When the mechanism is manually opened, the airflow is no longer restricted.

"J" valves were popular before *submersible pressure gauges* (SPGs) were commonly used. The reserve mechanism had to be placed in the up position at the start of the dive. The lever was moved to a down position by means of a cord or rod when the diver noticed

FIGURE 2-13. DIN VALVES ORIGINATED IN EUROPE AND ARE CAPABLE OF OPERATING AT PRESSURES GREATER THAN 200 BAR (3000 PSI).

FIGURE 2-14. YOUR SCUBA CYLINDER MUST BE VISUALLY INSPECTED AT LEAST ONCE PER YEAR.

difficulty breathing. These levers were easily bumped out of the up position during the dive and the diver would be using the last air without knowing it.

You will see "J" valves in use, but the valve is always used with the reserve lever in the down position. The mechanism is rarely used because divers now use submersible pressure gauges to monitor their air supply.

DIN Valves

The DIN valve system originated in Europe. The DIN valve has a large, threaded opening and the regulator first stage screws into the valve (figure 2-13). This system is also known as the *captured O-ring system*. While common in the rest of the world, DIN valves are not commonly seen in the United States. The DIN valve is capable of operating at pressures higher than 200 bar (3000 psi).

Burst Disks

 Every cylinder valve is equipped with an *over-pressure relief disk* or *burst disk*. This disk is designed to allow the cylinder to vent excessive pressure by bursting

the disk. This relief mechanism is designed to rupture and prevent an explosion if the cylinder becomes seriously over-pressurized.

Maintenance

Proper care of your cylinder includes rinsing the outside with fresh water after using the cylinder, having the cylinder visually inspected each year or if the cylinder is emptied, and having the cylinder hydrostatically tested as required by government standards.

Visual Inspection

Scuba cylinders must be inspected internally and externally at least once per year at a professional dive shop or a dive-equipment repair facility by a certified cylinder inspector. The cylinder is inspected for dents, marring, and fire or heat discoloration on the outside and for corrosion, water, and cracks inside (figure 2-14).

FIGURE 2-15 A VISUAL CYLINDER INSPECTION STICKER IS PLACED ON YOUR CYLINDER WHEN IT HAS PASSED ITS VISUAL INSPECTION.

If the cylinder passes the visual inspection, a visual cylinder inspection sticker is attached to the cylinder with the month and year of the inspection noted on the sticker (figure 2-15). If the cylinder does not pass the visual inspection, it might need to be cleaned or *tumbled* to remove oxidation. If the cylinder needs to be tumbled, it automatically needs hydrostatic testing.

Hydrostatic Testing

 In the United States, hydrostatic testing is required every five years or whenever the cylinder must be cleaned by tumbling. Hydrostatic testing tests the cylinder for metal fatigue. During hydrostatic testing, the scuba cylinder is filled with water and placed in a larger sealed cylinder full of water (figure 2-16). The pressure of the water in the scuba cylinder is increased to 5/3 the service pressure of the cylinder and then reduced to the pressure of the surrounding water. If the cylinder's size increases with the increase of pressure but does not

FIGURE 2-16. HYDROSTATIC TESTING STARTS BY FILLING THE SCUBA CYLINDER WITH WATER AND PLACING IT IN A LARGER CYLINDER OF WATER.

decrease back within set limits when the pressure is relieved, the cylinder can no longer be used.

Storage

You should store cylinders for any long term with some pressure in the cylinder. In steel tanks, keeping some air in your cylinder ensures that water cannot enter your cylinder and cause corrosion. With aluminum tanks, this is not as much of a concern. Aluminum tanks can be stored empty and with the valves open so that they will not be a hazard in a fire. You should store cylinders upright in a cool, dry, and protected location where they cannot be knocked over.

Never leave a cylinder standing by itself when you are not holding it. You should lay your cylinder down to prevent damage to it, the valve, or injury to someone. When transporting a cylinder in a moving vehicle, place the cylinder on its side and secure it to prevent damage to the cylinder, the valve, or the vehicle.

Backpacks

Backpacks are designed to hold a cylinder securely on a diver's back. Backpacks are now usually incorporated directly in the buoyancy compensator, but you might still see divers using a backpack and separate buoyancy control device. The backpack must be used with an easily adjustable harness with a quick-release buckle at the waist and at least one at the shoulder.

Verify What You Have Learned

Review the following questions about cylinders:

4. What is the difference between a "J" valve and a "K" valve?

_____

_____

_____

5. The two types of metal used to make scuba cylinders are _____ and

_____.

6. In the United States, a visual inspection is performed _____ and a hydrostatic test is performed _____.

FIGURE 2-17. YOUR SCUBA REGULATOR DELIVERS AIR TO YOU ON DEMAND AND PROVIDES EASY BREATHING UNDER WATER.

REGULATORS

The scuba *regulator* is a mechanical device that delivers air to you on demand (figure 2-17). One function of the regulator is to reduce the high pressure of the air in the cylinder to the *ambient pressure*, or the pressure surrounding your body, so you can breathe it. Regulators are composed of two main parts: the first stage and the second stage. Regulators also commonly have other pieces of equipment attached to them, including additional regulator second stages and gauges.

First Stage

The first stage of most United States type regulators fits over the post of the cylinder valve using a device combining the yoke and yoke screw (figure 2-18). Some use a DIN threaded fitting. In the first stage, the high-pressure air from the cylinder is reduced to approximately 10 bar (150 psi) above the pressure surrounding the cylinder. The air from the first stage is then delivered to the second stage through a low-pressure hose.

The first stage of your regulator has a number of

FIGURE 2-18. THE FIRST STAGE OF THE REGULATOR ATTACHES DIRECTLY TO THE SCUBA CYLINDER.

outlets or ports to which hoses and pieces of equipment are attached. The first stage must have at least one high-pressure port. This port bypasses the mechanisms that reduce the pressure from the cylinder. Your submersible pressure gauge is attached to this port so you can monitor your air supply. The following hoses might

FIGURE 2-19. THE MOUTHPIECE IS ATTACHED TO THE SECOND STAGE OF THE REGULATOR.

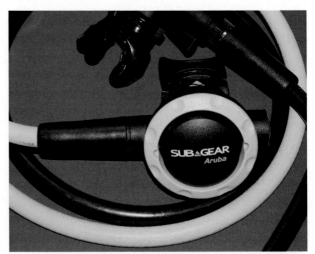

FIGURE 2-20. THE MOST COMMON ALTERNATE AIR SOURCE IS AN OCTOPUS REGULATOR.

be connected to low-pressure ports in addition to your primary second stage hose:

- A power-inflator hose for your buoyancy compensator.
- An alternate second stage or octopus regulator.
- A dry suit power-inflator hose, if used.

Second Stage

The second stage of your regulator has a mouthpiece attached to it (figure 2-19). The second stage further reduces the air pressure from approximately 10 bar (150 psi) above the surrounding pressure to whatever the ambient pressure is. Therefore, the air you breathe is always at the pressure needed by your body, no matter how deep you are under the water.

Some regulators offer higher performance than others and deliver a greater volume of air at deeper depths regardless of flow restrictions. This is important, because the deeper you go, the denser the air. If you plan to learn to do deep, wreck, cave, or ice diving or do underwater hunting, you will want a high-performance regulator.

Alternate Air Sources

It is standard practice that you and your buddy be

FIGURE 2-21. SOME ALTERNATE AIR SOURCES ARE COMBINED WITH THE POWER INFLATOR OF THE BUOYANCY COMPENSATOR.

equipped with alternate air sources in case of emergency. An alternate second stage can be attached to your first stage, or you can carry a source of air totally separate from your scuba cylinder.

Octopus Regulators

The most common alternate air source is an *octopus regulator* (figure 2-20). The octopus regulator is an additional second stage that allows you to share air from your cylinder with another diver. The hose for the

FIGURE 2-22. SMALL SCUBA CYLINDERS WITH THEIR OWN REGULATOR ARE CALLED PONY BOTTLES.

FIGURE 2-23. THIS IS ANOTHER TYPE OF CONTINGENCY SCUBA.

octopus regulator should be at least 10 centimeters (4 inches) longer than a standard regulator hose. The octopus regulator is inexpensive, convenient, and easy to use. However, it is not a source of air separate from your scuba cylinder, so your remaining air supply is depleted much faster when it is in emergency use by another diver and yourself.

 Another type of alternate air source is a combination regulator and power-inflator for your buoyancy compensator that fits on its power-inflator hose (figure 2-21). These units eliminate the extra hose for an octopus regulator and are easy to locate in case of an emergency. The air donor typically uses this alternate air source and gives their primary air source to the other diver.

Contingency Scuba

Contingency scuba or true alternate air sources provide a totally independent regulator and air supply. The two main types of contingency scuba are:

- A *pony bottle*, which is a small scuba cylinder with a separate regulator (figure 2-22). Pony bottles are commonly used by wreck divers and divers who dive deep.

- A smaller cylinder with an integrated first and second stage mounted directly on the cylinder (figure 2-23).

Contingency scuba provides an excellent backup for yourself if you and your buddy get separated under water. However, contingency scuba adds additional expense to your scuba equipment as well as extra bulk and weight.

Position of the Alternate Mouthpiece

The mouthpiece for your alternate air source should be located on the front of your body (figure 2-24). The mouthpiece for your alternate air source must be visible, easy to identify, and available for immediate use when it is needed. An alternate air source will not do you or your buddy any good if it cannot be located immediately during an emergency.

Gauges

Divers must rely on gauges and instruments to tell them depth, bottom time, direction, and air supply, just as a pilot relies on instrumentation to fly a plane. The gauges and instruments can be integrated into a console or worn separately.

A *dive console* streamlines your gauges into one unit. The console is an enclosure molded with slots to hold a submersible pressure gauge, depth gauge, and sometimes a compass.

FIGURE 2-24. YOUR ALTERNATE AIR SOURCE MOUTHPIECE SHOULD BE LOCATED ON THE FRONT OF YOUR BODY AND BE CLEARLY VISIBLE.

FIGURE 2-25. THE SUBMERSIBLE PRESSURE GAUGE IS A REQUIRED PIECE OF SCUBA EQUIPMENT.

Submersible Pressure Gauge

 The *submersible pressure gauge* (SPG) is a required piece of equipment for scuba diving. The SPG displays the amount of air pressure remaining in your scuba cylinder in the same way a fuel gauge shows how much gas you have left in your car's gas tank. By looking at your SPG frequently during your dive, you will know when your air supply is getting low and it is time to end your dive before you run out of air.

All mechanical SPGs perform the function of measuring the air pressure in your scuba cylinder (figure 2-25). SPGs give a reading in bar or pounds per square inch (psi). For a typical aluminum cylinder, the SPG reads 200 bar (3000 psi) when the cylinder is full, 100 bar (1500 psi) when the pressure is reduced to half, and so on.

SPGs are sensitive instruments and you should not subject them to shocks or abuse. If you notice a small leak from the hose or connection between the hose and SPG, it is not necessary to end your dive immediately. However, you should have the SPG and hose serviced as soon as possible to your NAUI Pro Center or dive-equipment repair facility. If you see water in your SPG, have it serviced as soon as possible and do not rely on it for diving until you do.

SPGs can also be integrated in dive computers and measure pressure electronically. In addition, some *air-integrated dive computers* can also monitor your breathing rate and predict how long the air in your cylinder will last based on your breathing rate (figure 2-27).

Depth Gauge

 Your depth and the duration of your dive at any particular depth are limited by a number of factors, so you need to monitor your depth when diving. A depth gauge gives you a way to measure your depth when you are under water (figure 2-28). There are four types of depth gauges:

- Capillary tube
- Bourdon tube
- Diaphragm mechanism
- Electronic gauge

The capillary tube is a simple, inexpensive instrument that consists of a clear piece of tubing sealed at

2800 - 3200

Rec. Starting Pressure

FIGURE 2-26. THE SPG'S INTERNAL MECHANISM.

FIGURE 2-28. A DEPTH GAUGE MEASURES YOUR DEPTH WHEN YOU ARE UNDER WATER.

FIGURE 2-27. MOST ELECTRONIC SUBMERSIBLE PRESSURE GAUGES ARE INTEGRATED WITH DIVE COMPUTERS.

one end. The tubing is marked with numbers that correspond to your depth. As you descend in the water, water enters the tube and compresses the air inside. You read your depth by looking at the air and water interface inside the tube. A capillary tube is very useful at shallow depths (above 12 meters or 40 feet), but is not recommended for deeper depths, as the scale size becomes too small for accurate readings.

A Bourdon tube uses pressure to straighten a curved metal tube. Bourdon tubes can be open or closed, although open tubes are rarely seen today. The closed tube is filled with air and is encased in a housing filled with oil. The pressure from the surrounding water is

transmitted through a flexible part of the housing to the oil and then to the tube. The tube is attached to a linkage and needle and as the pressure opens the tube, the needle moves to show your depth. Bourdon tubes measure depth reasonably accurately.

A diaphragm mechanism uses a metal diaphragm, which is attached to a linkage. The linkage is attached to a needle. As the pressure increases on the diaphragm, the needle moves to show your depth. Diaphragm gauges can often be adjusted for their zero point.

Electronic depth gauges are part of all dive computers and most electronic dive timers. An electronic depth gauge measures your depth using transducers, and then displays the depth digitally. Electronic depth gauges are extremely accurate and reliable.

You must have a means of recording the deepest depth you reach on a dive. Capillary gauges do not have a means of recording your deepest depth so you must remember to record it on a slate during your dive. Bourdon tube and diaphragm gauges might have a second needle that is pushed around the gauge by the depth needle attached to the linkage. The second needle stays at your deepest depth while the depth needle keeps showing your current depth. Electronic depth gauges record your maximum depth in their memory and then display the maximum depth when you surface or on demand.

Compass

When you are swimming under water and visibility is poor, a compass is an important reference instrument, if not essential. Some divers use a compass on every dive, including when diving in clear, tropical water. A compass can also be critical on the surface if it is foggy and you cannot see the beach or boat.

A compass consists of a magnetized needle that aligns itself with the earth's magnetic field. The needle will point towards magnetic north as long as there are no magnetic influences nearby that can cause the needle to *deviate* or turn away from its specified direction. This constant reference to magnetic north enables you to know your position or direction of travel under or above the water relative to the north-seeking needle.

A diving compass must:

- Be filled with liquid to withstand pressure and dampen needle movement under water.
- Have a reference line, called a "lubber line", used as the direction of travel.
- Have a means, such as a rotating bezel, to show a selected bearing or direction (figure 2-29).

Maintenance

Your regulator, alternate air source, and gauges are your life-support system under water and should be carefully maintained. Maintenance of your regulator first and second stages, alternate air source, and gauges can be divided into steps you can take as a user to keep your regulator in top condition, and steps that must be performed by a qualified repair technician.

You should replace the dust cap that fits over the inlet to the first stage whenever your regulator is off a cylinder. The dust cap must be dry before you fit it over the inlet to the first stage. The first stage contains precision moving parts and O-rings. If water, sand, or dust get into the first stage, they can damage the moving parts, affecting the performance of your regulator and making it difficult for you to breathe. Some dust caps use an O-ring to create a seal with the first stage. If the dust cap requires an O-ring and it is missing, you will see an empty groove in the cap. Be sure to replace the

FIGURE 2-29. DIVING COMPASSES ARE FILLED WITH LIQUID TO WITHSTAND PRESSURE, AND SHOULD HAVE A LUBBER LINE AND ROTATING BEZEL.

O-ring to ensure that you are sealing the inlet closed.

At the end of each diving day, you should rinse your regulator with fresh water to remove salt crystals or other impurities (figure 2-30). Always be sure to let water run through the mouthpiece and exhaust tees on the second stage. However, you should never press the *purge button* when running water through the mouthpiece. This could cause water to enter the hose to the first stage and get into the first stage of the regulator from there.

You should soak your regulator (if it does not have a DIN connector), alternate air source, and gauges overnight in fresh water at the end of a dive trip, and then rinse them thoroughly. Let the regulator dry completely and then store it in a cool, dry place. Do not coil the hoses tightly or allow them to hang at an angle with weight on them, which causes kinks at the hose ends. Hoses that have been stressed can spring leaks and must be replaced.

At least once per year, you should have your regulator serviced by a certified repair technician. Repair technicians are trained by the manufacturers in the proper methods to service their regulators and also to spot problems and correct them. The repair technician will take the first and second stages apart, clean all the metal parts, and replace the O-rings and other nylon or silicone parts of the regulator. The repair technician will also test and adjust the intermediate pressure of your first stage during the service. During an annual service, the repair technician will also inspect your submersible pressure gauge and high-pressure hose, depth gauge, and compass for proper operation.

Do not leave your gauges sitting in the sun. The sun can cause the oil in a compass or depth gauge to expand and leak. Also, if you will be traveling at high altitudes, be sure to transport your gauges in a pressure-proof container when at more than 300 meters (1,000 feet) above sea level.

Verify What You Have Learned

Review the following questions about regulators, alternate air sources, and instrumentation:

7. The most important criteria when selecting a regulator is _____ _____.

8. You must replace the _____ before you rinse your regulator.

9. What is an advantage to using an octopus regulator? _____

10. What is the primary advantage for using contingency scuba instead of an octopus regulator? _____

11. A _____ depth gauge is usable only at shallow depths.

12. The _____ measures the air pressure in your cylinder.

ADDITIONAL DIVING INSTRUMENTS

Some additional diving instruments that you might want to consider using include a timing device, a computer, and backup instrumentation.

Timing Devices

Along with keeping track of your depth under water, you must also keep track of the time you stay under water. You can keep track of your time under

FIGURE 2-30. YOU SHOULD RINSE YOUR REGULATOR AT THE END OF EACH DIVING DAY.

water by using a watch, an underwater timer, or a dive computer (figure 2-31).

Watches used for diving must be designed to withstand pressure. They should be rated for depths of at least 100 meters (300 feet). Your watch should also have a way to measure elapsed time with one of the following:
- A rotating bezel around the dial of the watch.
- A stopwatch feature.

Underwater dive timers are designed to measure elapsed time and have a valuable feature not found in most dive watches. A pressure-activated switch starts the timer when you leave the surface and shuts off automatically when you come back to the surface. The dive timer automatically records the elapsed time of your dive without action on your part. With most watches, you must remember to set the recording mechanism at the start of the dive and check it at the end of the dive.

Dive Computers

Dive computers measure the length of your dive time as well as many other items. Computers are the

Diving Equipment

FIGURE 2-31. WATCHES FOR DIVING MUST BE DESIGNED TO WITHSTAND PRESSURE.

most convenient method of keeping track of your dive time as well as your depth.

The dive computer combines your depth gauge, timing device, and sometimes your submersible pressure gauge in one unit. New dive computers are introduced every year, with more features available.

At a minimum, a typical dive computer records or displays the following information:
- Maximum depth
- Current depth
- Actual dive time
- Remaining allowable dive time

Between dives, the computer can display information from your previous dives as well as the amount of time that you have been out of the water. The computer can also help you plan your next dive by telling you how long you can stay at different depths.

See Chapter 5 for detailed information about dive computers.

Backup Instrumentation

Even the best instruments can sometimes fail or malfunction. Having an instrument fail does not necessarily mean an emergency, but it can end your diving day unless you have a backup. If you use a bottom timer, you should back it up with a watch. If you use a dive computer, you should back it up with a second computer or a watch and a depth gauge. If you use an air-integrated computer, you should back it up with a submersible pressure gauge, depth gauge, and watch.

Maintenance

Rinse your instruments in clean, fresh water at the end of each diving day and have your instruments inspected and serviced once per year by a qualified repair technician. Instruments are highly reliable, but they can go out of calibration. Also, O-ring seals can wear out and must be replaced or water can flood the instrument. If salt water gets into an instrument and stays inside, the instruments are quickly ruined.

Do not subject watches to extreme changes in temperature, such as by wearing them in a hot shower following a cold-water dive. The extreme change in temperature can cause condensation in the dive watch and ruin the mechanism. It is also possible to ruin the seals in a watch in this way, which will cause the watch to flood.

Verify What You Have Learned

Review the following questions about instrumentation:

13. A _____ calculates your remaining allowable bottom time while diving.
14. A diving watch must be _____ and measure _____ while under water.
15. Proper maintenance of instruments includes _____ and _____.

BUOYANCY COMPENSATOR

A buoyancy compensator (BC), enables you to control whether you float on the surface of the water, hover in the water, or sink to the bottom. You control this by adding air to or venting air from your BC. By controlling the amount of air in your BC, you can precisely control your buoyancy. Buoyancy control is one of the most important skills you will learn as a diver.

Features

All BCs are made of durable material that can hold air and are designed for rugged use. Alternatively, a

FIG 2-32. THE LOW PRESSURE INFLATOR DEVICE (POWER INFLA-TOR) IS ATTACHED TO YOUR CYLINDER WITH A LOW PRESSURE HOSE.

plastic bladder that is inside the BC might hold the air. The amount of air the BC can hold determines its available *lift capacity*. You use the lift capacity to offset any weight you and your gear might develop in the water.

BCs must be equipped with an *overpressure relief valve* to prevent damage to the BC from too much internal air pressure. The BC must also have an *inflator/deflator hose* that is at least 2 centimeters (3/4 inch) in diameter. At the end of the inflator/deflator hose is a *power-inflator mechanism* and a *deflator/oral inflator valve*. All BCs are also equipped with a mouthpiece at the end of the inflator/deflator hose that enables you to inflate the BC by blowing air into it (figure 2-32).

The power-inflator mechanism is attached to the regulator first stage with a low-pressure inflator hose. The power-inflator mechanism enables you to add air to the BC directly from your cylinder by pushing a button. If your power-inflator mechanism fails or you have no air in your cylinder, you can orally inflate your BC by pressing the deflator/oral inflator valve button and blowing into the mouthpiece at the same time. Stop pressing the

button before you stop blowing or take your mouth off the mouthpiece, or air will flow out of your BC.

On some BCs, you can pull down on your inflator/deflator hose or bleed valve activator to open the overpressure relief valve or *dump valve*. Some BCs have the dump valve located elsewhere on the BC. Pulling on a knob attached to a cable that hangs from the valve opens this valve. Alternatively, to deflate or bleed air from your BC, you can lift your inflator/ deflator hose over your head and press the deflator/oral inflator valve button. This allows air in your BC to flow up and out the inflator/deflator hose.

For Your Information

Some older BCs were equipped with carbon dioxide (CO_2) cartridge inflator mechanisms. These mechanisms were designed to be used in an emergency only, but the mechanisms could corrode easily if they weren't maintained properly and they were unreliable. You can still use a BC that is equipped to use a CO_2 cartridge inflator mechanism as long as it has been equipped with a plug to avoid air loss. Avoid using the mechanism.

Types

There are three general types of buoyancy compensators (BCs): back flotation, jackets, and horse collars. Some BCs have integrated weight systems. Some BCs combine features of more than one type.

Back Flotation

Back-flotation systems are designed so that the entire bladder of the BC is behind you. This leaves your chest and waist uncluttered. Back-flotation systems are popular for underwater photography for this reason.

Back-flotation systems provide good *trim* as you swim under water because the air in the bladder on your back counteracts the weights you wear around your waist. However, on the surface, the back flotation can tend to push you face down in the water unless you actively kick or recline to maintain a face-up position.

Jackets

Jacket-style BCs are the most popular buoyancy compensators. These BCs are designed so that the bladder wraps from your back around to your waist (figure 2-33). These BCs are comfortable to wear, provide good trim under water, and float you upright on the surface when your BC is inflated.

Horse Collars

The older horse collar design encircles your neck. You can use a horse collar for both skin and scuba diving. The adjustment of the harness is critical to keep the BC from riding up when it is inflated. You must don and remove the horse collar separately from your cylinder. Always remember to detach the low-pressure inflator hose when removing your cylinder.

Integrated Weight Systems

Some jacket-style and back-flotation BCs enable you to integrate or add your weights directly to the BC instead of wearing them on a weight belt. The BC must have a means of allowing you to quickly release the weights in an emergency. Some integrated-weight systems use pockets that you load with weights and then secure in your BC with Velcro™. In an emergency, you pull the entire pocket out of the BC and drop it. Other integrated-weight systems have pockets that are secured at the bottom with a threaded cable. You load your weights directly into the pockets in the BC. In an emergency, you pull the cable and the weights drop out of the pockets.

The advantages to an integrated-weight BC include:
- The need to wear a weight belt is eliminated.
- The weights cannot slide around your body.
- The weight is not supported solely by your lower back.

One disadvantage to an integrated-weight BC is that once it is assembled, it can be heavy and awkward to handle. If you need to carry the system for any distance, you must either remove the weights or wear the system. A potential major hazard is that it is impossible for a dive supervisor to tell at a glance approximately how

FIGURE 2-33. JACKET-STYLE BCS ARE THE MOST POPULAR STYLE OF BC.

much weight you are wearing (for example, whether you are obviously overweighted).

Selection

The best way to select a BC is to try on different models and see which one is the most comfortable for you. Also, the features and design of the BC should match the type of diving you will be doing. For example, if you are going wreck diving, rugged material is more critical.

If possible, try on the BC with a cylinder attached to the backpack and try the unit, or a rental like it, in the water. Ensure that you inflate the BC to see how it feels when full of air. The BC should not interfere with your body movement when it is full of air. The controls must also be easy to locate and operate.

Maintenance

You should rinse your BC internally and externally after each diving day (figure 2-34). Salt water, dirty

Diving Equipment

FIGURE 2-34. YOU SHOULD RINSE YOUR BC INTERNALLY AND EXTERNALLY AT THE END OF EACH DIVING DAY.

FIGURE 2-35. BE SURE TO DRAIN ALL THE WATER OUT OF THE BLADDER AFTER RINSING.

water, or chlorinated water inside your BC can cause damage. Every time you bleed air from your BC under water, some water gets into the BC.

Rinse the inside of your BC using the following procedure:

1. Fill the inside of the BC with fresh water through the oral inflator mouthpiece.
2. Slosh the water around inside the BC thoroughly, turning the BC upside down and right side up.
3. Drain the water by turning the BC so that the inflator/deflator hose outlet is the lowest point and pressing the deflator/oral inflator valve button to allow the water to drain out of the mouthpiece (figure 2-35).

Rinse the exterior of the BC thoroughly, as well as the power-inflator hose. Inflate the BC to allow it to dry completely. Store the BC in a cool, dry place with air in the bladder.

BCs must have their power-inflator mechanism inspected once per year. If it is not serviced, it can mal-

function. You should also inflate your BC completely to check for leaks before each dive trip.

Verify What You Have Learned

Review the following questions about buoyancy compensators:

16. The three main types of BCs are

_____,

_____, and

_____.

17. The two essential features found on all BCs are _____ and

_____.

18. Why should you rinse the inside of your BC?

_____

_____.

WEIGHTS AND WEIGHT BELTS

You wear lead weights when you are diving to offset the buoyancy of your body, your wetsuit, and other diving gear you are wearing. Weights are available in many configurations and as you gain diving experience, you will find the configuration that fits you best.

Types of Weights

Weights come in many different shapes and sizes (figure 2-36). Most commonly, you will find lead molded into cylinders or blocks with slits to enable a weight belt to be threaded through the weight. The block of lead can be uncoated or coated with a plastic covering. Some of the larger blocks of lead are curved to fit the hip and are known as *hip weights*. Solid lead weights come in sizes from 0.5 to 6.5 kilograms (1 to 14 pounds).

Lead can also be molded into cylindrical shapes with a slit in the middle to enable a weight belt to pass through. These are called *bullet weights*. Bullet weights typically come in sizes from 0.5 to 2.0 kilograms (1 to 4 pounds).

 Also, lead shot can be sewn into pouches of various sizes. This type of weight is known as a *soft weight*. Soft weights conform to the shape of your hip and are more comfortable to wear. Soft weights also cause less damage to a deck or injury to a person if they are dropped.

Weight Belts, Harnesses, and Weighting Systems

The simplest and most common weight belt is a 5-centimeter- (2-inch-) wide nylon web belt with a metal or plastic buckle (figure 2-37). *Weight keepers* are used on this type of weight belt to keep the weights from shifting on the belt.

Some weight belts are composed of a series of pockets attached to a nylon web belt. These pockets will hold either solid weights or soft weights.

There are also shot belts that have one continuous compartment filled with lead shot. The compartments are filled with different weights of shot and you simply choose the weight you need.

Another type of weight belt is a stretchable/ com-

FIGURE 2-36. WEIGHTS COME IN MANY DIFFERENT WEIGHTS AND SIZES.

FIGURE 2-37. WEIGHT BELTS COME IN MANY STYLES.

pensating belt with a quick release buckle. This type resists slipping, compensates for suit compression, releases cleanly, and *springs* off your body if you must *ditch* the weight belt.

A weight harness, usually used with dry suits, uses a belt and shoulder harness system to support the weights on your shoulders rather than around your waist. This helps reduce strain on your lower back and helps prevent the belt from sliding around your body.

A desirable safety feature of many weight belts is the ability to compensate for the compression of a wetsuit as you descend under water. Without a compensating feature, weight belts become looser at depth. A loose weight belt can slip down below your waist or can rotate to place the buckle at your side or back instead of in the front where it should be.

Diving Equipment

The length of your weight belt must be adjustable so there is not an excess of belt to pose a quick-release hazard. Your instructor will show you several methods of adjusting your weight belt so that you do not need to cut the end of the belt. The tail of the belt should not be longer than needed to provide a tightening grip of about 8 to 10 centimeters (3 or 4 inches). One advantage to the wire cam buckle is the complete absence of a tail.

Quick Release of Weights

No matter what type of weight system you choose, you must have a means of ditching the weights with one hand. This type of system is known as a quick release. The plastic or metal buckle on a weight belt must be a quick-release buckle that opens by pulling on the end of the weight belt or on the buckle. You can then pull the weight belt free from your body by grasping the buckle and pulling the belt away as needed. Integrated weight systems in BCs use either pockets that can be quickly pulled out of the BC and dropped or a cable that can be pulled to drop weights out of the bottom of the BC.

Verify What You Have Learned

Review the following questions about weight belts:

19. The most important feature of a weight belt is the _____.

20. A compensating weight belt

_____

_____.

21. Divers might prefer soft weights over molded lead weights because _____

_____ and

_____.

DIVING SUITS

Your normal body temperature averages about 37°C (98.6°F). Your skin will be cooler, but any time the water temperature is colder than your skin temperature, your body will lose heat to the water. Divers must wear a thermal-protection diving suit in all but the warmest waters (figure 2-38).

It is essential to wear the right thermal protection for the conditions where you dive. When you grow cold under water, you lose your ability to perform at your best. Heat loss under water affects your ability to think, and you fatigue rapidly. Cold water is a contributing factor in many diving accidents.

The amount of insulation you need to wear on a dive depends on the water temperature, your activity level during the dive, and other factors such as your build, body fat, and so on. In colder water, every diver needs to wear more insulation than they would wear in warm water. The harder you work under water, the more heat your body generates, and the warmer you are, unless you fail to wear adequate protection.

FIGURE 2-38. DIFFERENT DIVING SUITS ARE NEEDED TO ALLOW YOU TO DIVE IN WATER FROM FRIGID TO THE WARMEST TROPICAL WATERS.

Different ranges of temperatures feel comfortable to different divers. You might wear more or far less insulation than your dive instructor or buddy. It is essential to wear what feels right for you, rather than what someone tells you to wear. In the warmest tropical waters, you might be able to dive in just a skin suit. In colder water, you will need a wetsuit. In the coldest waters, dry suits are the most effective form of thermal insulation.

Dive suits also provide protection from cuts, scrapes, and stings. Even if the water isn't cold, you should wear some type of protective covering to avoid injuries and sunburn.

Dive Skins

Dive skins are thin, one-piece suits designed to protect your skin from cuts, scrapes, and stings that can occur when you dive in tropical waters. The term dive skins covers a wide range of products made from different materials. To determine what you are buying, it is important to ask what materials were used to make the suit. Two common materials are Lycra® and Polartec®.

Lycra®

By themselves, Lycra® dive skins provide only minimal thermal protection (figure 2-39), but Lycra® can be combined with polypropylene, which is a plush fabric, or other insulating materials to add some thermal capability. Lycra® dive skins, like wetsuits, provide almost no protection from the wind, especially when they are wet. This can be a problem on the surface with many suits, where heat is lost as water outside your suit evaporates and carries heat away from your body.

Polartec®

Polartec® is a combination of Lycra® and a velour fleece thermal lining that traps air and water as insulation. Dive suits made from Polartec® provide the warmth of a thin neoprene wetsuit without the need to wear as much weight to compensate for the buoyancy of the suit.

FIGURE 2-39. SKINS HELP PROTECT YOU FROM CUTS, SCRAPES, AND STINGS.

Wetsuits

Wetsuits are made from foam neoprene, which is a synthetic rubber filled with thousands of tiny gas bubbles. Neoprene provides good insulation in many diving situations. Wetsuits are the most widely used thermal protection for divers because of their simplicity and relatively low initial cost.

To work properly, a wetsuit must fit your body quite precisely, and snugly. Once you enter the water, a thin layer of water is trapped between your skin and the inner surface of your suit. The water is then warmed to your skin temperature and the insulating suit keeps you, and the water, warm.

If you do not dive deep or make multiple dives in very cold water, a wetsuit will provide you with reasonable insulation. As a wetsuit ages, it loses some of its insulating capability because some of the *cells* (gas bubbles) within the wetsuit break down on each dive.

Wetsuits come in a variety of colors. The color is usually in the nylon coating on the outside and inside of the neoprene material. Nylon provides better durability and makes the wetsuit easier to put on and take off, but it makes the wetsuit slightly thicker.

Thickness

Wetsuits are available in many thicknesses from 2 millimeters (mm) to 7 mm and in many different styles. The thicker the suit, the greater the insulation, although thick suits can be bulky and awkward to wear. The most popular thickness of a wetsuit for warm water to 27°C (80°F) is 3 mm. In colder waters, most divers prefer a suit thickness of 7 mm or greater.

Styles

Shorty wetsuits (wetsuits with short sleeves and thigh-length legs) and 2 mm or 3 mm full-body suits are popular for wear in tropical temperature water. For colder water diving, some divers prefer to wear a bib overall set of pants known as a *farmer john* and a *step-in* jacket combination. They also wear a hood, booties, and gloves.

You can adjust the warmth of your wetsuit by *layering*. For example, in the winter, you might wear a vest or a hooded vest underneath your farmer john to add insulation. In the summer, you might be able to dive without a hood.

Options

If you are tall, thin, very muscular, or otherwise differ from standard sizes, you might want to consider having your wetsuit custom made to your measurements. If you have a wetsuit custom-made, you can choose from a wide range of options. Options for wetsuits can include:
- Zippers at the wrists and ankles to make the suit easier to put on. However, water can enter and leave the suit through the zippers, chilling you.
- Knee pads to protect your knees and the suit from sharp rocks.
- A spine pad to cushion the cylinder and keep the spine warmer.
- Pockets inside the wetsuit to hold keys.
- Sheaths built into the leg to hold a dive knife.
- Attached hood for extra warmth.

Talk to your NAUI Pro Center and dive instructor about the types of suits used in your area or the area in

FIGURE 2-40. DRY SUITS KEEP YOU WARMER THAN WETSUITS IN COLD WATER.

which you will be doing most of your diving. Their recommendations will help you select the most appropriate type of suit.

Dry Suits

Dry suits are preferred for colder water. Dry suits are much more expensive than wetsuits, but are well worth the cost for the increased comfort in many diving situations. A dry suit is designed to keep you dry. The suit keeps you dry by using a combination of wrist seals, a neck seal, and a waterproof zipper (figure 2-40).

With some non-neoprene dry suits, you wear underwear under the suit to add insulation and keep you warm. The underwear traps air between your skin and the suit. You can layer the underwear to adjust your insulation for any water temperature. The water temperature, your body structure, and your activity level during the dive determine the amount and type of underwear that you wear beneath your dry suit.

Dry suits are easier to put on than wetsuits, but it does take specialized or additional training to learn how to use them properly. Most dry suits are bulkier than wetsuits. Depending on the fit of your suit and the type of insulating underwear you use, you might need to wear more weight with a dry suit than with a wetsuit.

Types

There are many different types of dry suits. Dry suits can be made from foam neoprene, solid neoprene, or a variety of heavy-duty nylons with waterproof materials laminated to them.

The foam neoprene suits are one-piece suits that have a waterproof zipper and seals at the wrists and neck. The suit itself provides insulation. This suit is warmer than a wetsuit made out of the same material because the inside of the suit is dry and the air in the suit as well as the suit itself provide insulation.

The solid neoprene suit requires that undergarments be worn under the suit for additional insulation. The amount of insulation worn can vary depending on the temperature of the water. This suit is less bulky than the foam neoprene suit.

The nylon-shell suit is loose fitting, which gives you greater mobility and comfort. The nylon shell suit also requires that undergarments be worn.

Features

Most of the options available for wetsuits, such as pockets, knife sheaths, and kneepads, are also available for dry suits. Other options made especially for dry suits include:

- Dry hoods
- Dry gloves
- Attached hard-sole dry boots

Because dry suits do not need to fit as closely as wetsuits, custom fitting is rarely necessary. However, the cost of dry suits is still greater because of the special watertight zipper and the other materials and labor needed to make the suit waterproof.

Buoyancy Control

While diving, you control the amount of air in your dry suit with an inflator valve, which allows you to add air to the suit, and an exhaust valve, which allows you to bleed air from the suit. The inflator valve is similar to the power inflator used on a BC. You add air to the dry suit as you dive deeper and then bleed air as you return to the surface. The most common location for the inflator valve is in the middle of the chest so it will not interfere with your BC jacket.

The exhaust valve is a low-profile valve that usually automatically vents air as you ascend. A common location for the exhaust valve is on the outside of your upper left arm. Different valve models bleed air at different rates. A valve that vents quickly is better, because it allows you to bleed air from your suit faster.

When you dive with a dry suit, you use the dry suit for buoyancy control and the BC for surface flotation. You use the BC for backup buoyancy control. You must be very careful if adding air to both your dry suit and the BC under water because it is difficult to control both pieces of equipment at the same time. You must always wear a BC with a dry suit.

If you are taking your NAUI Scuba Diver certification course in an area of the world that normally requires dry suits (for example, Alaska or Canada) you will probably be diving in dry suits from your very first class. If this is the case, your instructor will present supplemental material and training so you will understand how to use your dry suit. If your class does not include training in dry suits and you decide to buy one, you need to take a NAUI Dry Suit Specialty course to learn how to use the dry suit properly.

Hoods

You lose the greatest amount of heat from your head, hands, chest and armpits, and groin. Therefore, thermal protection for your head is critical when you are diving. In cold water, you can lose a significant amount of your body heat through your head alone.

For most cold-water diving, you can use a simple hood made from wetsuit material (figure 2-41). The hood can have an attached *bib* that tucks under the collar of your wet suit to keep your neck warm and help keep water from circulating in and out down the back of your neck. The warmest arrangement is to have

FIGURE 2-41. WEARING A HOOD HELPS YOU CONSERVE
BODY HEAT.

FIGURE 2-42. WETSUITS CAN BE DRIED AND SAFELY STORED ON
WIDE HANGERS MADE FOR WETSUITS.

your hood attached to your suit.

If you are diving in colder water, you might want to
use a dry hood attached directly to a dry suit. The dry
hood keeps your head completely dry.

Most hoods are fairly uncomfortable out of the
water. However, once you are under water they are
almost unnoticeable. Pressure equalization in your ears
when you wear a hood may require special attention.
Your instructor will address any special techniques
needed for the type of gear you are wearing.

Choosing the Correct Suit for the Conditions

Some insulation is required for most diving activities and having the correct suit for the conditions is one
of the keys to enjoying a dive. The correct suit for you
might not be the correct suit for your buddy because
your reaction to cold might be quite different. Also,
depending on the area of the world in which you live,

your resistance to cold might be less. For example, if
you live in a desert climate, you might have to wear
more insulation because your body is accustomed to
high temperatures. If you live in a cold climate, you
might be wearing less insulation in the water because
your body is accustomed to colder temperatures.

Use the following *general* guidelines when deciding
what type of diving suit to wear:

- **27°C (80°F) and warmer water.**
  A skin suit is recommended.
- **24°C to 27°C (75°F to 80°F) waters.**
  A 2 mm to 3 mm full wetsuit or shorty is
  recommended.
- **13°C to 24°C (55°F to 75°F) waters.**
  A 5 mm to 7 mm full wetsuit is suggested. As
  the water gets colder, you also need to wear a
  hood and gloves.
- **2°C to 13°C (35°F to 55°F) waters.**
  A full dry suit is recommended.
- **2°C (35°F) and colder water.**
  Special training and equipment are needed to
  dive in water this cold.

FIGURE 2-43. YOU SHOULD ATTACH YOUR DIVING INSTRUMENTS TO YOUR BC SO THEY DO NOT DRAG ALONG THE BOTTOM.

Maintenance

You should rinse a diving suit with fresh water after every diving day. Rinse dive skins and wetsuits inside and out. There are commercial products you can use at the end of a dive trip to clean your dive suits completely before storage.

You should store your wetsuits on wide hangers designed especially for wetsuits (figure 2-42), or unfolded, lying flat. If you get a hole in your wetsuit, you can repair it with wetsuit cement and neoprene patch material.

If the inside of a dry suit is completely dry, and it is worn with under clothing, you only need to rinse the out-side of the dry suit. You need to eliminate sweat, dead skin, and so on, from neoprene dry suits by rinsing the suit inside and out. All dry suits should be occasionally rinsed inside and out. You should lubricate dry suit zippers with only paraffin wax, beeswax, or preparations provided by the manufacturer. Your dry suit can be stored rolled up in a bag away from heat and ozone-producing machinery such as hot-water heaters and electric motors.

Your dry suit, with its valves, zippers, and seals, should be inspected annually by a qualified repair technician. Dry-suit valves can malfunction if they are not regularly serviced. Your dry suit owner's manual should be your primary guide and will list any special care instructions.

Verify What You Have Learned

Review the following questions about diving suits:
22. A _____ is suitable for only warm, tropical diving.
23. A _____ is made only from foam neoprene.
24. A _____ uses undergarments for insulation.
25. True or False. You do not need special training to use a dry suit.

ACCESSORY EQUIPMENT

Accessories are available that can make diving more enjoyable. There are also accessories for specialized activities. Some of the available accessories are described as follows.

Attachment Devices

Clips enable you to attach your instruments to your BC. Without clips, your gauges and octopus regulator will naturally hang at your side, and a foot or more below your waist, as you swim horizontally through the water. If you are swimming close to the bottom, your instruments can strike and damage marine life, or be damaged themselves. When corals and other delicate organisms are broken, they do not grow back. They die.

Remember to clip your instruments to your BC on every dive to avoid damage to them or the underwater environment. The clips you use must be fastened so you can remove your BC easily and quickly in an emergency (figure 2-43). Accessory clips and other holders are available at most dive stores.

Knives

A dive knife is a working tool used for many purposes. Its most important function might be to cut fishing line or nets if you get tangled in them under water. Knives are not used as weapons to fight sharks, as you might have seen on television.

Diving Equipment

FIGURE 2-44. SELECT THE KNIFE MOST APPROPRIATE FOR THE DIVING YOU USUALLY DO.

There are many different styles and sizes of diving knives and you should select the knife most appropriate for the diving you do (figure 2-44). For example, an underwater hunter might want a knife with a thin, sharp blade, while a wreck diver might want a heavy knife with a blunt tip for prying and pounding.

All dive knives should be kept sharp and have their blades coated with a thin layer of oil when they are not in use. Even stainless-steel knives can rust if they are not properly maintained.

Keep your dive knife in its sheath when it is not in use. Sheaths are usually made from plastic and can be mounted in different places including:
- On the inside of your calf.
- On the back of your instrument console.
- On your BC pocket or shoulder strap.

How and where you mount your knife depends on the design of the sheath, the size of the knife, and your individual preference.

Gear Bags

You need a gear bag to transport your gear to and from the dive site and keep it safe, clean, and out of the way at the site. Without a gear bag, it is difficult to handle your equipment and easy to drop delicate gear. On a charter dive boat, it is easy to lose your gear or have your gear accidentally picked up by other divers unless you have a bag to keep it in.

You can use almost any heavy-duty nylon or canvas

bag as a gear bag. Nylon is usually better because it does not rot or mildew as easily as canvas. Mesh bags or panels help any wet gear in the bag to dry. You should mark all your gear with some personal mark, and your bag with your name, address, and telephone number so it can easily be identified in case you accidentally leave it on a dive boat.

Special gear bags are available at dive shops. These bags are the easiest to use for diving because they usually have special compartments for fins, regulators, and instruments. Many of the bags are padded for airline travel and even have wheels so they roll through airports or on wharves. Some of the bags have special dry compartments for your logbook, clothing, and other items you do not want to get wet.

Dive Flags and Floats

When you are diving, it is almost impossible for a boat or jet ski moving at high speeds to see your bubbles or for their operators to know you are in the area. To avoid an accident, you should use a special *diver-down flag* to let others know you are under water.

The United States dive flag is a red flag with a white diagonal stripe running from the upper-inner corner to the lower-outer (fly) corner of the flag (figure 2-45). This flag must be flown from your surface support station or boat any time you have scuba divers in the area. Many states require, by law, that this flag be flown when divers are in the water. It is your obligation to stay within a set distance of the flag (no more than 30

FIGURE 2-45. ALWAYS HAVE A DIVE FLAG FLYING WHEN DIVERS ARE IN THE WATER.

Diving Equipment

FIGURE 2-46. A SURFACE FLOAT GIVES YOU A PLACE TO REST ON THE SURFACE.

FIGURE 2-47. YOUR LOGBOOK RECORDS YOUR EXPERIENCE IN THE WATER.

meters [100 feet], but local laws might require less). It is also your obligation to take the flag down when all divers are out of the water.

When appropriate, dive boats must fly the international blue and white *alpha flag* when divers are in the water (figure 2-45). This signal flag indicates that the boat's maneuverability is limited because of diving activities. This flag is also used as the *diver-down flag* in many countries. Your instructor will let you know what the local regulations are for dive flags.

If you are shore diving, your surface support station can be anything from an inflatable inner tube to an inflatable surf mat or kayak (figure 2-46). It does not matter what you use as long as some type of object appropriate for the conditions and area that can support you is nearby in case you need it.

Logbooks

A logbook is your record of experience in the water (figure 2-47). You should record the information from every dive you make in your personal logbook soon after you leave the water. In some parts of the world, there are laws requiring that you log your dives.

You will be required to use a logbook during your NAUI diver-training courses. In addition, some dive operators will want to review your logbook before they make diving services available to you.

If you decide to continue your education on to diving leadership, your logbook shows:
- That you have varied diving experiences.
- You have documented performing advanced diving skills under the supervision of an instructor.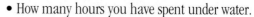
- How many hours you have spent under water.
- How many dives you have made.

Your training, diving, and hours will have to be documented before you can be accepted for leadership training. NAUI has an online dive log available at www.naui.org.

First Aid Kits

It is a good idea to have a first aid kit on any dive trip. All you need to do is add a few items to a standard first aid kit to meet the particular needs of diving and you are ready to deal with typical minor diving-related injuries. See Appendix C for the recommended items for a diving first aid kit.

Other Accessories

Some other useful accessories are:
- An *underwater slate* so you can record data and communicate with your buddy (figure 2-48).
- A *goodie bag* to hold game, specimens, artifacts,

FIGURE 2-48. WRITING ON A SLATE IS A GOOD WAY TO COMMUNI-CATE UNDER WATER.

Verify What You Have Learned

Review the following questions about accessory equipment:

26. What is the most likely use for a dive knife under water?

_____

_____

_____

27. When you fly a dive flag, you must

_____ and

_____ .

28. You should record all dives in your logbook because _____

and _____ .

29. Two additional accessories that will be useful to you when you dive are _____

and _____ .

trash, and other treasures.

- An underwater light, which is necessary for night diving, but is also good to have during the day to bring out colors and to peer into holes and crevices.
- A marker buoy to mark the location of a dropped item or a specific area.
- A spare parts kit that includes the items that can save a dive. The items can include a mask strap, a snorkel keeper, a fin strap, assorted O-rings, and a regulator mouthpiece with attachment strip.
- A checklist is a great way to remember all of the gear you need for diving as well as personal items. See Appendix C for samples of checklists.

CONCLUSION

Diving is an equipment-intensive activity. Remember that all this equipment helps you adapt to the underwater environment and function there as comfortably and safely as possible. The more you work with your gear, the easier it becomes to use. Once the gear is easy to use, you will be able to devote more of your attention to your surroundings and activities.

CHAPTER

3

Diving Skills

LEARNING GOALS

In this chapter you will:

- Be introduced to the snorkeling skills you will learn during your course.
- Learn the steps for assembling and testing your scuba equipment.
- Learn the steps for donning your scuba gear.
- Read about some of the methods for entering and exiting the water.
- Be introduced to the mask and regulator skills you will learn during your course.
- Learn about buoyancy control and buoyancy skills.
- Be introduced to the safety skills you will learn during your course.

It is one thing to use your diving gear in a swimming pool or other confined water setting, but exploring open water is the purpose of scuba diving. To enjoy diving, you must be able to combine your knowledge of the underwater environment with the ability to handle your equipment under a variety of conditions. You must have the confidence and ability to operate your gear by feel, because your mask will restrict much of your vision. In your NAUI Scuba Diver certification course, you learn the basics of diving, but you become a knowledgeable diver only through additional experience and further training.

If your training is occurring during the winter months in an area where the weather is cold, you still have the option of completing your open-water training immediately. You can complete your class through NAUI's Universal Referral Program by training at a tropical resort under the direction of another instructor. Ask your NAUI instructor for details about this program.

SNORKELING SKILLS

Developing good snorkeling skills is fundamental to being a good diver. You must know the proper use of your mask, snorkel, and fins.

Preparing Your Gear for Use

You need to prepare almost all of your new diving gear before you can use it. This is especially true with a new mask. New mask lenses are covered with a thin film of lubricant. You can use toothpaste to remove this lubricant by using the following procedure:

1. Put a dab of toothpaste on the inside of each lens of the mask.
2. Rub the toothpaste over the entire lens.
3. Rinse the mask well with fresh water.

Washing the lens with toothpaste helps keep the lens from fogging, which occurs when condensation forms on the inside of the lens. Each time you don your mask for diving, you will need to prepare it so that it will not fog because of the temperature difference inside the mask compared to the surrounding water. The most common way to prevent fogging is to use the following procedure:

1. Apply a few drops of antifog solution
2. Rub the solution on the inside of the lens.
3. Rinse the mask thoroughly.

An alternative is to use saliva, but many prefer commercial products. The commercially prepared products usually work more effectively than saliva. To prepare your mask properly, be sure to read the instructions enclosed with the product.

The snorkel is usually attached to the left side of your mask strap if your regulator comes around your right side (figure 3-1). Some snorkels are designed to be worn only on the left side. Some snorkels use a silicone snorkel keeper, while others have plastic clips. The snorkel should hang so that the mouthpiece comfortably reaches your mouth and the top is properly positioned behind your head when in use. Your instructor will show you the best way to attach your snorkel to your mask.

To prepare your fins for use, make sure you take any storage inserts out of the foot pockets and, if you are wearing heel-strap fins, adjust the straps around your heels for a snug, comfortable fit (figure 3-2). Have your booties on when you adjust the straps. Making the straps too tight can cause your feet to cramp. If the straps are too loose, your kick will be

Diving Skills

FIGURE 3-1. THE SNORKEL IS USUALLY ATTACHED TO THE LEFT SIDE OF YOUR MASK STRAP.

FIGURE 3-2. BE SURE THAT YOUR FIN STRAPS ARE ADJUSTED SO THAT THEY ARE SNUG BUT NOT TIGHT.

awkward and inefficient, your foot might cramp, and you might lose a fin.

If your fin straps are oily or slippery from a lubricant used in manufacturing, wash the straps in mild soap and water to remove the oil. Leaving the straps oily can cause the straps to slip in the water and loosen your fins.

Donning Your Gear

When you are ready to go diving, and you have completed your site survey and dive plan, you don or put on most or all of your gear at the dive site. Depending on your gear, your wet suit is usually the first piece of gear to put on. Sit down when you don your booties to avoid falling, especially if you are on a rocking boat. Your feet and your booties must be either completely dry or completely wet for the booties to slip on easily.

Your fins must be donned at the water's edge. If it is possible to put your fins on while sitting, you will be less likely to fall. However, most of the time, you will have to don your fins while standing. Always use a *figure-four position* when donning your fins as follows:

1. Steady yourself by putting one hand on your buddy's shoulder.
2. Cross the ankle of the leg closest to your buddy over the knee of your other leg (figure 3-3).

FIGURE 3-3. USE YOUR BUDDY FOR SUPPORT AND THE FIGURE-FOUR POSITION TO DON YOUR FINS.

3. Hold your fin by the side where the blade and foot pocket meet, or by the strap with the bottom facing away from you.
4. Put your foot in the foot pocket of the fin.
5. Slide the heel strap up and over your heel.
6. Turn around and repeat the process for your other leg.

Avoid walking more than a short distance while you are wearing your fins because you can easily lose your

Diving Skills

FIGURE 3-4. IF YOU MUST MOVE WHEN WEARING FINS, BE SURE TO WALK BACKWARD.

FIGURE 3-5. BE SURE THAT YOUR MASK IS POSITIONED COMFORTABLY ON YOUR FACE AND HEAD.

 balance and fall. If you must move when wearing your fins out of the water, be sure to move by shuffling your feet backward or by side stepping (figure 3-4). Never try to walk forward in your fins.

You might need to don your mask and snorkel last so that you will not restrict your vision when you are out of the water. One procedure to don your mask is:

1. Position the mask on your face.
2. Slide the strap down over the back or your head(figure 3-5).
3. Check the skirt of the mask to be sure that no hair or part of any suit hood are caught under the skirt (figure 3-6).

Be sure that your mask strap is not too tight. If the mask and strap are too tight, it will not be comfortable.

If you are going in the water to snorkel, place the snorkel in your mouth and adjust it along the strap so the snorkel fits easily into your mouth (figure 3-7).

Using Your Fins

Your fins provide you with thrust and stability in the water. When you are fully equipped for diving, you must use the large muscles in your legs for propulsion. Using your legs frees your hands to carry a camera and take pictures, a light for night diving, or use other items.

You can move your fins in a number of ways to cre-

FIGURE 3-6. BE SURE THAT YOU GET ALL YOUR HAIR OUT OF YOUR MASK.

ate propulsion. The most common kick is the flutter kick (figure 3-8). This kick differs in many ways from a swimmer's flutter kick. When you kick with fins, think of

FIGURE 3-7. THE SNORKEL SHOULD BE POSITIONED COMFORTABLY WHEN THE MOUTHPIECE IS IN YOUR MOUTH.

FIGURE 3-8. YOUR KICK SHOULD BE SLOW AND WIDE AND USE THE MUSCLES OF YOUR UPPER LEGS AND LOWER TORSO.

your legs as broomsticks and your fins as the bristles of the broom. You sweep up and down from the hip, keeping your knees almost straight and your toes pointed.

When kicking in fins, your kick must be slow, deliberate, and wide. If you bend your knees too much and pull your upper legs up towards your stomach, kicking as if you are pedaling a bicycle, your fins will slip back and forth in the water and produce very little thrust. If you kick too fast, you will tire quickly and your up and down strokes will be small and will not give you much propulsion.

On the surface, modify your kick so that you keep your fins in the water. Shorten the up stroke so that your fin does not come out of the water. You can also swim very efficiently on your back or your side while using the flutter kick on the surface. Swimming on your back (figure 3-9) or side (figure 3-10) keeps your fins in the water and is a good change of pace from swimming face down. Periodically check in the direction of travel, as you cannot see ahead while swimming on your back.

When you are kicking on the surface, make sure you have just enough air in your BC to make you buoyant or float. If you get tired, you can stop kicking and rest. As long as you are buoyant, you can rest without effort for as long as necessary.

FIGURE 3-9. MANY DIVERS PREFER TO SWIM ON THEIR BACKS ON THE SURFACE.

FIGURE 3-10. YOU CAN ALSO SWIM ON YOUR SIDE ON THE SURFACE.

FIGURE 3-11. WHEN YOU DO THE DOLPHIN KICK, YOU START BY BENDING FORWARD AT THE HIPS.

FIGURE 3-12. WHEN YOU ARCH YOUR BACK, YOUR LEGS RISE IN THE WATER.

You can also use the dolphin kick when diving. When doing the dolphin kick, keep your legs together and knees relaxed and alternately bend forward from your hips and then arch your back (figures 3-11 and 3-12). This movement causes your body to move through the water just like a dolphin.

You will learn these and other ways to kick with fins so you can change kicks if your legs get tired. Also, you will learn how to kick with one fin in case a fin strap breaks or you lose a fin.

If a strap on your fin works loose during a dive or pulls free, you must be able to remove the fin, correct the problem, replace the fin, and continue with your dive. It is usually easier to correct a fin problem under water than at the surface. If you need to fix a problem

at the surface, be sure to establish buoyancy by inflating your vest or buoyancy compensator (BC) so your need to kick is eliminated.

When replacing a fin in the water, use the same figure four position you used to don your fins. This position eliminates muscle strain on the large muscles in the back of your leg and might bring your foot into position where you can see what you are doing, though this is not essential. You should learn to don and remove gear by feel alone.

Breathing through Your Snorkel

Breathing through your snorkel while face down in the water will help you conserve energy, as well as the air in your cylinder. You breathe slowly and deeply when using a snorkel so you get good air transfer through the snorkel tube. Be sure that the end of the snorkel is positioned at the back of your head to keep the open end out of the water. Also, remember to keep your body in a horizontal position when swimming at the surface.

Surface Diving

There are a number of dives you can use to get under water. These dives are called *surface dives*. To perform a good surface dive, you must be weighted so you are neutrally buoyant at the surface. The key to a successful surface dive is to get as much of your body out of the water as possible. The weight of your body out of the water will help push you beneath the surface of the water.

Head First

There are two common headfirst dives: the pike dive and the tuck dive. The tuck dive causes less splash, and is less likely to scare fish. With either dive, you want to get your legs as far out of the water as possible in a straight, vertical line. The weight of your legs carries you well below the surface.

The steps for the pike dive are:
1. Lie horizontal at the surface.

FIGURE 3-13. THE KEY TO A SUCCESSFUL PIKE DIVE IS TO GET AS MUCH OF YOUR BODY OUT OF THE WATER AS POSSIBLE.

2. Point your hands, palms together, and arms straight, at the bottom or your target for the dive.
3. Bend forward at the hips until the trunk of your body is vertical in the water.
4. Snap your legs up in the air until they are in a straight line with the rest of your body.
5. Kick to continue your descent as soon as your downward momentum begins to decrease (figure 3-13).

The steps for the tuck dive are:

1. Position yourself upright in the water.
2. Tuck your legs to your chest in a tuck position and, at the same time, use your hands and fins to rotate your body to a head down position.
3. Quickly and smoothly, extend your arms down as you extend your legs up into the air so your body is in a straight vertical line.
4. Kick to continue your descent as soon as your downward momentum begins to decrease (figure 3-14).

Both dives should be carried out in one smooth, continuous motion.

FIGURE 3-14. A TUCK DIVE IS A GOOD DIVE TO USE FROM A STATIONARY POSITION.

Feet First

Feet-first dives are particularly useful for skin divers. On scuba you usually settle gently below the surface and continue your descent feet first. The steps for a feet-first dive are:

1. Position yourself upright in the water.
2. Hold your head upright and breathe through your snorkel or regulator.

FIGURE 3-15. A FEET-FIRST DIVE IS A GOOD DIVE TO USE TO CONTROL YOUR DESCENT AND CLEAR YOUR EARS.

3. Stretch your arms out to your sides.
4. Spread your legs forward and back into a split position.

Diving Skills

5. Kick your legs together and bring your arms forcefully down to your sides at the same time.
6. Stroke your arms up over your head as your head goes under water.
7. After you have cleared your ears, tuck your knees to your chest and turn your body so you are facing down.
8. Continue your descent to the bottom (figure 3-15).

A feet-first dive is also called a kelp dive. There are variations to this dive that your instructor will show you.

Shallow Water Blackout

If you are free diving, before you do a surface dive, you want to breathe in and out deeply a few times before you take in a deep breath of air and hold your breath to do your dive. If you take in more than three or four breaths, you are *hyperventilating* excessively and this can be a problem.

If you breathe in and out deeply and rapidly for more than three breaths, you lower the level of carbon dioxide (CO_2) in your body. However, the deep, rapid breathing cannot raise the level of oxygen (O_2) in your body. Most people do not realize that it is higher levels of carbon dioxide that gives the stimulus to breathe. When you do your dive, you use up the O_2 in your system, but if you over-hyperventilate, the amount of CO_2 in your body may be lowered to the point that you will not feel the need to breathe as you exhaust your available oxygen. This can cause you to lose consciousness or black out under water. Because you are most likely to black out at, or as you near, the surface on your ascent, the problem is called *shallow water blackout*.

Shallow water blackout is easy to prevent. Just breathe in and out deeply two to four times, and on your next breath, do your dive. This will not excessively lowering the level of carbon dioxide in your body.

Clearing Water from Your Snorkel

Water can enter your snorkel through the open end from waves, from accidentally dipping the end of the snorkel in the water, and from doing a dive. There are two ways to clear your snorkel quickly and efficiently

FIGURE 3-16. EXHALING THE AIR IN YOUR LUNGS FORCEFULLY CLEARS THE WATER OUT OF YOUR SNORKEL.

and with minimal effort. They are the *blast clear* and the *displacement clear*.

You can also obviously clear your snorkel at the surface by lifting your head completely out of the water, removing the snorkel mouthpiece, and allowing the water to drain out of the snorkel. This technique uses a lot of your energy, is a signal of a novice (new) diver or a problem, and is not recommended.

Blast Clearing

You perform the blast clear by exhaling air from your lungs forcefully as you surface from a dive. The air will blow the water out of your snorkel (figure 3-16). Take in your next breath cautiously in case any water is left in the snorkel. You can breathe past water left in the bottom of your snorkel as long as you breathe slowly. Then you blast clear again to get rid of the remaining water. Each time you take a breath following a blast clear you should be cautious to avoid inhaling water.

Displacement Clearing

The displacement clear is an alternative technique. It uses the least amount of energy and removes the water from your snorkel by the expansion of a very small amount of air you exhale into the snorkel as you surface (figure 3-17).

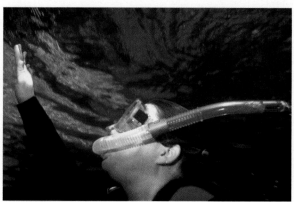

FIGURE 3-17. THE DISPLACEMENT CLEAR REPLACES THE WATER IN THE SNORKEL WITH AIR, IN PART, BECAUSE THE AIR EXPANDS AS YOU ASCEND.

You perform the displacement clear by using the following steps:

1. Tilt your head back so you are looking straight up when you are ready to ascend from your dive.
2. Swim to the surface, keeping your head tilted back.
3. Exhale slowly into your snorkel as you approach the surface. The air displaces the water as you ascend.
4. Tilt your head forward to look face down into the water as your head breaks the surface.
5. Inhale. You should not have any water left in your snorkel.

Verify What You Have Learned

Review the following questions about using your mask, snorkel, and fins:

1. If you must walk in fins, you must walk

_____.

2. To prevent losing your balance when donning fins, you can _____ or

_____.

3. Two recommended methods of clearing your snorkel are _____ and _____.

4. The _____ clear of your snorkel requires the least amount of energy.

ASSEMBLING SCUBA EQUIPMENT

You must know how to assemble your own gear for diving. Your gear includes your cylinder, buoyancy compensator (BC), and regulator as well as your weight belt. Remember that as a responsible diver, no one is responsible for the proper assembly and operation of your equipment except you.

Assembling Your Scuba Unit

Your scuba unit consists of your cylinder, BC, and regulator. By using the following steps, you will soon be able to set up your scuba unit correctly and efficiently. An instructor or divemaster can easily tell whether someone is an experienced diver just from the way they set up their gear.

To assemble your scuba unit, use the following steps:

1. Place your cylinder in front of you with the on/off knob to your right, and the opening where the air comes out of the valve facing away from you.
2. Pull the dust cap off of the scuba cylinder valve and check for the presence of the O-ring in the cylinder valve.
3. Wet the tank strap of your BC if water is easily accessible.
4. Pick up your BC with the shoulder straps in your hands and the tank strap facing you.
5. Slip the tank strap over the cylinder and move it down the cylinder until it is at the correct height. Your instructor will show you the correct placement for your BC's tank strap (figure 3-18). If the strap is too low, your first stage will hit your head during your dive. If the strap is too high, the cylinder will be too low on your back. This position might throw you off balance, and it will be difficult for you to reach your second stage hose at the first stage to recover a lost regulator.
6. Tighten the tank strap and secure it. Your instructor will show you the correct operation of your tank strap fastener.

FIGURE 3-18. YOUR BC MUST BE POSITIONED AT THE CORRECT HEIGHT IN RELATION TO THE CYLINDER.

FIGURE 3-19. BE SURE THAT YOUR CYLINDER DOES NOT SLIP IN THE TANK STRAP.

7. Pick your BC up by the shoulder straps to see if the cylinder slips in the tank strap (figure 3-19). If the cylinder moves, you must tighten the strap around the cylinder.

8. Pick your regulator up and turn it so that the second stage hose extends to your right and, for most regulators, the gauges and low-pressure inflator hose to your left. Make sure that the knurled (ridged) knob of the yoke screw is facing your stomach.

9. Attach the regulator to the cylinder using one of the following methods:
   - For a United States-made regulator, slip the yoke down over the cylinder valve (figure 3-20). The inlet for the first stage will match up with the outlet from the cylinder valve. The inlet for the first stage of the regulator will fit right into the indentation on the cylinder valve and against the cylinder's O-ring. Tighten the yoke screw only until it is finger tight.
   - For a DIN valve regulator, screw the first stage into the DIN valve only until it is finger tight.

10. Tighten the yoke screw only until it is finger tight (figure 3-21). Do not use force. The O-ring will form an airtight seal when you turn on the cylinder.

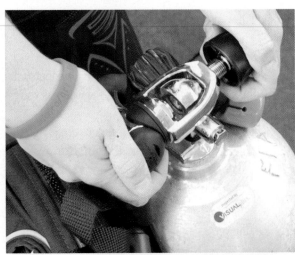

FIGURE 3-20. THE OUTLET FROM THE CYLINDER VALVE MATCHES UP WITH THE INLET FROM THE FIRST STAGE WHEN YOU HAVE THE REGULATOR POSITIONED CORRECTLY.

11. Connect the low-pressure inflator hose from your first stage to the power-inflator hose on your BC (figure 3-22).

12. Hold your console so that your submersible pressure gauge (SPG) is facing away from you, anyone else, or other gear. It is best to point the face down when you turn on your cylinder. There is a very slight chance that the glass face of the SPG could pop off, should the inner workings and the pressure relief fail.

FIGURE 3-21. THE YOKE SCREW SHOULD ONLY BE TIGHTENED UNTIL IT IS SNUG. DO NOT USE ANY FORCE.

FIGURE 3-23. CHECK THE SUBMERSIBLE PRESSURE GAUGE TO BE SURE THE CYLINDER IS FULL.

14. Open the cylinder valve completely by turning the on/off knob counterclockwise until it stops. Then turn the knob back about one-quarter turn.

This completes the assembly of your scuba unit. However, before you can use the unit, you must test it to be sure it is operating properly.

Testing Your Scuba Unit

Testing your scuba unit includes making sure that your primary and back-up second stages work and that your BC is inflating and deflating properly. The steps to test your scuba unit are:

1. Look at your SPG to see how much air you have in your cylinder (figure 3-23). If you are using a 200 bar (3000 psi) cylinder, your SPG should reflect about 200 bar (3000 psi). If your gauge reads less than about 165 bar (2500 psi), you should switch your equipment to another cylinder if you are planning a normal full-length dive.

2. Put your primary regulator in your mouth, breathe out, and then breathe in to be sure that

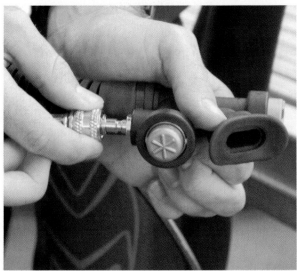

FIGURE 3-22. BE SURE TO CONNECT THE LOW-PRESSURE INFLATOR HOSE TO THE POWER-INFLATOR HOSE ON YOUR BC.

13. Slowly turn on the cylinder by turning the on/off knob counterclockwise. You will hear air pressurizing the hoses of the regulator. If you hear a loud hissing sound from the cylinder valve, you may have a problem with the seal between the cylinder valve and the first stage. This indicates that the valve O-ring needs to be replaced. Air leaks elsewhere indicate other problems that must be corrected before diving.

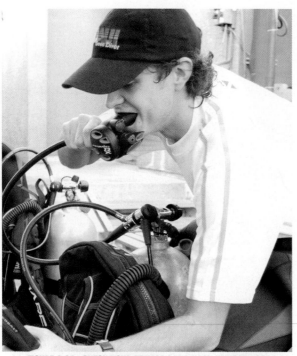

FIGURE 3-24. CHECK YOUR PRIMARY AND BACK-UP REGULATORS TO BE SURE THEY ARE DELIVERING AIR ON DEMAND.

FIGURE 3-25. ONE WAY TO SECURE YOUR EQUIPMENT IS TO LAY THE CYLINDER ON ITS SIDE IF YOU WON'T BE USING IT IMMEDIATELY.

the regulator is delivering air on demand (figure 3-24). Do not forget and breathe out first, as you might inhale debris, sand, or small pebbles. Even insects have been found in regulator second stages after storage.

3. Repeat the process in step 2 with your back-up or alternate air source regulator.

4. Press your power-inflator button to be sure that air is flowing into your BC on demand.

5. Press your deflator/oral inflator valve button to be sure that air flows out of your BC on demand.

When you have finished assembling your gear, you must make sure that the unit is secured and not in danger of falling over and injuring you or someone else or damaging the cylinder valve or regulator. If you are on a boat, place the unit back in the cylinder rack and secure the cylinder with the supplied elastic or other tie cord. If you are beside a pool, place your second stages and gauges inside the BC and lay the cylinder down on the tank strap (figure 3-25). If you are on a sandy beach, push the tank bottom deeply into the sand to make a secure base and wrap your hoses around the valve.

Assembling Your Weight Belt

How you set up your weight belt is important because it affects your comfort and safety. You want to have the correct amount of weight, and you want the weights to be balanced on the belt. With training and experience, you will know how much weight you need to wear based on the diving suit you are wearing. As a new diver, your instructor will help you determine how much weight you should wear. A rule of thumb for the amount of weight an average size person needs in salt water with a full 7 mm (1/4 inch) wetsuit is 10% of your body weight plus 2 kg (5 lbs).

The length of your belt is also important. The excess tail of the belt that hangs out of the buckle must be long enough for you to grab it with your entire hand, and only that long.

If you are using a flat 5-cm- (2-inch-) wide nylon web belt, with no elastic, and blockweights, string the weights on your belt using the following procedure:

1. Lay the weight belt out straight on a flat surface with the buckle facing up.

2. Bring the end of the weight belt up through a slit in the first weight and down through the other slit.

3. Position the weight so it will be over or slightly

forward of your hip.

4. Repeat the process in steps 2 and 3 until you have all the weights strung on the belt.

5. Try the belt on to see the position of the weights. Be sure that you distribute the weights evenly on each side and leave the area of the belt that spans your middle back clear of weights.

To keep the weights from shifting, you can put *weight keepers*, which are metal or plastic clips, between the slits in the weight to keep the weights from sliding. You can also put a twist in the belt as you thread it through your last weight to keep the weights from sliding off the belt. Ask your instructor for tips to keep your weights securely positioned on the weight belt.

If you are using soft weights in a weight belt with pockets, distribute the weights evenly throughout the belt. If you have too much weight on one side and not enough on the other, you will tend to roll and not be able to easily stay in control in the water. The weights will keep pulling you to one side.

DONNING SCUBA GEAR

There is a specific order to donning all of your scuba gear before you get in the water. Your instructor will show you the way they want you to don your gear. One order is as follows. For obvious reasons, your diving suit must be put on first. Your scuba unit is next, followed by your weight belt. And finally your mask and fins. Putting your gear on in this order makes the process easy and fast, and ensures that your weight belt can be readily ditched, if necessary.

Donning Your Diving Suit

Depending on where you learn to dive, you might use anything from a dive skin to a dry suit. There are different specific procedures for donning each type of diving suit. Your instructor will show you the proper techniques for the suit you will be using.

No matter which type of suit you are wearing, be sure you sit down when donning the bottom portion. This is especially important if you are donning your diving suit

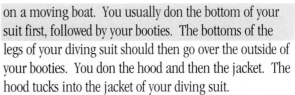

on a moving boat. You usually don the bottom of your suit first, followed by your booties. The bottoms of the legs of your diving suit should then go over the outside of your booties. You don the hood and then the jacket. The hood tucks into the jacket of your diving suit.

If the weather is warm, you want to be sure to set up your scuba unit and weight belt before donning your diving suit. If the weather is cold, you might want to don the diving suit first before you set up your scuba.

If you get too warm with your suit on, be sure to cool yourself down by getting in the water or pouring cool water over your head and suit.

Donning Your Scuba Unit

A buddy pair must don scuba units as a team (figure 3-26). It is easier to don scuba gear when you work together because of the extra hands that are available to position hoses and straps.

FIGURE 3-26. YOU AND YOUR BUDDY ALWAYS DON YOUR SCUBA UNITS AS A TEAM.

FIGURE 3-27. BE SURE THAT YOUR BACK-UP REGULATOR AND
GAUGES ARE CLIPPED TO YOUR BC.

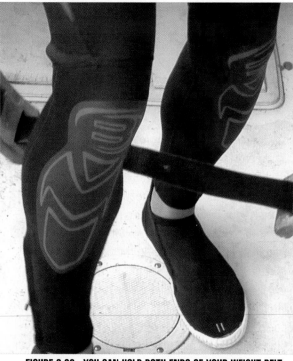

FIGURE 3-28. YOU CAN HOLD BOTH ENDS OF YOUR WEIGHT BELT
AND THEN STEP OVER IT.

To don your scuba unit while standing, use the
following procedure:

1. Stand your cylinder upright and face your BC
   towards you.
2. Grasp your BC by the shoulders as your buddy
   grasps the scuba unit by the first stage and the
   bottom of the cylinder.
3. Lift the cylinder together with one smooth
   motion and help your buddy steady the cylinder
   on his/her thigh.
4. Put your arms through the armholes.
5. Fasten your waistband and clips.
6. Let your buddy know you are ready to support the
   weight of the cylinder so they can let go.
7. Secure your back-up regulator and gauges to the
   front of your BC (figure 3-27).
8. Repeat the process so your buddy can don
   their BC.

After you have both donned your gear, check to be
sure that your shoulder straps are comfortably positioned. The cylinder should feel secure on your back.
Also, if your weight belt is already in place, be sure that
the buckle of your weight belt and the free end of your
weight belt can be easily reached without obstructions.

Donning Your Weight Belt

One way to don your weight belt is to use the following procedure if your dominant hand is your right hand:

1. Hold the buckle of the weight belt in your
   left hand and the free end of the belt in your
   right hand.
2. Step over the belt with both legs (figure 3-28).
3. Slide the belt up your legs and over your hips.
4. Bend over and let your back support the weight of
   your belt.
5. Slide the free end of the belt through the buckle
   and fasten the belt securely around your waist.

If your left hand is your dominant hand, you can
use the previous procedure with your left hand holding
the free end of the weight belt so that your dominant
hand will open the quick release buckle.

Always be sure to pick up a weight belt by the
free end, which is the end without the buckle, to prevent
the weights from sliding off the belt. It is best to securely fasten your weights on your own belt to further prevent this possibility.

Verify What You Have Learned

Review the following questions about assembling your scuba gear:

5. How should your regulator be oriented when you mount it on your cylinder?

_____

_____

6. A scuba cylinder valve is turned on when you rotate it in a _____ direction.

7. How should you and your buddy don your scuba units?

_____

_____

8. To ensure that it is clear to be ditched if necessary, you should put the weight belt on _____.

FIGURE 3-29. DO A GOOD EQUIPMENT INSPECTION BEFORE YOU GET IN THE WATER. YOU MUST BE FAMILIAR WITH YOUR BUDDY'S GEAR.

ENTERING AND EXITING THE WATER

Because you will be diving at many different sites, you must know different ways of getting in and out of the water. There are general rules that apply to all entries and some rules that are specific to each type of entry.

You will become familiar with a number of entries during your confined-water and openwater training. Your instructor will also teach you specific techniques for your local diving area.

This section of the book introduces some of the common entries and exits that divers use. It would take an entire book to describe all of the entry and exit techniques used worldwide. You will learn local methods from your instructor. Never assume that you know how to enter and exit the water everywhere. Always get an orientation from a NAUI diving professional to the diving procedures for every new site and region.

Checking Your Equipment

Once you and your buddy have your equipment on, you must check one another's equipment one last time

before getting in the water (figure 3-29). You must know how your buddy's equipment works and they must know how to operate yours in case of an emergency.

The acronym, **SEABAG**, is an easy way to remember the series of steps that you follow to plan a dive and check each other's equipment. SEABAG stands for:

- **S**ite survey
- **E**mergency planning
- **A**ctivity planning
- **B**uoyancy
- **A**ir
- **G**ear and go

See Chapter 6 for the steps for site survey, emergency planning, and activity planning. The steps for buoyancy, air, and gear and go are covered in this section. A checklist for the steps is included in Appendix C.

To check for *buoyancy*, use the following steps:

1. Check your own and your buddy's weight system to be sure that you can easily release the weights, if necessary. Note the type of system they are wearing and the type and direction of release.

2. Check your own and your buddy's BC to be sure that you know how to power inflate, orally inflate, and deflate the BCs. Also note the number and types of releases on the BC.

To check for *air*, use the following steps:

1. Check to be sure that your buddy's and your cylinder valve are almost fully open and only back 1/4 turn.
2. Check that your buddy's and your primary regulators and back-up regulators are delivering air on demand. Remember to exhale before inhaling.
3. Check that your buddy's and your SPG reflect that the cylinder is full while breathing from the second stage.
4. Check that all cylinders are secure in their tank straps.

To check for *gear and go*, use the following steps:

1. Check that you both have your mask, snorkel, and fins ready to don.
2. Check that your hoses are free, not tangled, and properly secured.
3. Check to be sure that you both have any necessary accessory equipment such as lights or cameras.
4. Proceed to your entry point.

No matter how experienced and skilled a diver you become, you always want to have your buddy inspect your equipment and be sure that you inspect your buddy's equipment in addition to self-checks. It is much easier to correct a problem **before** you get in the water.

Boat and Platform Entries

There are general rules that apply to most boat and platform entries:

- Your BC should be partially inflated to provide buoyancy.
- You should hold your mask firmly in place to avoid flooding it or having it come off.
- You should breathe from your regulator during the entry.
- You should make sure that the entry area below you is clear and sufficiently deep for the type of entry you are using.

The only objective for an entry is to get into the water with minimal effort and effect on both you and your equipment. Any entry that accomplishes this objective is a good entry.

FIGURE 3-30. YOU USUALLY DO A GIANT STRIDE ENTRY FROM A LARGE BOAT.

Giant Stride Entry

You can use the giant stride entry from a boat or dock where the distance to the water is no more than about 2 meters (6 feet) (figure 3-30). This entry keeps you near the surface. It is appropriate when the water is deeper than 2 meters (6 feet), there are no objects under water that you might strike while entering, and you want to stay on the surface.

The steps to a giant stride entry are:

1. Have your fins on and your mask and regulator in place.
2. Place your fin blades and the balls of your feet off the edge of the platform.
3. Look at the water below you to ensure that there are no divers below you.
4. Hold your mask and regulator with one hand and any loose items with your other hand and arm.
5. Step out from the platform with one bold stride. As you step out, your trailing leg will follow behind you.
6. Bring your legs together once you are under water to propel you back to the surface.
7. Quickly check that all your gear is still in place once you resurface.

FIGURE 3-31. YOU DO A BACK ROLL ENTRY FROM A SMALL BOAT.

FIGURE 3-32. THE SEATED SIDE ENTRY IS EASY AND CONTROLLED.

8. Turn back to the boat or platform and signal to the divemaster that you are okay. Do not signal that you are okay until you know that you are.
9. Swim clear of the entry area so the next diver can enter the water.

The key to doing a good giant-stride entry is to be in the stepping position (one leg behind you and the trunk of your body upright) as you enter the water. Then, as you go under water, bring your legs together to propel yourself back to the surface.

A variation to this entry involves putting your feet together before you hit the water. This will take you deeper, and can be used in special cases where you do not wish to resurface immediately. This variation can also place less strain on the legs if you enter from a height greater than about 2 meters (6 feet).

Back Roll Entry

You use the *back roll* entry when a boat is so small that if you stood to enter the water you could injure yourself by falling or fall out of the boat (figure 3-31). This entry is also used if you are entering the water from the side of a boat with high gunwales.

The steps to a back roll entry are:
1. Have your fins on and your mask and regulator in place.
2. Seat yourself with your back facing the water and your rear end partially over the edge.
3. Look behind you at the water below to ensure that there are no obstacles or divers below you.

4. Hold your mask and regulator with one hand and your weight belt and any loose items with your other hand and arm.
5. Lift your legs and let the weight of your cylinder roll you into the water. Your body should be in an "L" shape with your legs straight. Maintain an "L" shape as you are going into the water, or tuck your legs to your chest.
6. As you go under water, swim away from the boat or platform and back to the surface.
7. Be sure to turn back to the boat or platform and signal to the divemaster that you are okay, if appropriate.
8. Swim clear of the entry area so the next diver can enter the water, if appropriate.

You might experience some dizziness as you roll into the water. This results from upending or agitating the fluids in your inner ears as you turn. You will reorient in a few seconds. Also, be sure to recheck your mask strap, because it has a tendency to slip off your head during this type of entry.

Seated Side Entry

You can use the seated side entry from the side of a swimming pool, a ledge at water level in a quarry, or from a boat dock (figure 3-32). This is a good entry whenever you can sit at the water's edge, make your final preparations, and then lower yourself into the water.

The steps for a seated side entry are:
1. Sit at the edge of the water with your legs in the water.

2. Don your fins and mask and put your regulator in your mouth.

3. Place both of your hands on the same side of the entry edge and turn and lower yourself into the water. You should perform this step in one continuous movement.

The seated side entry is simple, easy, and effective. You are close to the water so the impact of your entry is minimal. Also, because you are seated, you are not as likely to lose your balance as you are when standing.

Beach Entries

Beach or shore entries can be very different depending on your location. They can range from wading into calm water to climbing down rocks to get to the water's edge. Each type of entry takes some precautions.

Calm Water

When you can walk into shallow, calm water to begin your dive (figure 3-33), it is usually an easy entry, but some precautions are necessary:

- Shuffle your feet along sandy bottoms, rather than stepping. This detects holes and rocks or obstructions, helps prevent loss of balance, and chases bottom-dwelling animals from your path.
- Step carefully along rocky bottoms. Rocks can be covered with algae, which makes them slippery. Be sure to have solid footing and maintain your balance as you take each step.
- Don your fins when you get to waist-deep water. If necessary, inflate your BC and float on your back while donning your fins. Lie down and begin swimming as soon as possible.
- If you lose your balance during the entry, do not try to stand up again. Crawl forward on your hands and knees and begin swimming rather than using your energy to try and stand again.

Surf

Entries through surf require special training. If your training does not include entries through surf, you

FIGURE 3-33. WADING ENTRIES ARE EASY WHEN THE CONDITIONS ARE CALM.

should receive additional training before you dive in an area with surf. Some precautions for surf entries include:

- All of your equipment must be securely in place.
- You must watch the waves continually.
- You must time your entry to coincide with a low point in the wave action.
- As a wave approaches, if you are not yet in water deep enough to swim, keep your knees bent and duck under the wave as it passes.
- Avoid stopping in the surf zone.

As you approach thigh-deep water, or if a wave is going to break over you, have your regulator in your mouth and go underwater into the base of the wave. Your BC must be deflated when doing a surf entry so you can easily get under water. If you are using a float, it must be trailed behind you.

Rock Jetties or Breakwaters

Steep rock entries from jetties or breakwaters also require some special training and considerations. Depending on your comfort level moving about in full gear, you might use a procedure similar to the following to get in the water only if it is calm without surge or surf:

1. Find a rock at the water's edge that will be good to sit on to don your mask and then push off into the water.

2. You and your buddy carry your scuba units and weight belts down close to the entry rock near the water's edge.

3. One buddy dons their mask and pushes off into the water. They then roll onto their back and don their fins. Donning your fins after leaving the rocks avoids the possibility of having a fin get stuck in the rocks and twisting or breaking an ankle.

4. The other buddy passes the first buddy their scuba unit to don and then the weight belt to don.

5. The buddy on land then passes their scuba unit and weight belt to the buddy in the water to hold while they get in the water.

6. Once the second buddy is in the water, they don their gear and start the dive.

If both buddies prefer, or if surge is washing over the jetty, they can don their gear at their set-up point and then climb down the rocks and into the water. However, you must be careful to maintain your balance and move slowly.

Boat and Platform Exits

Procedures for getting out of the water and back onto a boat or platform vary, depending on the situation. You might climb up a ladder into a boat or onto a platform or have to take your gear off in the water and then push yourself up onto a platform.

Some general rules apply to all boat and platform exits:

- Evaluate the exit area before getting out of the water. Conditions can change during a dive.
- Make sure all of your equipment is in place and is secure as you approach the exit.
- Think out the steps of your exit in advance.
- Keep your fins in place as long as you are in the water.

Ladder

If a dive boat has a ladder, you might be asked to climb the ladder with your scuba unit and weight belt in place. Use the following steps when using a ladder to exit from the water:

1. Stay to one side of the ladder or the other until it is your turn to exit. Never get under another diver trying to exit.

2. Swim to the ladder when it is your turn.

3. Hold on to the ladder and use the figure four position to remove your fins. If possible, climb out of the water before removing the fins.

4. Slip your fin straps over your wrists or hand your fins up to the divemaster.

5. Place your feet on the bottom rung of the ladder and stand up.

6. Climb the ladder one step at a time, being sure to maintain your balance and support the weight of your scuba unit.

7. Take your fins from the divemaster and move away from the exit area.

Always remember to stay away from the ladder when someone is using the ladder. If they fall, you could be seriously injured, especially if they are wearing their cylinder.

It might also be possible in some situations to also remove your weight belt and scuba unit at the exit point. Observe, listen, and ask the divemaster for the procedure they want you to use.

Boat Transom Platform

You must coordinate your approach to a swim platform with the wave action. The water movement will help lift you onto the swim platform. Sometimes you can use the following steps when exiting the water onto a swim platform:

1. Hand any items you are carrying up to the divemaster (figure 3-34).

2. Remove your weight belt and hand it up to the divemaster.

3. Remove your scuba unit and let the divemaster pull it out of the water.

4. Place your hands, shoulder-width apart, on the swim platform.

5. Kick your legs together and push up with your arms at the same time to bring your body out of the water.

6. Swivel around and sit on the swim platform.

7. Remove your fins using the figure four position.

FIGURE 3-34. WHEN YOU EXIT ONTO A SWIM PLATFORM, IT IS EASIER TO HAND YOUR GEAR UP FIRST.

FIGURE 3-35. IT IS SOMETIMES NECESSARY TO CRAWL OUT OF THE WATER THROUGH SURF.

8. Leave the swim platform area.

An alternative method is to leave all of your gear in place, remove your fins, and climb up a ladder and onto the deck.

Beach Exits

Procedures for beach exits vary greatly depending on the situation and the conditions. You must evaluate the condition of the exit area and the steps of your exit before you proceed with your exit.

Calm Water

When you do a beach exit in calm water, swim towards shore until you are about waist deep. Stand up and use your buddy's shoulder and the figure four position to remove your fins. Walk out of the water.

Surf

When you are exiting through surf, you must concentrate on your exit procedures. Keep your regulator in your mouth. Hold your mask on. Never stop in the surf zone. If the surf is rough, swim until you can crawl out of the water on your hands and knees (figure 3-35). Once you are clear of the water, you can roll over and remove your fins.

Rock Jetties or Breakwaters

With rock exits, you reverse your entry procedure. If you put your gear on in the water, you need to take it off in the water and hand it out to your buddy. When approaching the rock you are going to use to exit, use the wave action so that the water movement will help you get onto the exit area.

Verify What You Have Learned

Review the following questions about entries and exits:

9. Which pieces of equipment must you check before you get in the water?

_____
_____.

10. Three general rules that apply to entries are:

_____
_____
_____.

11. The objective of an entry is to

_____
_____.

12. State one example of when it is appropriate to use each of the following entries:

a. Giant stride

_____

b. Back roll

_____

c. Seated

_____

MASK SKILLS

There are a number of ways that water can get in your mask during your dive. For example:

- Your mask fogs while under water. The easiest way to remove the fog is to let water into your mask and swish it around.
- You laugh or smile under water, which causes the muscles of your face to create channels that will let water into your mask.
- Your mask gets knocked to the side by the careless movement of another diver.

In any of these situations, you need to know how to get the water out of your mask and feel comfortable doing it.

If you are skin diving and water gets into your mask, you can wait to get back to the surface to pour the water out. You can also easily clear your mask under water while skin or scuba diving.

Clearing Water from Your Mask

To clear water from your mask or replace your mask underwater, you must replace the water in the mask with air. When you exhale air into the mask, the air rises to the top and the water flows out the bottom (figure 3-36). Replacing the mask underwater is the same process as on land.

The steps to clearing water from your mask are:

1. Point your chin toward the bottom whenever you have water in your mask to prevent water from getting up your nose.
2. Inhale a breath of air if your lungs are empty and you are on scuba.
3. Put your finger tips on top of the mask frame and push in to maintain the seal at the top of the mask.
4. Start exhaling through your nose. As you exhale, tip your head back slowly. The air will force the water out of the bottom of the mask.
5. If you have a purge valve in your mask, do not tip your head back, look toward the bottom, and simply exhale into the mask.

When you are breathing from scuba, you must perform the steps to clearing your mask deliberately and slowly (figure 3-37). You must consciously think about

FIGURE 3-36. THE AIR YOU BREATHE OUT YOUR NOSE REPLACES THE WATER IN YOUR MASK.

FIGURE 3-37. CLEARING WATER FROM A MASK IS SOMETHING EVERY DIVER MUST BE ABLE TO DO.

what you are doing and you must concentrate on inhaling through your mouth and exhaling through your nose. This pattern is different from normal breathing and is different from the normal pattern of breathing on scuba. If you do not concentrate on what you are doing, you might forget and inhale water through your nose, which will cause you to choke and cough.

A single, sustained exhalation is more effective than short or strong bursts of air. It does not take much air to clear a mask completely. When you become proficient at mask clearing, you will be able to clear your mask several times on a single breath of air.

Removing water from your mask is an important diving skill. You must repeat this skill until you are completely comfortable with it and can do it automatically. Initially, your instructor will have you practice this skill in shallow water and then will have you repeat the skill in deeper water.

Removing and Replacing Your Mask

You might wonder why you would want to take your mask off under water. Generally, you don't, but someone else might inadvertently remove it for you. Your mask can be bumped and dislodged, or it can catch on something and be pulled free. In these cases, you must be able to calmly locate your mask and put it back on.

Your vision without a mask will not be good, but you will be able to see. Learn to open your eyes without a mask on, because they are more useful than you might think.

 When you are wearing contact lenses, you run the risk of losing the lenses if your mask floods or comes off your face under water. In this situation, keep your eyes closed unless you need to see to locate your mask. If your mask is lost, you will have to rely on your buddy to find it or help you surface, to avoid losing your lenses.

One way to replace your mask under water is to use the following steps:

1. Orient your mask so that the inside of the mask is facing you and your snorkel is on the side on which you wear it.
2. Position the mask over your eyes and nose and place the mask strap on the back of your head.
3. Run a finger around the mask seal and make sure that all of your hair or your hood (if you are wearing one) is out of the mask.

4. Clear the water from your mask as described in *Clearing Water from Your Mask* on page 67.

Verify What You Have Learned

Review the following questions about mask skills:

13. What are the recommended steps to replacing your mask under water?

_____

_____

_____

_____

14. Which way should you tilt your head when clearing water from a mask with a purge valve?

_____

REGULATOR SKILLS

Learning to scuba dive includes more than just learning how to breathe from a regulator. You can do that already! Some of the regulator skills you will master during your NAUI Scuba Diver certification course include:

- Breathing underwater if your mask comes off your face.
- Finding your regulator if it comes out of your mouth while you are swimming under water.
- Sharing air with another diver.
- Breathing from a free-flowing regulator.

Breathing Underwater

When you breathe on scuba, you do all of your breathing through your mouth. However, you must exhale small amounts of air into your mask as you descend to prevent mask squeezes. You must always remember to keep breathing so that you will not trap expanding air in your lungs during an ascent.

Breathing with a Flooded Mask or without a Mask

If you lose your mask under water, or if your mask floods, you must concentrate on your breathing and maintain air pressure in your nose to avoid inhaling water through your nose until you correct the problem. You must be able to do this without needing to hold your nose closed, because in many situations, you will need to use both your hands for other purposes.

Clearing Your Regulator

Whenever the mouthpiece of your regulator is out of your mouth, you must continually exhale a small stream of bubbles (figure 3-38). This helps keep your airway open. You do not want to *lock off* your throat. If you do rise in the water, the air in your lungs will expand, and the air must be able to escape through your mouth instead of over expanding your lungs and causing damage.

Your regulator should remain in your mouth as much as possible, but there are a few situations in which you must remove it.

If the mouthpiece of your regulator comes out of your mouth for any reason, the regulator second stage will automatically fill with water. When you put the regulator back in your mouth, you must be able to clear the water from the second stage before you can breathe. There are two primary ways to clear your regulator second stage of water: the blast clear and the purge clear.

Blast Clear

The quickest and easiest way to remove water from the second stage of your regulator is to do the *blast clear*. The blast clear is not truly a "blast" of air, just a simple exhalation. To perform the blast clear, you put the regulator mouthpiece in your mouth and exhale the air remaining in your lungs out of your mouth. The air from your lungs forces the water out of the one-way exhaust valve located on the bottom or side of your second stage. Most regulators require that you be in an upright position or facing slightly down to clear all the water out of the second stage. Some regulators require you to tilt to the side opposite the hose to fully clear the regulator.

FIGURE 3-38. YOU MUST EXHALE A SMALL STREAM OF BUBBLES WHENEVER THE REGULATOR IS OUT OF YOUR MOUTH.

Purge Clear

If you do not have enough air in your lungs to perform the blast clear, you can use the *purge clear* to get the water out of your second stage. To perform the purge clear, use the following steps:

1. Put your tongue up to the roof of your mouth and against your teeth to prevent water from the second stage from going into your mouth and throat.
2. Lightly press the purge button located on the front or side of the second stage to replace the water in your second stage with air from your cylinder.

Recovering Your Regulator

There will be times when your second stage will be out of your mouth during a dive. For example, if you are diving in kelp, the kelp might wrap around your hose and it might be convenient to take the regulator out of your mouth to untangle it. Also, you might get so relaxed that you forget to bite on your mouthpiece to hold the regulator in your mouth. There are two ways to recover your regulator: the sweep method and the reach method.

Sweep Method

Use the following steps to find your regulator using the *sweep method*:

1. Get into a vertical position, right side down or lean to the right.
2. Bring your right elbow into your side.
3. Touch your right hand to your thigh and then move it back to touch your cylinder.
4. Sweep your right arm out from your cylinder in a big circle around to the front of your body. Your primary regulator should be in the bend of your arm (figure 3-39).
5. Put your primary regulator in your mouth and either blast or purge clear the second stage.

Always remember to blow a steady stream of small bubbles whenever the regulator is out of your mouth.

Reach Method

Use the following steps to find your regulator using the *reach method*:

1. Reach over your right shoulder with your right hand and grasp the first stage of your regulator. It might be necessary to lift your cylinder from the bottom with your left hand.
2. Feel for the primary regulator hose on the upper or front right side of your first stage (figure 3-40).
3. Follow the hose down to the end. Your primary regulator will be at the end of the hose.
4. Put your regulator in your mouth and either blast or purge clear the second stage.

Remember, if you happen to recover your back-up second stage or cannot immediately locate your primary second stage, you can always use your own back-up regulator or redundant scuba system for breathing until you find your primary second stage. Use the alternate air source only until you can find your primary regulator or you can get your buddy's attention and assistance to locate your primary regulator.

Breathing from a Free-Flowing Regulator

When a regulator begins delivering air continuously, it is *free-flowing* (figure 3-41). To stop a free-flow, turn the regulator so the mouthpiece opening is down. Fortunately, this is about the only problem you will ever have with a regulator, and it is usually not serious.

FIGURE 3-39. SWEEPING YOUR RIGHT ARM AROUND IN A LARGE CIRCLE IS ONE WAY TO FIND YOUR REGULATOR.

FIGURE 3-40. FEELING OVER YOUR RIGHT SHOULDER WITH YOUR RIGHT HAND FOR YOUR REGULATOR HOSE IS ONE WAY TO FIND YOUR REGULATOR.

However, you should not dive with a free-flowing regulator.

If the regulator starts to flow continuously during your dive, you can continue to breathe from the regulator by using the following procedure:

1. Using your hand, hold the mouthpiece loosely in your mouth.
2. Breathe the air you need from the stream of air escaping from the mouthpiece.
3. Perform a safe ascent.
4. It is a good idea to turn off, or have your buddy

FIGURE 3-41. MOST REGULATORS WILL FREE FLOW IF THEY ARE TURNED UPRIGHT UNDER WATER.

FIGURE 3-42. YOU MUST BE ABLE TO USE THE ORAL INFLATOR OF YOUR BC UNDER WATER OR AT THE SURFACE IF YOUR POWER INFLATOR FAILS.

turn off your cylinder when you reach the surface so you do not drain all the air from your cylinder. Be sure to allow the excess air to escape through the sides of your mouth. Most will purge through the exhaust port and prevent the pressure of the air escaping to force too much air into your lungs.

Orally Inflating Your Buoyancy Compensator

If your BC's power inflator fails, you must orally inflate your BC during your dive to maintain proper buoyancy. To orally inflate your BC, use the following steps:
1. Inhale a breath of air.
2. Remove your regulator mouthpiece.
3. Put the BC's oral inflator mouthpiece in your mouth.
4. Press the deflator/oral inflator valve button as you blow into the mouthpiece (figure 3-42).
5. Release the deflator/oral inflator valve button.
6. Stop blowing into the mouthpiece.
7. Remove the oral inflator mouthpiece and put your regulator in your mouth.
8. Clear the regulator and take a breath.
9. Repeat steps 1 to 8 until you have achieved your desired state of buoyancy.

Switching from Your Regulator to Snorkel

When you surface, you will usually take your regulator out of your mouth and switch to snorkel (figure 3-

FIGURE 3-43. SWITCHING FROM REGULATOR TO SNORKEL SHOULD BE SMOOTH AND EASY.

43). When you get ready to descend, you must take your snorkel out of your mouth and replace it with your regulator. You will practice regulator/snorkel exchanges at the surface until they are simple and easy for you to perform. You must remember to inhale before the switch and to exhale before you inhale after the switch to clear any water out of either the regulator or the snorkel.

Monitoring Your Air Supply

You must monitor your air consumption during your dive by frequently checking your submersible pressure gauge (SPG). At a minimum, you should check your SPG every 5 minutes when you are in shallow water (less than 9 meters [30 feet]) and more frequently when you are in deeper water (figure 3-44). You must also begin checking your SPG more frequently when your cylinder pressure drops below 70 bar (1000 psi).

When you begin diving, your air consumption will be high and you will be surprised at the shortness of your dives. As you gain experience and your comfort level in the water increases, your air will last longer. When you are cold, diving deep, or breathing rapidly on a dive, your air consumption will increase. When you are diving in these conditions, you must monitor your air supply more frequently.

On dives to 18 meters (60 feet) or less, begin your ascent when your cylinder reaches a minimum pressure of 50 bar (800 psi) or more. On deeper dives, begin your ascent when your cylinder pressure reaches a minimum pressure of 70 bar (1000 psi) or more, depending on the conditions.

FIGURE 3-44. YOU MUST CHECK YOUR SPG FREQUENTLY DURING YOUR DIVE.

Verify What You Have Learned

Review the following questions about regulator skills:

15. You should _____ whenever your regulator is out of your mouth.
16. Two methods to clear water from your regulator are the _____ method and the _____ method.
17. What should you avoid when breathing from a free-flowing regulator?

_____

_____

BUOYANCY SKILLS

If there is one skill that determines a person's diving ability, it is buoyancy control. Buoyancy control consists of numerous skills that you can learn quickly by understanding and applying some basic principles. Proper buoyancy control makes diving easier, adds to your enjoyment, and helps protect the underwater environment.

Many factors affect your buoyancy in the water. You must be aware of all of them and you must know the various means that are available to you for remaining in control of your buoyancy at all times. The four major ways you affect your buoyancy are through:

- The type of protective suit you wear.
- The amount of weight you wear.
- The amount of air in your BC or dry suit.
- The amount of air in your lungs.

You must begin your dive properly weighted if you want to easily adjust your buoyancy under water. You fine-tune your buoyancy by the amount of air you have in your lungs. You must always keep breathing, but you can take shallower breaths to be less buoyant or deeper breaths to be more buoyant.

If you are learning to dive using a dry suit, you will use the dry suit instead of your BC to control your buoyancy at depth. You use the BC for surface flotation and as a backup for buoyancy under water.

When you pick up objects under water and carry them with you, it will probably be necessary for you to increase your buoyancy to offset their weight.

Checking Your Buoyancy at the Surface

If you are properly weighted, you should be able to hover at 4 meters (15 feet) with 34 bar (500 psi) or less of air in your cylinder. You must test your buoyancy at the surface before you begin your dive. To test your buoyancy for scuba diving, use the following steps:

1. Make sure that your BC is completely deflated.
2. Assume an upright position in the water.
3. Take in a deep breath and hold it while you hang in the water motionless. If you are properly weighted, you will float at eye level.
4. Exhale completely. If you sink, you are properly weighted.
5. As soon as you sink, kick back to the surface and inflate your BC.

This procedure gives you an approximation of correct buoyancy adjustment. You will fine-tune your buoyancy adjustment as you gain experience in using different types of equipment (for example, exposure suit worn, type of cylinder used, and size of cylinder used) and diving in salt and fresh water.

Your buoyancy will change during your dive because of the compression of your diving suit, the amount of air in your BC, the items you collect during your dive, and the use of air in your cylinder. You will control your buoyancy during your dive by adding to or removing air from your dry suit or BC.

Descending

Being able to descend easily in the water is one of the important skills of diving. Diving is not much fun if you have to struggle to get to the bottom. Some of the general steps for descending are:

1. Have your regulator in your mouth.
2. Note the exact time that you leave the surface. If you are using a dive computer, it will automatically start timing your dive when you leave the surface. However, a dive computer does not always record the time of day you leave the surface. Having a slate or your dive table in your BC pocket is a good place to record the time.
3. Deflate your BC. If you are weighted correctly,

FIGURE 3-45. REMEMBER TO EQUALIZE EARLY AND OFTEN DURING YOUR DESCENT.

you will slowly sink when all the air is removed from your BC and you exhale. Remember to hold the power inflator hose over your head and watch its mouthpiece to see the air coming out as you go under water. Stop pressing the deflator/oral inflator valve button when you do not see any more air to prevent large amounts of water from entering the BC.

4. Equalize your ears as you start your descent and continuously throughout your descent (figure 3-45). **Never** continue descending if you feel pressure in your ears and you cannot equalize them. You will not feel discomfort if you are equalizing properly.

5. Exhale and begin your feet-first descent (figure 3-46). Remember to breathe out completely and then take in a small breath of air. The less air you have in your lungs during the first few feet of descent, the easier your descent will be. If you descend feet first, you can maintain better contact with your buddy and it will be easier to equalize pressure in your ears, mask, and sinuses.

6. Stay with your buddy as you descend. Remain close enough to touch each other and maintain eye contact throughout the descent. If one buddy is having trouble equalizing, the other buddy must be patient and wait with them until the problem is corrected.

Diving Skills

FIGURE 3-46. DESCENDING FEET FIRST GIVES YOU BETTER CONTROL OF YOUR SPEED, BUOYANCY, AND ABILITY TO CLEAR YOUR EARS.

Your rate of descent should not be rapid. The recommended rate of descent is no faster than 23 meters (75 feet) per minute.

When you are wearing a wetsuit and make descents in open water, you will lose buoyancy as the pressure of the water compresses your wetsuit. You will need to add small amounts of air to your BC to compensate for the compression of the wetsuit. You must never sink out of control. You should be able to stop your descent at any time just by inhaling a full breath of air. If you are wearing a dry suit, you will add air to the dry suit instead of your BC to control your buoyancy.

As your wetsuit compresses, it can also loosen your weight belt if the weight belt is not a compensating type. Your wetsuit loses thickness as it compresses and causes your weight belt to become loose around your waist. When this happens, the buckle can shift position, making it difficult to locate. The weight belt could even slide down around your legs or fall off. Remember to check your belt as you descend and then check it again as you reach the bottom. Tighten the weight belt if necessary.

Use your fins as little as possible during your descent. You should control your descent by your buoyancy, not by kicking. As you get close to the bottom, kicking can stir up clouds of silt, ruin the visibility and harm the environment. If you take in a deep breath of air and continue to descend, you are too heavy and you need to add air to your BC to help slow your descent.

Controlled Descents

Because so many things are happening at once during a descent, your first one will be a *controlled descent*. This means you will descend on a line or along the contour of the bottom. Doing a controlled descent will allow you to concentrate on equalizing pressure, maintaining buddy contact, and controlling your buoyancy.

Free Descents

Once you are comfortable with controlled descents, your instructor will introduce you to *free descents*. Free descents are vertical descents in open water without a line. When you can execute free descents in a controlled manner, you will be well on your way to becoming a capable diver.

During the Dive

During your dive, your goal is to maintain what divers call neutral buoyancy (figure 3-47). Neutral buoyancy is a state in which you neither sink nor float

FIGURE 3-47. MAINTAINING NEUTRAL BUOYANCY WHILE UNDER WATER IS THE KEY TO ENJOYABLE DIVING.

when at rest. As you go deeper in the water, you will add small amounts of air to your BC to offset wetsuit compression or to your dry suit to achieve neutral buoyancy. You add just a small amount of air to your BC (or dry suit) and then check to see if you are still sinking by slowing your activity and breathing normally. If you are still sinking, add another small amount of air to your BC (or dry suit).

As you ascend or you feel yourself rising in the water because of the expansion of air, you will need to vent small amounts of air from your BC (or dry suit) to maintain neutral buoyancy. How much air you need to vent and how often you need to vent it depends on your situation and your depth.

To vent air from your BC (or dry suit), you must get into the necessary position first. Dump valves are usually located on the upper left shoulder of your BC and on the upper left arm of a dry suit. Some BCs have extra dump valves on either the lower back or top right side of the BC. If you have an extra dump valve, ask your instructor how to operate it.

Slow your activity and your kicking from time to time to test your buoyancy. If you float up without kicking, you are too buoyant and need to vent some air. If you sink, you need to add a little air. You should strive to control your buoyancy so well that you can stop at any depth any time and remain suspended there without using your fins or hands. This technique is how you evaluate your buoyancy control and will be a part of your open-water training.

Ascending

For every descent you make, you must also make an ascent. Some of the general procedures for doing an ascent are:

1. Stop a minute and secure any accessories you are carrying. For example, if you are carrying a goody bag, close it and clip it to your BC.
2. Make sure your automatic exhaust valve will open if you are wearing a dry suit.
3. Find your power-inflator hose and your deflator/oral inflator valve button and hold the hose up over your head. If you are wearing a dry

FIGURE 3-48. IF YOU ARE WEARING A DRY SUIT, YOU MUST VENT AIR FROM THE SUIT AS YOU ASCEND.

suit, raise the exhaust valve until it is level with or above your shoulder (figure 3-48). Holding the hose over your head also ensures that your hand will run into an overhead object before your head will.
4. Give your buddy the up signal.
5. Start swimming slowly towards the surface with your buddy. Remember to look up and around as you are surfacing and breathe normally (figure 3-49).
6. Control your buoyancy and your ascent by venting air from your BC (or dry suit). Your rate of ascent must not exceed a speed of 9 meters (30 feet) per minute if you are using dive tables.
This is only 15 centimeters (6 inches) per second and is much slower than you naturally want to proceed. If you are using a computer, following it will control your rate of ascent, and it might be slower than 9 meters (30 feet) per minute.
7. Slow your ascent when you get to 9 meters (30 feet).
8. Stop at a depth of 4 meters (15 feet) for 3 min-

FIGURE 3-49. YOUR NORMAL ASCENT SHOULD ALWAYS BE SLOW AND CONTROLLED.

FIGURE 3-50. IF YOU ARE PROPERLY WEIGHTED, YOU SHOULD BE ABLE TO HOVER AT 4 METERS (15 FEET) WITH 34 BAR (500 PSI) OR LESS OF AIR IN YOUR CYLINDER FOR A PRECAUTIONARY DECOMPRESSION STOP.

utes to do a precautionary decompression stop (figure 3-50). If you can perform the stop while hanging onto a line or by following the contour of the bottom, it makes the stop easier.

9. Proceed to the surface, inflate your BC, switch from your regulator to your snorkel if desired, and record the time you surfaced.

When you first start diving, it will help if you time your ascents and compare the ascent time with your depth gauge so you can determine your rate of ascent. You must develop a feel for the correct rate. Your instructor will help you do this. A slow ascent rate is important because the dive tables are based on a slow ascent rate. If you rise too quickly, decompression sickness can result.

Verify What You Have Learned

Review the following questions about buoyancy:

18. What are three steps you should take to prepare for a descent?

_____

_____

_____

_____

19. What three actions do you perform on every descent?

_____

_____

_____

20. What three actions do you perform on a normal ascent?

_____

_____

_____

_____

21. Four major factors that affect your buoyancy are

_____,

_____, _____,

and _____.

22. On ascent, as the air in your BC or dry suit starts to expand, you must

_____

_____.

SAFETY SKILLS

There are some important safety skills you must master to be a responsible diver. Your goal is to never have to use these skills, but you must always be prepared in case you or your buddy have a problem. The important safety skills are:

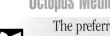

- Sharing air with another diver.
- Being able to perform independent controlled emergency ascents.

Sharing Air with Another Diver

If your buddy forgets to check their pressure gauge at depth and runs out of air, you must know how to share air with your buddy. If you have a contingency air supply, such as a *pony bottle*, that is the best method of sharing air with your buddy.

If you do not have a contingency air supply, there are two major ways to share your air supply with your buddy: the alternate air source or octopus method and the buddy breathing method. These methods are called dependent ascents because your buddy is dependent on your air supply.

Octopus Method

The preferred method of sharing air with another diver is for your buddy to breathe from two separate regulator which you supply. This might be a secondary regulator attached to your air supply (an octopus regulator or other alternate air source regulator). This technique is the *octopus method* of breathing (figure 3-51).

The exact procedure you use for sharing air with an alternate air source depends on your equipment configuration and personal preference. You must work out how you will share air in an emergency before you start your dive. Your buddy must know which regulator to use, where to find it, and how it is attached to your BC or your equipment. If they don't, and they run out of air during the dive, they might grab for the first regulator they see – usually the one that is in your mouth! Although this regulator might be the one you plan to pass, you want to pass it in a controlled manner.

FIGURE 3-51. SHARING AIR WITH A BACK-UP SECOND STAGE IS THE PREFERRED DEPENDENT METHOD OF SHARING AIR.

FIGURE 3-52. ASCENDING IN AN EMERGENCY REQUIRES COORDINATING. SIGNAL YOUR BUDDY WHEN READY.

Your buddy will find that breathing from your extra regulator is just as easy as breathing from their own regulator. However, ascending will take some coordination (figure 3-52). You and your buddy must ascend at the same speed by maintaining physical and eye contact.

The general steps to the octopus method of sharing air are:

1. Give your buddy the appropriate regulator for your equipment configuration when they signal that they are out of air.

FIGURE 3-53. MAINTAIN PHYSICAL CONTACT THROUGHOUT YOUR ENTIRE OCTOPUS ASCENT.

2. Hold on to them with one hand and position your buddy in front of you. This position allows your buddy to keep the mouthpiece of the secondary regulator easily in their mouth and allows you both to maintain physical and eye contact (figure 3-53).

3. Ask your buddy if they are okay and wait for a reply.

4. Give your buddy the up signal and wait for their reply before starting your ascent. Once your buddy is breathing and is okay, you should carry out your normal ascent procedure. The normal ascent rate is 9 meters (30 feet) per minute if you are using dive tables.

If you are using a redundant contingency scuba system, you should still perform the steps of ascending together after you pass the system to your buddy.

Buddy Breathing Method

The other method of sharing air with your buddy is the *buddy breathing method*. If you do not have a secondary regulator or redundant contingency scuba system, you share air by passing your primary regulator back and forth. This procedure is simple, but requires a higher level of skill from you and your buddy. Buddy breathing and ascending at the same time can be done successfully with training and practice in confined water. However, you must frequently review the steps if buddy breathing is to be successful when it might be needed.

If your scuba is not set up with a secondary regulator, you should rehearse buddy-breathing techniques before entering the water. You should practice again in shallow water at the beginning of every dive to renew your skills and coordinate procedures.

Use the following steps for buddy breathing:

1. Take a deep breath of air and start exhaling when your buddy gives you the out of air signal.

2. Grasp your buddy's right shoulder strap with your left hand.

3. Hold your regulator by the hose and near the mouthpiece and remove it from your mouth, using your right hand. Turn the mouthpiece down so the regulator does not freeflow. Keep exhaling a small stream of bubbles.

4. Pass the regulator to your buddy by the hose and let them guide the regulator into their mouth. Always give them access to the purge button so they can clear the second stage of water.

5. Continue to use your left hand to hold your

buddy by the right shoulder of their BC.

6. Allow your buddy to take two breaths of air from the regulator and then pass the regulator back to you. Never let go of the hose. You must maintain contact and control of your air supply at all times.

7. Take two breaths of air from the regulator and then pass the regulator back to your buddy.

8. Give your buddy the up signal and wait for their up signal back and begin your ascent when the situation is stabilized.

9. Repeat the exchange process while doing a slow, controlled ascent to the surface. Once you start buddy breathing and ascending, do not try to change rhythm or techniques during the ascent.

During buddy breathing, you must remember to exhale small bubbles whenever the regulator is out of your mouth. You and your buddy must control your buoyancy and you must maintain physical contact.

Unless you practice buddy breathing on a regular basis, it is unrealistic to expect that you could perform it in an emergency. Divers who are not skilled in buddy breathing but attempt to do it anyway during an emergency risk serious injury.

FIGURE 3-54. KEEP THE REGULATOR IN YOUR MOUTH WHEN DOING AN EMERGENCY ASCENT.

Independent Emergency Ascents

If you run out of air and you cannot obtain air from your buddy, you must make an independent ascent to the surface. There are two types of emergency ascents: swimming and buoyant. The one you do depends primarily on your status at the time you realize you are out of air.

Swimming

You do an *emergency swimming ascent* when you run out of air at shallower depths (about 18 meters or 60 feet). They can be done from greater depths but contingency air supply is superior and recommended for deeper water diving. You simply look up to maintain an open airway and swim to the surface while exhaling a continuous stream of bubbles from your regulator (figure 3-54). You always keep the regulator in your mouth during an emergency swimming ascent, because as the water pressure decreases, you will get another small breath of air from your cylinder. You must also remember to be ready to vent air from your BC to control your buoyancy during the ascent.

During your NAUI Scuba Diver certification course, you will practice emergency swimming ascents (ESAs) during your confined-water training sessions. During these sessions, your instructor will tell you to inhale and then start your ascent. You must remember that in a real emergency, you will exhale and then try to take a breath but little or no air will be available. You will also discover that the expanding air flows out from your lungs almost naturally with very little effort on your part.

Buoyant

You do a *buoyant emergency ascent* when you run out of air at greater depths. You drop your weight belt and gently exhale all the way to the surface.

If you are wearing a wetsuit and drop your weight belt, you must get yourself horizontal in the water and be facing up to create as much surface area as possible to slow your ascent as you approach the surface. You

Diving Skills

must also remember to vent air from your BC to slow your ascent. Your ascent rate will increase due to the buoyancy of your wetsuit and its expansion.

If you are in warm water and drop your weight belt, you will have to swim to the surface. However, not having the extra weight will help make your ascent easier.

General Guidelines

If you find yourself without air, you might wonder which method of ascent you should use. The method you should use depends on the situation, but the following general guidelines should help you decide which method to use:

- Discuss and agree on emergency procedures with your buddy before your dive. This discussion should include the signals you will use in an emergency and your respective equipment configurations.
- The optimal method of knowing that you have air in an emergency is to carry a contingency air supply like a pony bottle. This is the easiest and safest method for reaching the surface if you find that your primary scuba unit is not providing air. Simply place the backup regulator in your mouth, clear it, and continue breathing as you ascend.
- A dependent ascent, breathing from your buddy's air supply, is better than an independent swimming or buoyant ascent because you have a supply of air during the ascent. Breathing from your buddy's back-up regulator is better than trying to perform buddy breathing. Remember that buddy breathing takes practice and you and your buddy must both be comfortable with buddy breathing.
- You should consider doing an independent ascent only if your buddy is not available.

It should be obvious that not running out of air in the first place is the best course of action. Monitor your submersible pressure gauge frequently during your dive to avoid running out of air. Making this one of your diving habits will ensure that all of your ascents will be normal ascents and you will not need to worry about decisions regarding emergency ascents.

Verify What You Have Learned

Review the following questions about safety skills:

23. Each diver should take _____ breaths when sharing air with one regulator.

24. How do you know which of your buddy's two regulators to use during an assisted ascent?

_____

_____

25. If you are planning to use buddy breathing in an emergency, you should

_____

_____

26. When is it appropriate to choose a buoyant emergency ascent?

_____

_____

BUDDY SYSTEM

It is easy to keep track of your buddy in controlled conditions where the visibility is good and the area is limited. Maintaining contact with your buddy in open water is not as easy. Diving is fun, but it is not as fun if you spend most of your time looking for your buddy.

If you use the following points to keep track of your buddy, diving will be very enjoyable:

- Agree on a leader for each dive.
- Discuss the dive before you get in the water and agree on the location, purpose, activity, and general course you will follow under water.
- Maintain your same position relative to one another for your entire dive. If you start out on the right side of your buddy, stay on the right side for the entire dive. It is more enjoyable to dive side by side than for one of you to be in front and the other buddy following behind.
- Establish your direction of travel under water and then follow that heading until you or your buddy suggest a change or stop with a clear signal. Make sure your buddy acknowledges the signal before you change direction. If you do get separated from your buddy, you will

have a general idea of where to locate your buddy.

- Use the lost buddy procedure if you do lose your buddy. The common procedure is:

  1. Get yourself vertical in the water and look in all directions for your buddy or their bubbles (figure 3-55). If you are in low visibility water (3 meters or 10 feet or less), return to where you last saw your buddy and start your search there.

  2. Rise about 3 meters (10 feet) in the water and look again for your buddy or their bubbles if you did not find them the first time.

  3. Ascend slowly to the surface after a minute if you do not see your buddy. Keep turning as you ascend and look for your buddy or their bubbles.

  4. Surface, note your position relative to two points on the shore, and wait for your buddy. When your buddy surfaces, get back together and continue your dive.

  5. Use one of the following options, depending on your circumstances:

     - If you are diving where help is readily available to assist you in a search for a lost buddy, signal for help if your buddy does not surface within 5 minutes. It is your role in the emergency to contact and guide the help.

     - If you are diving in a remote location, you might be your buddy's only source of help if your buddy is in trouble under water and minutes are critical. You will have to search for your lost buddy within your capability to do so, and be prepared to render aid as needed. Before you put yourself in this type of situation, prepare by taking the NAUI Advanced Scuba Diver course and the NAUI Scuba Rescue Diver course.

As you and your buddy gain experience together and get to know one another, it will become easier to stay together. You will become familiar with each other's diving styles and you will be able to function as a true team with minimal effort. Developing this harmony should be your goal, because diving with a good buddy is diving at its best.

Your buddy also makes working with equipment easier. For example, if your cylinder slips out of its tank strap under water, it is easier for your buddy to refasten the cylinder than for you to take off your BC and fix the cylinder yourself (figure 3-56). A good buddy is more likely to notice developing problems, such as a loose tank strap, before you do.

FIGURE 3-55. BE UPRIGHT IN THE WATER AND LOOK IN ALL DIRECTIONS FOR YOUR LOST BUDDY.

FIGURE 3-56. IT IS MUCH EASIER TO SOLVE PROBLEMS UNDER WATER IF YOU WORK WITH YOUR BUDDY.

Verify What You Have Learned

Review the following questions about the buddy system:

27. Three recommended techniques that help maintain buddy contact while diving are

_____,

_____, and

_____.

28. The steps to the recommended lost buddy plan are: _____

_____

_____

_____

_____

_____

_____

COMMUNICATION

There are standard signals you need to know to communicate under water as well as on the surface. The NAUI Diving Hand Signals are standard in the United States diving community and are usually recognized in other countries as well (figure 3-57). As a certified diver, you must be able to correctly identify and use each signal. Once you start using them, they are easy to remember.

Remember, for a signal to be effective, all concerned must discuss it and agree upon it before you start the dive. Proper use of signals is necessary for every dive. Be sure to discuss the signals you are accustomed to using with any new buddy.

Underwater Communication

You probably realize by now that communication is not easy under water. When you give a hand signal, you must display it distinctly and you must wait for a response from your buddy. Your buddy acknowledges the signal by either repeating the signal or giving you the okay signal (figure 3-58). Along with the standard hand signals, divers create their own hand signals. Some divers even learn American Sign Language to expand their vocabulary for underwater communication. Always remember to review your hand signals with your buddy before each dive.

You can write messages to your buddy on an underwater slate (figure 3-59). This is a handy way to give detailed messages. You can also use the sense of touch to communicate. You can touch your buddy to gain their attention or to let another diver know you are nearby. Try to avoid touching another diver when you are behind them, especially if they are not aware of your presence. It is easy to frighten someone in this situation.

You can use and hear audible signals under water although you cannot determine sound sources by direction under water. You or a boat can produce sound signals. Diver-produced audible signals include rapping on your cylinder with a knife or other hard object, or using special full-face masks or devices that allow you to speak to your buddy under the water.

FIGURE 3-57. EVERY DIVER SHOULD USE THESE STANDARD SIGNALS.

FIGURE 3-58. THE OKAY SIGNAL IS BOTH A QUESTION AND AN ANSWER. YOU WILL USE THIS SIGNAL REPEATEDLY.

FIGURE 3-59. UNDERWATER SLATES ARE AN EASY WAY TO SHOW YOUR BUDDY A DETAILED MESSAGE.

Most charter boats have an underwater recall device that sounds like a siren. If you hear the recall signal while you are under water, you must surface and look to the boat for instructions. They might need to reposition the anchor and just want to see where all their divers are, or they might need to have everyone return to the boat because of an emergency.

Surface Communication

At the surface, you can use different types of audible and visual signals to communicate. You use some of the standard hand signals at the surface. For example, if you wave to someone from the surface, it is a sign of distress, **NOT** a way to say hello.

FIGURE 3-60. IF YOU SEE THE RECALL FLAG FLYING ON YOUR CHARTER BOAT, YOU MUST RETURN IMMEDIATELY TO THE BOAT.

Dive boats have a blue and white flag that they fly when they want divers to return to the boat (figure 3-60). When you surface and see this flag, return immediately to the boat.

Audible communication is possible at the surface, but yelling is not effective at a long distance over the water. A whistle produces a loud sound that you can hear at a considerable distance. Also, using a whistle does not take a lot of energy. A repeated series of four short blasts on a whistle is a standard distress signal.

Verify What You Have Learned

Review the following questions about communication:
29. The four ways of communicating under water are _____, _____, _____, and _____.
30. The two ways of communicating at the surface are _____ and _____.
31. When you are given a hand signal under water, you must _____.
32. What is the most important point to remember regarding diving communication?

_____

_____

Diving Skills

HANDLING YOUR SCUBA EQUIPMENT IN THE WATER

Usually you don your scuba equipment out of the water, go diving, and then remove your equipment after you get out of the water. There will be times when you need to don or remove your equipment in the water. For example, the boat you are using might be too small to permit much equipment handling while you are on board.

You might also need to adjust an item of gear in the water and will need to remove it to adjust it. If your scuba unit is caught in fishing line or kelp, you can remove the unit so you can see the problem and correct it.

Removing and Replacing Your Scuba Unit on the Surface and Underwater

Removing your scuba unit in the water is as easy as removing a jacket (figure 3-61).

Use the following steps to get out of your scuba unit:

1. Unclip any buckles you have on the front of the BC.
2. Undo the waistband.
3. Pull your left arm out of the left armhole of the BC and use your right arm to pull the scuba unit around to your right.

There are many ways to don your scuba unit (figure 3-62). Your instructor will show you the way they want you to don your unit.

One method you might be shown is to don the unit over your head. To don your scuba unit by passing it over your head, use the following steps:

1. Position your BC in front of you with the cylinder under the BC. The first stage of the regulator is toward you and the second stage is in your mouth.
2. Keep the hose for your second stage between your arms. If you do not have the hose between your arms, the hose will be trapped under your shoulder strap when you lower the cylinder in place.
3. Slip your arms into the armholes of the BC until the unit is above your elbows. It will seem like

FIGURE 3-61. REMOVING YOUR SCUBA UNIT IN THE WATER IS AS EASY AS REMOVING A JACKET.

you are putting the unit on upside down.
4. Grasp either side of the tank with each hand.
5. Slide the unit over your head and down your back as you arch your back.
6. Feel around your waist for the two ends of your waistband or strap.
7. Fasten your waistband or strap snugly and re-clip any buckles at the front of your BC.
8. Straighten out your second stage regulator hose and reposition the mouthpiece comfortably in your mouth.

If you are on the surface, you want your scuba unit to be buoyant so it will float. If you are on the bottom, you want the scuba unit to be negative while donning it.

FIGURE 3-62. REMEMBER TO WORK AT A SLOW AND STEADY PACE WHEN DONNING YOUR SCUBA UNIT IN THE WATER.

Always breathe from your regulator when you are donning the scuba unit. When you are at the surface, you will slip under water as you pass the cylinder over your head and the regulator will give you a source of air.

You must learn to refasten your waistband and buckles by feel. Before you refasten your waistband and clips, feel to be sure that your straps are not twisted and your hoses are not trapped.

Work at a slow and steady pace when removing and replacing your scuba unit. You should be able you handle your equipment independently, but there is nothing wrong with asking your buddy for assistance if you have difficulty. An extra set of hands and eyes is useful and saves time.

Removing and Replacing Your Weight Belt on the Surface and Underwater

Handling a weight belt in the water can be awkward, but with practice, working with a weight belt is not as difficult as it seems.

There are a few important points to remember when working with weight belts:
- Always handle a belt by the free end to prevent the weights from slipping off the belt.
- Gravity will pull the belt towards the bottom unless you support the belt with your body.

- Keep your body in a horizontal position at all times when removing and replacing the weight belt.
- Work at a slow and steady pace when removing and replacing the weight belt.

To remove the weight belt to discard it or to hand it out of the water, use the following steps:
1. Undo the buckle and pull the tail of the weight belt free of the buckle.
2. Hold the free end of the weight belt in one hand and pull the belt completely away from your body. The weights will hang in a direct line towards the bottom (figure 3-63).
3. Release the weight belt. If you are handing the weight belt out of the water, be sure that the person you are handing it to has a firm grip on the weight belt before you let go.

You use the same procedure to remove and replace your weight belt on the bottom as you do on the surface. Your instructor will show you the procedure they want you to use.

If you use a right-hand release to your weight belt, one method to remove and replace your weight belt in the water is as follows:
1. Assume a facedown position in the water.
2. Undo the buckle and pull the tail of the weight belt free of the buckle.

FIGURE 3-63. ALWAYS PULL THE WEIGHT BELT COMPLETELY CLEAR OF YOUR BODY BEFORE DROPPING IT.

3. Hold the free end of the weight belt in your right hand and pull the weight belt around your right side to your front as you are rotating in the water to your left. Remember that you want to keep your body between the weight belt and the bottom.
4. Make your modifications to your weight belt.
5. Hold the weight belt with the buckle in your left hand, the free end in your right hand, and be sure that there are no twists in the belt.
6. Transfer the buckle to your right hand and move the entire weight belt down so that your right thigh supports it.
7. Drop the buckle and rotate your body to the left. The weight belt will drape across your thighs.
8. Reach down your left side with your left hand and feel for the buckle.
9. Slide the weight belt up your back and position it under your cylinder and BC at your waist.
10. Re-buckle the weight belt securely.

If you use a left-hand release to your weight belt, you can use the previous procedure with the opposite hand and rotating in the opposite direction.

Verify What You Have Learned

Review the following questions about handling your scuba equipment in the water:

33. The primary difference between donning your cylinder at the surface and donning your cylinder under water is

_____

_____.

34. You can keep your regulator hose from becoming trapped when you don your cylinder over your head by

_____

_____.

35. Handling your weight belt is easier if you remember to _____

and _____.

NAVIGATION SKILLS

When you are out of the water, you are constantly using navigation skills. Maps, street signs, and land-marks help you locate a destination and return you to your starting point. There are no street signs under water, but you can use a combination of natural and compass navigation to keep track of your location and travel during a dive. This section will introduce you to some of the fundamentals of underwater navigation. You can learn more about this necessary skill in a NAUI Underwater Navigation Specialty course.

Natural Navigation

You can avoid long surface swims by ending your dives at predetermined locations. To know where you are and be able to get where you want to go and back, is the objective of underwater navigation. By recognizing and using natural aids to navigation, you can achieve this objective.

Natural aids under water will soon become as useful to you as street signs. Ripple marks in the sand on the bottom form parallel to the shore. As you get closer to shore, the ripple marks get closer together. This fact gives you one useful reference. The positions of the sun and shadows at the start of your dive are another useful reference.

The back-and-forth movement of water close to shore is known as *surge*. The movement is usually toward and away from shore, so this gives you another clue to your location.

The water gets deeper as you go further away from shore and shallower as you return to shore or approach reefs. You will see underwater *landmarks*, such as rock formations, large and unique plants, crevices, and wrecks (figure 3-64).

You and your buddy can keep track of your position under water and be able to return to your starting point without surfacing by paying attention to all of these natural aids.

FIGURE 3-64. REEF FORMATIONS ARE EXCELLENT NATURAL AIDS FOR NAVIGATION.

Compass Navigation

When you dive at night or in water with limited visibility, natural aids are not as helpful to you. You must rely more on a compass and your depth gauge. Using a compass allows you to navigate by *dead reckoning*, which can be very accurate. The compass shows you directions and your depth gauge tells you your vertical position in the water.

A diving compass must be filled with liquid to withstand pressure underwater, have a reference line called a *lubber line* and have a means, such as a *rotating bezel*, to show that you are on a selected bearing or direction (figure 3-65). Because a compass is magnetic, *ferrous metal* (iron or steel) objects close to it will affect it.

When you use a compass, you keep the lubber line aligned with the centerline of your body. You can wear your compass on your wrist or mount it on your console with the rest of your diving instruments (figure 3-66). Where you carry the compass is not critical; having it aligned with your body is. When you reference your compass, always be sure that you are lined up with the lubber line and that the compass is level.

The compass needle always points to magnetic north. If you point the lubber line towards shore, the compass needle points to one point. Rotate the index

FIGURE 3-65. THE UNDERWATER COMPASS MAKES NAVIGATION ACCURATE DURING A DIVE.

FIGURE 3-66. YOU MUST ALWAYS ALIGN THE COMPASS WITH THE CENTER OF YOUR BODY.

FIGURE 3-67. YOU MUST ALWAYS ALIGN THE LUBBER LINE WITH YOUR BODY AND WITH THE DIRECTION YOU WANT TO SWIM.

marks on the bezel to mark the position of the needle, and you will know that whenever the compass needle is pointing in between the marks, you are swimming towards shore. If the compass needle points opposite the marks, you know you are heading away from shore.

When you decide to begin your dive in a certain direction, you sight over the level compass and set the index marks on the rotating bezel so that they line up with the compass needle. Then, by keeping yourself aligned with the lubber line, and the compass needle aligned with the index marks, you can maintain your course very accurately (figure 3-67). Usually, you only need to reference the compass occasionally to make sure you are on course. If you need to navigate precisely, you must reference the compass frequently.

A *reciprocal course* is made when your outbound course is a straight line and halfway through your dive, you make a 180° turn, which the compass enables you to do precisely. To make a 180° turn, you swivel around until your compass needle is directly opposite your original reference marker.

Even if you do not follow a specific pattern during your dive, the compass can still be helpful. You and your buddy can surface near the end of your dive, line up the lubber line with your body and the direction of your exit point, set your bearing with the index marks on the bezel, submerge, and follow that heading to your destination. Swimming under water is usually easier than swimming on the surface.

Simple navigational techniques make diving more enjoyable. Knowing where you are underwater will help you avoid long surface swims and help you to relocate interesting areas. You will save time, air, and be able to spend more time enjoying the objective of your dive.

You must be able to perform the basics of navigation that you will learn in your NAUI Scuba Diver certification course. To learn more about underwater navigation, enroll in a NAUI continuing education course, such as the NAUI Advanced Scuba Diver certification course, or a specialty course such as Search and Recovery Diving.

Verify What You Have Learned

Review the following questions about navigation:

36. Three natural aids to navigation are

_____, _____, and _____.

37. When you are using a compass for navigation, you should_____ and _____.

38. A reciprocal course is a

_____.

DISASSEMBLING YOUR SCUBA GEAR

After diving, you must disassemble your scuba gear and rinse it with fresh water. To disassemble your scuba unit, use the following steps:

1. Turn off your air. The cylinder valve turns off in a clockwise direction.

2. Push and hold the purge button on one of your second stages or power inflator to relieve all the air pressure in the hoses of your regulator (figure 3-68).

3. Unscrew the yoke screw from the cylinder valve (figure 3-69) or unscrew the DIN regulator from the DIN valve.

4. Dry the dust cap attached to the first stage of your regulator (figure 3-70).

5. Replace the dust cap over the inlet to the first stage of your regulator and tighten the yoke screw until

FIGURE 3-68. PURGE THE AIR FROM YOUR REGULATOR AFTER YOU HAVE TURNED OFF YOUR CYLINDER.

FIGURE 3-69. THE YOKE SCREW UNSCREWS EASILY ONCE YOU HAVE PURGED YOUR REGULATOR.

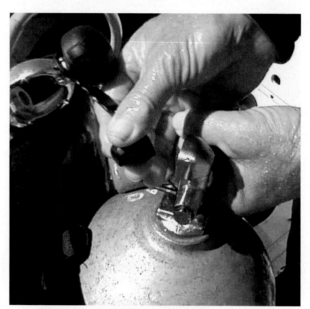

FIGURE 3-70. BE SURE TO DRY THE DUST CAP.

FIGURE 3-71. REPLACE YOUR DUST CAP OVER THE FIRST STAGE AND TIGHTEN THE YOKE SCREW FINGER TIGHT.

it is finger tight (figure 3-71). If you have a DIN regulator, screw in the dust cap.

6. Remove your BC from the cylinder.
7. Turn the BC upside down so that the power-inflator hose attachment point is the lowest point. This will allow any water in the BC to drain down into the power-inflator hose.

8. Press the deflator/oral inflator valve button to allow the water to drain out of the power-inflator hose.
9. Rinse your equipment with fresh water and allow it to dry completely before storing it.

Diving Skills

CONCLUSION

Breathing under water is not difficult. The hardest part of scuba diving physically is putting the gear on, and even that becomes easy with experience. You need to develop certain breathing habits for some circumstances, but other than that, there isn't much to learn about breathing on scuba.

You will soon find yourself feeling confident about handling your equipment in the water. The more practice and experience you have, the easier it will become. Your goal is to make working with your equipment as easy as your instructor makes it look.

If you find yourself struggling with your gear, this indicates that you do not understand something about how your gear works. Learn to work slowly and deliberately. Think of the steps involved in performing a skill with an item of gear and then execute them one at a time. Practice will help make the steps blend together into a natural motion for you.

Learning the other skills of diving, such as buoyancy control, entries, and emergency procedures requires more training and practice. You will start to develop these skills during your NAUI Scuba Diver certification course and will polish them with additional NAUI continuing education courses (figure 3-72).

FIGURE 3-72. DIVING IN OPEN WATER REQUIRES YOU TO USE ALL OF THE SKILLS YOU WILL LEARN DURING YOUR NAUI SCUBA DIVER CERTIFICATION COURSE.

CHAPTER

4

Diving Science

LEARNING GOALS

In this chapter you will:

- Learn about some of the characteristics of air and water.
- Be introduced to the concept of buoyancy and how if affects you under water.
- Understand the concept of pressure and how it affects the volume and density of air in a closed container.
- Learn how the pressure of the water affects the air spaces in your body and how to prevent problems occurring from the pressure changes.
- Be introduced to different types of lung overexpansion injuries and how to prevent them.
- Learn about the indirect effects of pressure on your body by means of the gases you breathe while diving.
- Understand the thermal effects of the air and water temperature and your body.

The underwater world presents a new and totally different environment from the air world in which you live. As you descend below the surface, the increased pressure will have direct and indirect effects on your body. However, most of your time underwater, you will not be aware of or feel these effects.

This chapter addresses physical properties of air and water and ways specific parts of your body are affected while diving. The better you understand these differences, the easier it will be for you to function as a diver.

DIRECT EFFECTS OF PRESSURE

When you descend in water, the force from the combined weight of air and water will increase. This force is called *pressure*. In this chapter, you will learn how pressure increases under water and how it affects your body.

Density and Its Effects

If you pick up one scuba cylinder with air in it at 1 bar (1 atmosphere) and another just like it filled with air to its rated pressure, the second is about 2-4 kg (4-8 lb.)

heavier than the first. This is because the compressed air is more *dense*. *Density* is the mass of an element per unit of volume. The density of a gas depends on its pressure and temperature. The density of a liquid, like water, is constant over a wide range of temperature and pressure.

As you can see from the above example, air has weight. One liter of air weighs 1.25 grams. In the Imperial Measurement System this is usually expressed as 0.08 pounds per one cubic foot of air. One liter of fresh water weighs 1.0 kilogram and one liter of salt water, because of it dissolved salts and minerals, weighs 1.025 kilograms. Again in the Imperial System these are commonly expressed as pounds per cubic foot, that is, 62.4 pounds per cubic foot for fresh water and 64 pounds per cubic foot for salt water.

On the Air You Breathe

Most of the time, we do not think about air, because breathing is an automatic activity and we cannot see or feel the air around us.

Composition

Air is a mixture of different gases. The gases in air are colorless, odorless, and tasteless. Air is composed of approximately 20.9% oxygen, 78% nitrogen, and 1.1% miscellaneous gases, such as argon and carbon dioxide (figure 4-1).

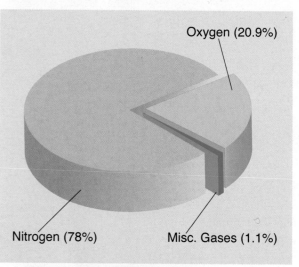

Oxygen (20.9%)

Nitrogen (78%)

Misc. Gases (1.1%)

FIGURE 4-1. AIR IS A MIXTURE OF GASES.

The **most** important component of air to us is oxygen. We cannot survive without oxygen. You can breathe pure oxygen for limited periods, but pure oxygen can be extremely hazardous above and underwater.

Nitrogen is a metabolically *inert* gas. It does not react in our bodies when we breathe it under normal conditions. However, dissolved nitrogen is present in your body, and additional nitrogen is absorbed in your body when you are under increased pressure underwater.

Some divers use special mixtures of gases, such as nitrox, for diving. These mixtures contain different percentages of oxygen and nitrogen than air. Diving with special gas mixtures requires additional training and specialized equipment. The NAUI Enriched Air Nitrox (EAN) Diver Specialty course provides the additional training you will need to dive with nitrox.

Characteristics

Air can be easily compressed. When pressure is applied to a volume of air, it can be forced to occupy a much smaller area. With a compressor, we can squeeze a large amount of air into a smaller space, making it denser than normal and therefore heavier than normal. For example, the compressed air in a scuba cylinder, when released, would fill a space equivalent to a small closet at atmospheric pressure. This is why a full scuba cylinder weighs more than an empty scuba cylinder (figure 4-2).

The air surrounding the earth at sea level is compressed by the weight of the air above it. In other words, the air at sea level is denser than the air at higher levels.

In the Water

Water cannot be significantly compressed. When pressure is applied to water, the pressure is transmitted throughout the water. The density of water at any depth is the same as the density of water at the surface, though the pressure it is under will be greater because of the weight of the water above it. But water is about 800 times denser than air. This and other factors have several effects on us as divers.

Water affects our vision, our ability to distinguish

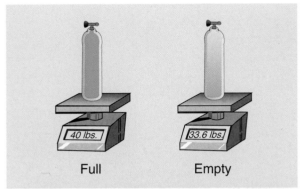

FIGURE 4-2. AIR HAS WEIGHT AS YOU CAN SEE BY THE DIFFERENCE IN WEIGHT BETWEEN AN EMPTY AND FULL SCUBA CYLINDER.

colors, our hearing, our ability to retain heat, and our ability to move through it, compared to air.

Vision

The human eye is designed to focus light rays in air. This is why objects appear blurry when you open your eyes under water. The mask allows you to put an air space in front of your eyes to see without the blur.

As light rays pass from air to water, they slow down and bend. This bending is called *refraction* and it changes the way you see objects under water. Objects appear 1/3 closer and larger than they do in air. Objects are actually further away and smaller than they appear to be under water. Remember this when you are reporting the sighting of an animal or an object. As a new diver, you will find that you reach in front of an object until you learn to compensate for refraction.

Colors

Colors also look much different underwater. Sunlight is composed of a spectrum or a rainbow of visible and invisible colors ranging from infrared to ultraviolet. As light passes through the water, the water absorbs the colors of the spectrum of the sunlight. The first visible color to be absorbed is red, followed by orange, then yellow, then green, then blue, then indigo, and finally violet. At greater depths, the only colors you can see without a dive light are blues and purples.

Diving Science

FIGURE 4-3. THE COLORS SEEN WITH NATURAL LIGHT ARE MUTED.

FIGURE 4-5. SOUND TRAVELS FASTER IN WATER THAN IN AIR.

FIGURE 4-4. ARTIFICIAL LIGHT ALLOWS YOU TO SEE THE TRUE COLOR OF OBJECTS UNDER WATER.

If you take a dive light with you on your dive, and shine it on objects at depth, you will be amazed at the colors you will see. Most underwater photographs are made with artificial light (an electronic flash or strobe) to bring out the magnificent, true colors of the underwater world (figures 4-3 and 4-4).

Hearing

Noises sound different underwater than they do in air. In air, you can tell where a sound is coming from because the sound waves hit one ear slightly before the other. Although the time difference is very short, it is enough for your mind to tell and be able to locate the source of the sound.

Because of the greater density of water compared to air, sound waves travel about four times faster in water than they do in air. The sound waves move so quickly that it is difficult to determine the source of a sound. You can hear the sound getting louder or softer, but you cannot tell its direction. When you hear a noise, you must look all around you to see where the noise is coming from (figure 4-5).

Boat motors, propellers, and jet skis have distinctive sounds underwater. If you want to surface, but hear a boat or jet ski, stay under as long as safely possible or until you hear the boat or jet ski leaving the area. Remember to always fly a *diver down flag* and stay within its perimeter to avoid surfacing in the same area as a boat or jet ski.

Heat Loss

When the air is 27°C (80°F), you think it is warm and comfortable. When you jump into 27°C (80°F) water, the water also feels comfortable at first, but you will notice you start to feel chilled if you remain motionless for a short time.

Because water is much denser than air, water can absorb a great deal of heat without changing its temperature. Also, heat can be conducted out of your body by direct contact with water at a rate nearly 25 times faster than by air.

Your body is transferring heat to the water touching your body to try to get the water as warm as you are. When your body is drained of enough heat, you will be chilled and start to shiver. Shivering is your body's signal to tell you that it can no longer generate enough heat to keep your internal organs warm. When you start to shiver on a dive, you must end your dive and get out of the water to rewarm.

Drag

Have you ever tried to run in water even up to your waist? If so, you know how difficult it is compared to running in air. The water resists your movement. This resistance to movement is called *drag*. Drag is something that you must deal with when diving.

The total frontal area of your body and equipment and its surface configuration also affect your resistance to movement in the water. If your equipment is sleek and compact, it will be easier for you to swim than if your gear has dangling hoses and loose straps. The more you can streamline yourself and your equipment, the easier it will be for you to move through the water. If you are in a horizontal position, you have much less resistance to forward movement than if you are in a semi-upright position (figure 4-6).

Verify What You Have Learned

Review the following questions about density and its effects:

1. Air is approximately _____ oxygen and 78% _____.
2. True or false: Air is denser in the mountains (at altitude) than at sea level.
3. True or false: Water is denser at 30 meters (99 feet) than it is at 3 meters (10 feet).
4. One way you can reduce drag under water is by _____.
5. When you look at objects under water, they appear _____ and _____ than they really are.
6. True or false: Sound travels slower under water.

FIGURE 4-6. STREAMLINING YOUR EQUIPMENT AND YOURSELF MAKES IT MUCH EASIER TO MOVE THROUGH THE WATER.

BUOYANCY

When different objects are placed in water, some float, some sink, and some remain suspended between the surface and the bottom. These objects all have varying densities and this affects their buoyancy. By understanding buoyancy, you can control it to your advantage for diving.

Archimedes Principle

Archimedes, a Greek philosopher, noticed that the level of water in a tub rose when he sat in it. From that observation and other experiments, he found that *an object in a fluid is buoyed up (lifted) by a force equal to the weight of the fluid it displaces.*

FIGURE 4-7. BUOYANCY IS ALWAYS AN UPWARD FORCE TENDING TO CAUSE YOU TO FLOAT, RISE, HOVER, OR SINK LESS QUICKLY.

FIGURE 4-9. YOU WANT TO BE NEUTRALLY BUOYANT DURING YOUR DIVE.

You can observe displacement by filling a glass to its brim with water. If you push a ping-pong ball into the glass, the water runs over the side. The *volume* or amount of water that overflows the glass is the volume that has been displaced.

FIGURE 4-8. YOU WANT TO FLOAT, OR BE BUOYANT WHEN YOU ARE AT THE SURFACE.

If you weigh the water that overflows and the ping-pong ball, you find that the water weighs more than the ping-pong ball. If an object displaces an amount of water weighing more than it does, it floats. If an object displaces an amount of water weighing less than it does, it sinks. If an object displaces an amount of water weighing the same as it does, it hovers.

States of Buoyancy

Buoyancy is always an upward force tending to cause you to float, rise, hover, or sink less quickly (figure 4-7). As a diver, you control your buoyancy primarily by the amount of weight you wear and the amount of air you have in your buoyancy compensator (BC) or dry suit.

Positive

If an object floats, it means the object displaces an amount of water that weighs more than the object does. In other words, the object is less dense than the water. You want to have enough buoyancy to float when you are at the surface before and after you dive (figure 4-8).

Neutral

If an object is neutral, it hovers. This means the object displaces an amount of water that weighs the same as it does. You want to be neutrally buoyant throughout your dive (figure 4-9).

Negative

If an object displaces an amount of water that weighs less than the object does, it sinks. Because the object is denser than the water, the water does not provide sufficient buoyancy to make it hover or float. You want to overcome any buoyancy you have when you begin your dive to be able to get beneath the surface.

Factors Affecting Buoyancy

Your weight and your volume affect your buoyancy. Your weight includes the weight of your body and the weight of your gear (diving suit, weight belt, and scuba unit). Your volume depends on your body size, the thickness of your diving suit, and your gear. Remember, density is mass per unit volume.

Wetsuits are much less dense than water because of the thousands of nitrogen gas bubbles trapped in the neoprene material. If you wear a full 6 mm thick wetsuit and jump in the water without any other gear, it will be impossible for you to sink below the surface. You cannot dive with a heavy wetsuit and a standard 12-liter or 80 cubic foot aluminum cylinder without wearing additional weights.

If you can imagine making a dive in a wetsuit, you can begin to understand how your buoyancy changes over the course of a dive. As you descend, the pressure of the water increases and compresses the gas bubbles in your wetsuit. As the bubbles compress, the wetsuit displaces less water and therefore, loses some of its buoyancy (figure 4-10). You will notice that you are sinking faster and faster the deeper you go. To compensate for the loss of buoyancy, you must add air to your BC, which increases your volume to regain the lost buoyancy.

As you ascend at the end of your dive, the bubbles in your wetsuit and the air in your BC will expand because the pressure of the water is reduced. You will notice that you are rising faster and faster. To compensate for the additional buoyancy, you must vent air from your BC to control your ascent. Uncontrolled ascents are extremely dangerous.

FIGURE 4-10. AS YOU DIVE, THE PRESSURE COMPRESSES YOUR WETSUIT AND MAKES YOU LESS BUOYANT.

The density of the water in which you dive also affects your buoyancy. Salt water is about 2.5% denser than fresh water because of the weight of the minerals dissolved in it. Therefore, you displace more weight in salt water than in fresh water, so you have greater buoyancy in salt water. If you are weighted to be neutral in salt water and you dive in fresh water with the same amount of weight, you will sink. You must recheck your buoyancy if you change from diving in salt water to fresh water and vice versa.

As a diver, you usually want to avoid having so little buoyancy that you must work to maintain your depth or to keep from sinking (figure 4-11). Neutral buoyancy beneath the surface is your constant goal, and it is important to help protect marine life. Divers who land,

Diving Science

FIGURE 4-11. IT IS ACCEPTABLE TO KNEEL IN SAND, BUT IT IS
NOT ACCEPTABLE TO KNEEL ON CORAL, OR OTHER
UNDERWATER CREATURES.

sit, or stand on coral reefs or other marine life can damage or kill these creatures. Diving without buoyancy control is tiring, hazardous, and a sign of an unskilled, unthinking, and uncaring diver.

Buoyancy Checks

Different people have different amounts of personal buoyancy. Some people float higher, some float lower, and some people actually sink, even with their lungs full of air (figure 4-12). You must check to determine your buoyancy in the water.

To check your personal buoyancy, use the following steps, wearing a bathing suit in fresh water:

1. Assume a vertical position in the water. You must remain motionless.
2. Inhale a deep breath of air and hold it. If you can hang motionless at any level, totally submerged, you are neutral. If any part of your head is out of the water, you are buoyant. If you sink, you are not.

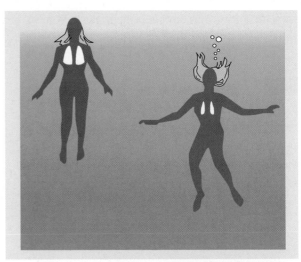

FIGURE 4-12. THE AVERAGE PERSON CAN FLOAT MOTIONLESS AT
THE SURFACE WITH THEIR LUNGS FULL OF AIR.

3. Exhale the air in your lungs. Your chest deflates and you displace less water so you will start to sink, unless you are very buoyant.
4. Kick back to the surface.

You can also try this experiment in salt water to see the difference. Your instructor will recommend how much lead weight you should put on a weight belt based on your personal buoyancy and gear. The lead weights divers wear to adjust buoyancy are many times more dense than water. By selecting the right amount of weight, you can adjust your buoyancy to be neutral at depth.

Before you begin a dive, you must check to see how buoyant you are with your gear on. To check your buoyancy for diving, use the following steps:

1. Assume a vertical position in the water. You must remain motionless.
2. Inhale a normal breath of air and hold it.
3. Vent or dump all of the air from your BC. If you float at eye level, you are properly weighted. If your head is higher out of the water, you are too buoyant. If your head is in the water, you are too heavy.
4. Exhale the air in your lungs. Your chest deflates and you displace less water so you will start to sink.
5. Kick back to the surface and inflate your BC.
6. Change the weight on your weight belt, if neces-

sary. If you were too buoyant, you need to add weight. If you were too heavy, you need to take weight off your weight belt.

If you change equipment or if you lose or gain weight (more than 2.4 kilograms or 5 pounds), you must recheck your buoyancy before you start your next dive.

Verify What You Have Learned

Review the following questions about buoyancy:

7. The three factors affecting buoyancy are

     _____, _____,
     and _____.

8. You can change your buoyancy by

     _____,
     _____, or
     _____.

9. An ocean diver needs to _____ weight to dive in fresh water.

10. During descent, a diver's buoyancy tends to

     _____.

WHAT IS PRESSURE

When you descend in water, the force from the weight of the air and water above you affects you. This force is called pressure and is measured in *bar* or *pounds per square inch (psi)*.

Air

If you weighed a column of air that was 1 centimeter by 1 centimeter and extended all the way to the edge of the atmosphere, you would find that it weighed about 1 kilogram. If it were 1 inch by 1 inch, it would weigh about 14.7 pounds. In other words, this column exerts a pressure of about 1 bar or 14.7 pounds per square inch (psi). This constant pressure is called 1 atmosphere of pressure (figure 4-13).

This atmosphere of pressure is constantly pushing on your body from all directions. However, you usually do not notice it for two reasons. First, your body is com-

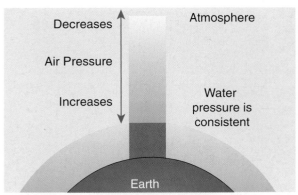

FIGURE 4-13. ONE ATMOSPHERE OF PRESSURE IS ABOUT 1 BAR (14.7 PSI).

posed of mostly fluids, which cannot be compressed. Second, most air spaces in your body, such as your lungs and sinuses, are open to the surrounding atmosphere and its pressure. As long as the pressure in a body's air spaces matches the surrounding atmospheric pressure, the pressure is equalized and you do not feel any effects from your surrounding atmospheric pressure.

Fresh Water

If you took a column of fresh water that was 10.3 meters (34 feet) tall and weighed it, you would also see that it exerted a pressure of about 1 bar (14.7 psi). This equals the pressure exerted by the atmosphere at sea level. Therefore, 10.3 meters (34 feet) of fresh water is also equivalent to 1 atmosphere of pressure.

Because water is not compressible and transmits pressure freely, pressure in water increases at a constant rate, and pressure is cumulative. In other words, 10.3 meters (34 feet) of fresh water is 1 atmosphere, 20.7 meters (68 feet) of fresh water is 2 atmosphere, 31 meters (102 feet) of fresh water is 3 atmosphere, and so on.

Salt Water

If you took a column of salt water that was 10 meters (33 feet) tall and weighed it, you would also see that it exerted a pressure of about 1 bar (14.7 pounds per square inch). This equals the pressure exerted by the atmosphere at sea level. Therefore, 10 meters (33 feet) of seawater is also equivalent to 1 atmosphere of pressure.

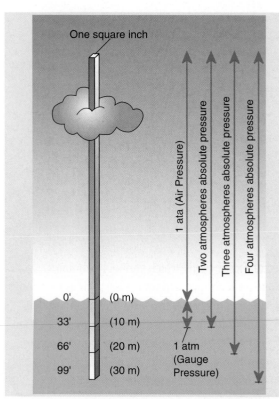

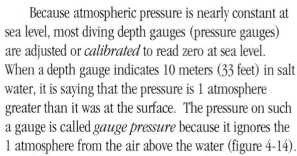

FIGURE 4-14. WATER PRESSURE ALONE IS CALLED GAUGE PRES-
SURE. WATER PRESSURE AND ATMOSPHERIC PRES-
SURE COMBINED ARE CALLED ABSOLUTE PRESSURE.

Because water is not compressible and transmits pressure freely, pressure in water increases at a constant rate, and pressure is cumulative. In other words, 10 meters (33 feet) of salt water equals 1 atmosphere, 20 meters (66 feet) of salt water equals 2 atmosphere, 30 meters (99 feet) of salt water equals 3 atmosphere, and so on.

Units of Pressure

You can refer to pressure in two different ways: *absolute* and *gauge*. When you dive, the pressure of the water as well as the pressure of the atmosphere push on you. At sea level, you are already under 1 atmosphere of pressure absolute (ata). At a depth of 10 meters (33 feet), you are under 2 atmosphere of pressure absolute: 1 atmosphere from the air plus 1 atmosphere from the salt water. At 20 meters (66 feet), you are under 3 atmosphere of pressure absolute (ata): 1 atmosphere from the air plus 2 atmosphere from the salt water.

Because atmospheric pressure is nearly constant at sea level, most diving depth gauges (pressure gauges) are adjusted or *calibrated* to read zero at sea level. When a depth gauge indicates 10 meters (33 feet) in salt water, it is saying that the pressure is 1 atmosphere greater than it was at the surface. The pressure on such a gauge is called *gauge pressure* because it ignores the 1 atmosphere from the air above the water (figure 4-14).

You always use absolute pressure when determining the total pressure being exerted on your body at any depth. For example, if you descend from the surface to 10 meters (33 feet) of salt water, you are doubling the pressure on your body. If you continue to 20 meters (66 feet), you are tripling the pressure on your body. As a diver, you must be concerned with pressure and how it can affect the volume of your air spaces under water.

Verify What You Have Learned

Review the following questions about pressure:
11. One atmosphere of pressure is equal to about _____ meters (_____ feet) of fresh water or _____ meters (_____ feet) of seawater.
12. The pressure is _____ times greater at 40 meters (132 feet) in salt water than it is at the surface.
13. The absolute pressure is _____ ata at 20.7 meters (68 feet) in fresh water.

How Pressure Affects Volume

To understand the direct effects of pressure, you must consider the effects of pressure on an open system and on a closed system.

Open System

If you invert a bucket, force it below the surface of the ocean, and take it to depth, the pressure surrounding the bucket increases and compresses the air in the bucket. The water level rises into the bucket. As the air compresses, its volume decreases. No air is lost from the bucket. When you take the bucket back to the

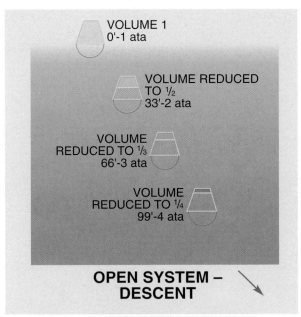

FIGURE 4-15. AS THE PRESSURE ON AIR INCREASES, THE VOLUME DECREASES.

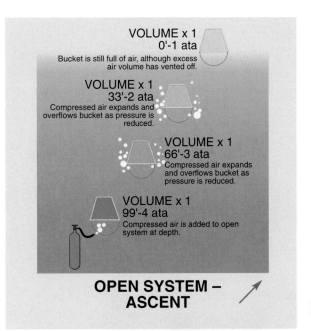

FIGURE 4-16. IF YOU FILL AN OPEN BUCKET WITH AIR WHILE AT DEPTH, THE AIR EXPANDS AND BUBBLES OUT OF THE BUCKET AS YOU BRING THE BUCKET BACK TO THE SURFACE.

surface, the pressure decreases, and the air expands to its original volume.

When the bucket gets to 10 meters (33 feet) of seawater or 2 ata, the pressure has doubled on the bucket. The volume of air in the bucket has decreased to half of the original surface volume. When the bucket descends to 20 meters (66 feet), which is 3 ata, the pressure has tripled on the bucket and the volume of air in the bucket will have decreased to a third of the original surface volume (figure 4-15).

This inverse relationship between pressure and volume is known as *Boyle's Law*, which is named for the scientist who first recognized the relationship. Knowing the name of the law is not as important as understanding the concept of the relationship between pressure and volume. When one increases, the other decreases, if it can.

Now consider a situation where you have the ability to maintain the volume of air in the bucket during its descent. As you take the bucket to depth, you add air to the bucket through a hose. You keep the volume constant by adding enough air to match the original volume.

You take the bucket to 10 meters (33 feet), fill it with air, and raise it to the surface. As the pressure decreases from 2 ata to 1 ata, the volume of air

doubles. The bucket cannot hold this increased volume, so the excess air bubbles out around the rim of the bucket. If you took the bucket to 30 meters (99 feet), filled it with air, and then raised it to the surface, a volume of air equal to 3 buckets would escape and the volume equal to one bucket would remain (figure 4-16).

Closed System

The effects of pressure on a closed system can be much more dramatic. If you take a sealed plastic bag filled with air down to depth, the bag becomes smaller and smaller as the air compresses and the volume decreases. When you return the bag to the surface, the air expands and the volume increases back to its original size (figure 4-17).

Now imagine that you take the same bag down to depth, open it, fill it with air back to its original volume, and close it again. When you bring the bag back to the surface, the air expands, but it cannot escape because the bag is sealed. The bag will expand slightly, but will finally burst to release the expanding air (figure 4-18).

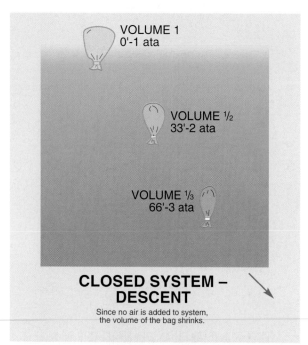

FIGURE 4-17. AS THE VOLUME DECREASES IN A CLOSED SYSTEM, THE FLEXIBLE CONTAINER ALSO DECREASES IN SIZE.

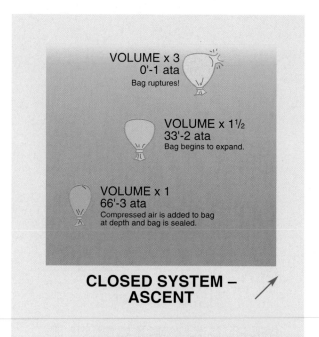

FIGURE 4-18. IF YOU ADD AIR TO A CLOSED SYSTEM AT DEPTH AND THEN ASCEND WITH IT, THE FLEXIBLE CONTAINER WILL BURST TO RELEASE THE EXPANDING AIR.

The only way to prevent the bag from bursting is to vent the excess air from the bag during its ascent.

The same thing would happen to your lungs if you took a deep breath from a scuba regulator at depth, held it, and then swam toward the surface, even at a few feet below the surface. **You must NEVER hold your breath when breathing compressed air under water**.

The greatest change in pressure is between the surface and 10 meters (33 feet) when you are diving in salt water or the surface and 10.3 meters (34 feet) when you are diving in fresh water. The pressure doubles from 1 ata to 2 ata. As you read further on in this chapter, you will learn how this change in pressure affects your body's air spaces.

How Pressure Affects Density

The increasing pressure under water not only affects the volume of air, it also affects the density of the air. As the pressure increases, the air compresses to a smaller volume. As the air compresses, it becomes denser. At 10 meters (33 feet) or 2 ata, air is twice as dense as it is at the surface. At 20 meters (66 feet) or 3 ata, air is three times as dense as it is at the surface (figure 4-19). This explains why you use air faster when you dive deeper and why breathing resistance increases with depth – you are moving denser air through your lungs with each breath.

When you add air to your lungs from scuba at 2 ata to maintain their original volume, your lungs contain twice as much air in the same physical space. When you scuba dive to 3 ata, your lungs now contain three times as much air in the same space compared to sea level. The overall effect is that the deeper you dive, the denser the air inside an air space becomes. Those air spaces include your lungs, middle ears, and sinuses.

As the air you breathe becomes denser, it does not flow as easily. When you scuba dive, you breathe air that is compressed to the ambient pressure at your depth, which is much denser than the air you breathe on the surface. The deeper you dive, the more resistance there is to the flow of compressed air through your regulator hose (and through your air passages). This resistance makes it more difficult to breathe, the deeper you dive. The combined resistance of breathing compressed

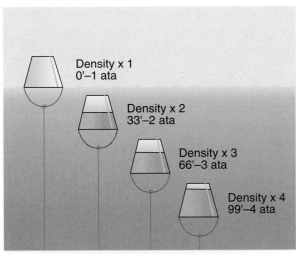

FIGURE 4-19. THE DENSITY OF AIR INCREASES AS THE PRESSURE INCREASES.

Density x 1
0'–1 ata

Density x 2
33'–2 ata

Density x 3
66'–3 ata

Density x 4
99'–4 ata

air and the restrictions of the equipment you wear to dive puts limitations on how hard you can exert yourself while under water.

You can function almost normally while under the pressure of water. To be comfortable, you must keep the pressure in the air spaces inside your body equal to the pressure surrounding your body. One of the important lessons you will learn in your NAUI Scuba Diver certification course is how to equalize pressure under water.

Verify What You Have Learned

Complete the following chart for a given quantity of air in a balloon:

Pressure	Volume	Density
Doubles	Halves	Doubles
	One third	
Halves		
		Quadruples

How Pressure Affects Air Consumption

The deeper you dive, the greater the surrounding pressure. The greater the surrounding pressure, the denser the air that you breathe and the faster you empty your cylinder. The rate at which you consume the air in your cylinder is directly proportional to the depth of your dive. You consume your air twice as fast at 10 meters (33 feet) as you do on the surface, three times as fast at 20 meters (66 feet), and so on. This is readily seen by considering these depths as multiples of atmospheres of pressure.

Air Consumption Factors

Other factors also affect the rate at which you consume air on your dive. These factors include:

- Your activity level during the dive.
- Your mental state.
- Your body size.
- The warmth of your diving suit.
- Your level of physical fitness.

Besides depth, physical activity has the greatest effect on your air consumption under water. You can use up to 4 times more air when you are exerting yourself than when you are resting. Improving your air consumption is not the only reason to avoid exertion under water, but it is certainly one that good divers keep in mind.

Beginning divers tend to be more active than necessary, but they quickly learn how to relax under water. During the first few dives after training, a new diver's air consumption rate decreases significantly because they learn how to relax. With experience, these divers also learn how to move through the water more efficiently. The sooner you can do this, the more enjoyable your diving will be.

As a diver, you need to think about developing a slow and relaxed breathing pattern as well as a slow rate of breathing. When you swim fast under water, you breathe more deeply and more often. Therefore, you use more air. You can waste a lot of air if you breathe shallowly and rapidly. If you limit your exertion and relax during your dive, you will be able to maintain a slow, deep pattern of breathing with long inhalations and long exhalations. This is the best way to breathe under water.

 Another factor in air consumption is your physical size. Larger people have larger lungs and use more air than smaller people who have smaller lungs and smaller overall metabolic needs. To compensate for these differences, sometimes larger divers will use larger cylinders. There is usually no reason for a small person to carry the same size tank as a larger person unless it is needed for a specific purpose.

Body temperature also affects your breathing. The colder you are, the more you breathe. This is unfortunate because heat is also lost each time you exhale. Therefore, you need to be sure to wear the proper amount of insulation for the conditions.

Divers who are physically fit breathe less and use their air more efficiently. They also do not have to oxygenate excess body fat.

These factors, or combinations of these factors, can significantly affect your breathing rate under different conditions. Through experience, you will learn to estimate the amount of air you will use based on all these factors.

Monitoring Air Consumption

Most sport divers do not calculate their air consumption before each dive. Instead, as they gain experience diving, they keep a record in their logbooks of how long their air lasts at different depths and in different conditions. This enables them to make rough predictions of the time they will be able to dive at a given depth, based on their air supply. They monitor their submersible pressure gauges, dive timers, and dive computers and use the information from these instruments to determine when to begin their ascent.

Even if you calculate your air consumption mathematically, which is possible, any combination of the air consumption factors can change your predicted air consumption rate. If you work harder than planned or the water is colder than you thought, your air consumption rate will be affected.

In certain specialty areas of diving, it is essential that you predict your air consumption to avoid running out of air. This is especially important if you participate in deep diving, cave or cavern diving, or wreck diving. Anyone who participates in this type of diving must know how much air they will need for any given dive.

Your rate of air consumption will change quite a bit during the first 10 or 20 dives you make. Recording every dive in your logbook will help you to estimate how long your air will last on most dives at different depths. Be sure to record the size of cylinder you use on each dive if you use different size cylinders. This is a good practice to continue even beyond your early dives, because you will learn how much your usual rate is affected by exertion, temperature, and other factors. You will also be able to estimate not only the duration of your air supply for a given depth, but will be able to adjust it for other factors as well.

Verify What You Have Learned

Review the following questions about air consumption:

14. Two factors that affect your air consumption rate under water are

    _____ and

    _____.

15. Divers monitor their air supply under water by checking their

    _____.

YOUR BODY

When you dive, the pressure of the water affects your air spaces as well as your breathing.

How Pressure Affects Your Air Spaces

The air spaces in your body include your lungs, sinuses, and middle ears. You can also have air spaces in your stomach, intestines, and teeth (figure 4-20). There are also two air spaces outside your body that you need to consider when diving. Those are your mask and dry suit (if you are wearing one). Pressure can affect these spaces in dramatic ways, called the direct effects of pressure.

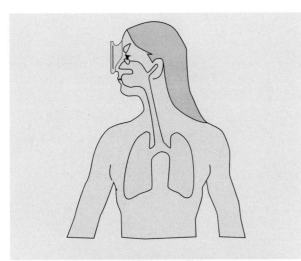

FIGURE 4-20. THE AIR SPACES IN YOUR BODY INCLUDE YOUR LUNGS, SINUSES, AND MIDDLE EARS. YOU CAN ALSO HAVE AIR SPACES IN YOUR STOMACH, INTESTINES, AND TEETH.

Squeezes

When you descend, the pressure on your body increases at a rate of about 0.1 bar per meter or about 0.5 psi per foot of depth. If any air space in your body is closed off so that the pressure inside the air space cannot stay equal to the surrounding pressure, the surrounding pressure tries to compress the air in the air space. Whenever the pressure outside an air space is greater than the pressure inside an air space, the situation is called a squeeze and it can cause damage to your body. Doctors also call this type of injury a *barotrauma*, which means *pressure injury*.

Divers can experience many different types of squeeze. You must be specific when you discuss this type of condition. For example, you can get squeezes in your sinuses, middle ear, or mask. You can avoid each of these squeezes by using proper equalization techniques.

Blocks

A reverse block is the opposite of a squeeze. It occurs when the pressure inside an air space is greater than the surrounding pressure. Blocks can occur during ascent. Air is trapped inside an air space and the air tries to expand as the surrounding pressure decreases.

Middle Ear

The air spaces inside your middle ears are especially important when you dive. You must be able to equalize the pressure inside your ears to comfortably and safely dive.

Anatomy

Your ears are divided into three sections: the outer ear, the middle ear, and the inner ear (figure 4-21). The outer ear is your ear canal. The eardrum separates your outer ear from your middle ear. The eardrum is a flexible membrane that vibrates when sound waves hit it.

Your middle ear contains a series of three small bones that transmit sound waves from the eardrum to the inner ear. Your middle ear also has an airway linking it to the back of your throat. This airway is called the *Eustachian tube*. Your middle ear transmits sound waves from your eardrum to the auditory nerves of your inner ear.

Your body's balance mechanism is also contained in the inner ear. If you have a sudden change in pressure or temperature in one ear and not the other, you can get dizzy or experience *vertigo*.

Middle Ear Squeezes

A middle ear squeeze occurs when the air or water pressure in your outer ear is greater than the air pressure in your middle ear. You equalize your middle ear by moving air from your throat through the Eustachian tube into your middle ear.

For most people, equalizing the pressure inside their ears is not an automatic process. To pass air through the Eustachian tubes usually requires a deliberate action to open the tubes and allow air to flow through them. If you cannot equalize your ears during a dive, you must end the dive and return to the surface.

As you descend in the water, the pressure on your outer ear increases and pushes in on the eardrum. If the pressure continues to increase and is not equalized in the middle ear by passing air through the Eustachian tube, pain will be felt; and the eardrum flexes in to help equalize the pressure. Finally, the eardrum can rupture

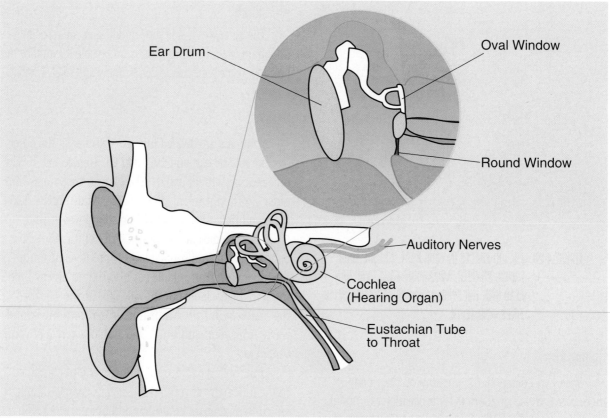

Ear Drum

Oval Window

Round Window

Auditory Nerves

Cochlea
(Hearing Organ)

Eustachian Tube
to Throat

FIGURE 4-21. THE MIDDLE EAR SPACE IS CONNECTED TO THE THROAT BY THE EUSTACHIAN TUBE. AIR PASSES THROUGH THIS TUBE
TO EQUALIZE PRESSURE IN THE MIDDLE EAR.

to allow water to flow into the middle ear to equalize the
pressure. **BEFORE** you feel the slightest pressure in your
ears, you need to equalize.

The Eustachian tube opening in the throat is normally closed. Most people can open the tube by *flexing* the
muscles at the back of their throat or jaw. If you listen
closely, you can hear a slight crackling sound inside your
head when you yawn, swallow, or move your jaw forward.

Some divers are fortunate and can equalize or clear
their ears by swallowing or wiggling their jaw. Most
divers require a bit more effort to open the tube and
equalize the pressure.

The most common method for equalizing pressure
in the middle ear is simple. You close your mouth tightly or block it with your tongue (on scuba), close your
nostrils by pinching them shut, and then exhale lightly
(figure 4-22). As you build a slight pressure in your
head, you should hear the pressure open the tube with a

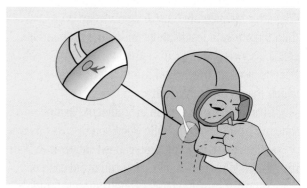

FIGURE 4-22. THE MANEUVER MOST COMMONLY USED FOR
EQUALIZING THE PRESSURE IN YOUR EARS IS A
SIMPLE BLOWING EFFORT.

gentle *pop*, which signals that air has flowed into the
Eustachian tube. You must never force this technique.
You could seriously damage your ears.

This maneuver works well for most divers. The key

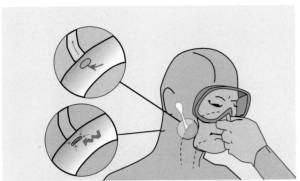

FIGURE 4-23. IF YOU DESCEND TOO FAR WITHOUT EQUALIZING, YOU MIGHT HAVE TIGHTLY CLOSED EUSTACHIAN TUBES.

to successful ear equalization is to keep the pressure difference between the water and the middle ear to a minimum. **This means that you must equalize early and often, starting at just beneath the surface.**

If the pressure difference between the inside of your ear and the water becomes marked, the pressure will hold the Eustachian tube closed (figure 4-23). Once this happens, it is unlikely that you can do anything at that depth that will open the tubes. Your better choice is to ascend a few feet and reduce the pressure difference until the tubes will open, and then attempt to equalize again. In some cases, divers will need to return to the surface and start their descent from the beginning.

Never try to equalize pressure in a squeezed ear by performing forceful blowing. Blowing hard against a closed nose and mouth will not open your Eustachian tubes if they are held shut by pressure. When the tubes are closed by pressure, they can actually seal tighter when you blow harder. This increases the pressure on your inner ear, which can permanently damage your hearing. Never try to force the Eustachian tubes open by blowing hard.

It is much better to equalize your ears continually during descent than it is to repeatedly descend too far, have trouble equalizing, and have to rise a few feet in the water. Most divers have no problem if they begin equalizing just beneath the surface and then equalize continually on descent. Descending feet first also makes equalizing much easier for most people. **Always remember to equalize early and often!**

Some other techniques you can use to equalize

your ears while closing your nose and mouth include wiggling the jaw, tilting the head from side to side, and putting your tongue to the roof of your mouth and compress the trapped air with your tounge. Any of these methods are acceptable and should help to keep the pressure in your ears equalized.

If an eardrum ruptures because you carelessly ignored the pain that signals an ear squeeze, water will enter your middle ear. Even if you are diving in the tropics, this water will be colder than the temperature inside your ear. When the water enters your middle ear, it shocks your balance mechanism and can cause vertigo (dizziness). If this occurs, hold on to any stable object that is close by, or hug yourself to provide stability. You must allow time for the water that has entered your ear to warm to body temperature. This will happen quickly and your sense of orientation and balance will return.

If you do suffer rupture of an eardrum, you must surface and seek medical attention immediately to minimize the possibility of infection. You will not be able to dive again until your eardrum has healed and your doctor permits you to get back in the water. Remember that this injury normally only occurs to divers who disregard pressure in the ears.

If you have a head cold, you must not attempt to dive and equalize by any method. Equalizing when you have a cold can force mucous and bacteria into the middle ear space, which could lead to infection. Using decongestant drugs is not the answer. Decongestant drugs might be only partially effective, or might lose their effect when you are under water, with a variety of adverse consequences.

Never use earplugs for skin or scuba diving. Earplugs trap air between themselves and the eardrum. Because there is no way to equalize this air space, the earplugs can be driven into the outer ear canal by the surrounding pressure. This is a painful and serious injury.

Middle Ear Blocks

A reverse block can occur, affecting your middle ear, if your Eustachian tube becomes blocked while you are at depth. If you begin to ascend and your ear hurts and feels "full," stop your ascent and descend until the

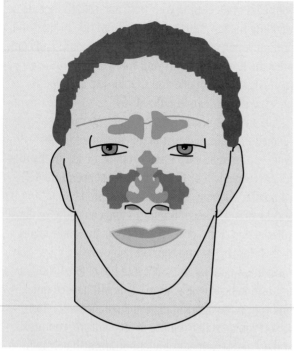

FIGURE 4-24. YOUR HEAD CONTAINS FOUR SETS OF SINUSES THAT MUST EQUALIZE WHEN DIVING.

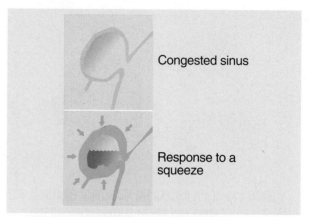

Congested sinus

Response to a squeeze

FIGURE 4-25. THE EFFECT OF A SQUEEZE ON A SINUS IS TO FILL THE VOLUME WITH TISSUE AND BLOOD TO EQUALIZE THE PRESSURE.

Sinus Squeeze and Blockage

If air is trapped inside a clogged sinus, and you attempt to dive, you will feel pressure on your sinuses because the air pressure inside the sinus is less than the surrounding pressure. If you continue to descend when the pressure within your sinuses is less than the surrounding pressure, the soft tissue surrounding the sinus will be pushed into the sinus as the tissues react to equalize the pressure (figure 4-25). This is quite painful and can cause blood to flow into the sinus to fill it.

If you cannot equalize your sinus normally during descent, it will fill with body fluids. Then, during ascent, the air in the sinus will try to expand to its original volume but it cannot because of the fluid. Pressure builds in the sinus and pain results. Blood can be forced out into your nose, mouth, or mask.

A sinus block traps air in a sinus cavity at depth. The air tries to expand on ascent, but cannot, causing pain (figure 4-26).

If your sinuses equalized during descent because of medication you had taken to clear your sinuses, and that medication wore off at depth, the openings to your sinuses would close off and trap air inside. As you ascend, the air in the sinus will try to expand, pressure will build, and you will feel pain. You can relieve the pain by descending again, but if you are running low on air, this might not be an option. Try breathing in with a closed mouth and nose. If this does not help, surface as slowly as possible.

feeling goes away. Swallow, wiggle your jaw and start to ascend slowly. You might need to repeat this technique throughout your ascent. If the block does not equalize, and you must surface, close your nose and mouth and breathe in. If nothing works, ascend as slowly as possible.

In some cases, a block might release quickly. If this occurs, the sudden change in your middle-ear pressure might cause some dizziness. The dizziness will pass quickly. Remember to hold on to something if you experience vertigo.

Sinuses

Your sinuses are air cavities lined with mucous membranes and surrounded by the bones of your head (figure 4-24). Your head has four sets of sinuses. One set is above your eyes, and the other three sets are behind your nose and cheekbones. Each of your sinuses is connected to your nasal airway by an air passage. Under normal conditions, the passages to your sinuses are open. However, when you have a cold or congestion due to allergies or other reasons, the sinuses will clog.

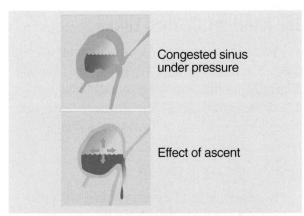

Congested sinus under pressure

Effect of ascent

FIGURE 4-26. IF SWELLING OR MUCUS CLOSES A SINUS WHILE DIVING, PRESSURE WILL DEVELOP INSIDE THE SINUS DURING ASCENT.

Prevention is the best way to avoid a sinus squeeze or block. Never dive when you have a cold or sinus congestion. Also, do not dive if you must use medication to open your sinuses or clear your ears.

Decongestant Drugs

You might think that the answer to preventing a squeeze is to take medication before you dive. Many sprays and tablets are available to relieve congestion. But none of these drugs are designed or tested to perform under water. The effects of any drug might be modified under pressure, and little is known about the potential problems that can occur when medications are used under water.

A drug that causes drowsiness on the surface can be worse under water. For this reason, you should consult a doctor who knows about diving before you use any medication during a dive — even any regular medication you might be taking. Also, avoid taking any medication that you know produces side effects when you use it.

Stomach and Intestines

Any gas that forms in your stomach or intestines during your dive will expand during ascent. This can cause discomfort by creating pressure. To prevent this situation, avoid eating gas-producing foods before you dive. If you have problems from stomach or intestinal

gas while ascending, stop or slow your ascent until the gas works its way out of your system.

Teeth

If you have an imperfect filling in one of your teeth, air can get under the filling. When you descend, the air in the space can compress and cause pain in your tooth. If you continue to dive, compressed air can fill the space in the tooth and loosen the filling or fracture the tooth on ascent. There is nothing you can do to equalize air pressure in a tooth. You must ascend back to the surface and have your tooth examined by a dentist.

Mask Space

Although it might seem obvious, divers often forget that their mask creates an air space attached to their body. This air space is also affected by pressure. As the water pressure increases during your descent, the mask is pushed against your face and the air inside the mask compresses.

Because the mask is rigid, it compresses only slightly. If you do not add air to your mask, the low air pressure inside the mask will cause your mask to suck tightly on your face. The soft tissue of your face will squeeze into the mask, causing tissue damage. This type of injury is known as a mask squeeze. Bloodshot eyes can result.

You should never have this type of injury because you can easily equalize the pressure inside your mask. Simply exhale a small amount of air through your nose into the mask every time you feel pressure pulling on your face and eyes.

Dry Suit

If you wear a dry suit, you have an air space surrounding your body. As you descend, the air inside the dry suit will compress. To keep the suit from squeezing, simply add air to the suit using the power-inflator valve. If you are wearing a dry suit during your training, your instructor will give you specific instructions in the use of your dry suit.

Verify What You Have Learned

Review the following questions about squeezes and blocks:

16. Which air spaces in your body are affected by changes in pressure?

_____

_____

_____

_____

17. What problems might occur if you attempted to dive with a cold?

_____

_____

18. If you feel pressure on your face when descending, you should

_____.

19. When the pressure outside an air space is greater than the pressure in an air space, you have a condition called a

_____.

20. What are three consequences of ignoring an ear squeeze?

_____

_____

_____

_____

21. What is the most likely cause of a sinus squeeze?_____

22. Which type of squeeze is the easiest to prevent?

_____

23. When the pressure inside an air space is greater than the outside pressure, you have a condition known as a _____.

THE ANATOMY OF YOUR LUNGS

Your lungs are inside large cavities within your chest. When you breathe in, they inflate, and when you exhale, they deflate. Your lungs consist of millions of tiny air sacs, called alveoli. The alveoli are surrounded by capillaries, which are tiny blood vessels (figure 4-27).

Lung Overexpansion Injuries

Whenever you breathe compressed air under pressure, you are exposed to the risk of a *lung overexpansion* injury. These injuries are rare and most divers never experience them, but they are life threatening and you must understand their causes and how to prevent and deal with them.

Under normal conditions, as you ascend, you breathe in and out in a relaxed manner. You exhale the compressed air from your lungs before it can expand as a result of the decreasing pressure. If you hold your breath, you can suffer a serious lung injury. With your airway closed, the air expanding in your lungs will cause the alveoli to rupture soon after they reach their full volume. **There is no sensation of discomfort that warns you when this rupture is about to occur.**

This type of accident most commonly occurs when divers panic under water and make a rapid ascent holding their breath. One cause is running out of air. It is instinctive to hold your breath when you cannot breathe under water. You must train yourself to exhale in any situation that would force you to ascend with no air to breathe.

A lung overexpansion injury can occur in as little as 1.1 meters (4 feet) of water and is actually **most** likely to occur in shallow depths. You must understand the importance of not holding your breath at any time while under water. If a lung overexpansion injury occurs, it is extremely serious and can be fatal.

You might think it would be a good idea to keep your lung volume as low as possible by forcefully blowing out all the air you can during an ascent. In reality, forcing air out during an ascent is not the best thing to do. Some small airways in your lungs can collapse when your lung volume is too low and the air trapped behind the collapse can expand and cause alveoli to

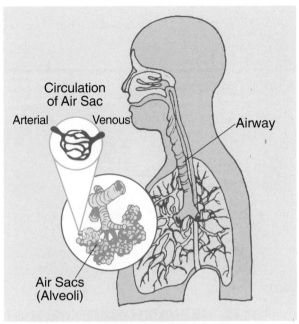

FIGURE 4-27. THE INSIDE OF YOUR LUNGS RESEMBLE STALKS OF BROCCOLI.

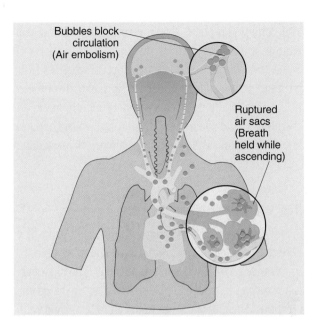

FIGURE 4-28. IF A LUNG RUPTURES AND INTRODUCES AIR INTO THE BLOODSTREAM, IT CAN CAUSE A BLOCKAGE CALLED AN AIR EMBOLISM.

 rupture. The best technique is to maintain normal lung volume during your ascent by breathing normally.

 As long as you breathe normally during ascent, there is little danger of suffering a long overexpansion injury. It is essential that you always breathe whenever you are under water on scuba. During your course, you will learn a variety of techniques for dealing with out-of-air emergencies. Knowing how to deal with an out-of-air emergency will help avoid a lung overexpansion injury.

Note

Divers who smoke have a higher risk of suffering a lung overexpansion injury due to lung damage from smoking.

 There are three general types of lung overexpansion injuries: air embolism, pneumothorax, and tissue emphysema.

Air Embolism

The most serious result of a lung overexpansion injury is an *air embolism* or *arterial gas embolism*

(AGE). The word *embolism* means plug and an air embolism refers to a plug of air in the bloodstream (figure 4-28). The greatest danger in this situation is that a plug of air will block the flow of blood to the brain. An air embolism can cause unconsciousness, paralysis, permanent brain damage, and even death. It is one of the most serious of all diving accidents.

Pneumothorax

If a lung ruptures, and the escaping air gets into the *pleural lining* surrounding the lungs, the escaped air can cause a condition known as a *pneumothorax*, which is a collapsed lung. This is not fatal by itself, but it is painful, can lead to serious complications, and requires immediate medical attention.

Tissue Emphysema

If air from a ruptured lung escapes into the chest cavity below the breastbone, it causes a condition known as a *mediastinal emphysema* (air in the middle tissues). In this case, the air is around the heart, and expansion of the air will cause pressure on the heart and the large blood vessels leading into and out of the heart.

This condition is obviously dangerous, painful, and also requires immediate medical attention.

A *subcutaneous emphysema* occurs when air from a ruptured lung collects under the skin, usually of the neck. This condition can cause swelling in the neck, a crackling sound when the skin is probed, voice changes, and difficulty in swallowing. It also requires immediate medical attention.

Hyperbaric Treatment

If you do suffer an arterial gas embolism, you will need to be treated in a *recompression chamber* or *hyperbaric chamber* as soon as possible. The chamber is pressurized to reduce bubble size and restore blood circulation. Then, the pressure in the chamber is released slowly, allowing the gas to move from your bloodstream and out of your body with each of your exhalations.

If you have any signs or symptoms of an air embolism, you must seek medical attention at an operational chamber immediately. You should never go back under water to try to relieve the symptoms.

Breathing and Circulation

Transporting oxygen through your body is a vital function of the circulatory system, and proper gas exchange in the lungs is critical. Each breath begins when your *diaphragm* moves and your chest muscles pull your ribs out. These motions expand your chest and draw air into your lungs.

Breathing in causes the alveoli to fill with fresh air. Oxygen is absorbed through the walls of the alveoli and then through the walls of your capillaries into your bloodstream. This oxygen-rich blood is pumped by the heart through your arteries to your tissues.

Your body *metabolizes* (uses) the oxygen and converts it to carbon dioxide and other waste products. Your circulatory system moves the carbon dioxide through your veins and back to your lungs, where it passes through the walls of the alveoli and out into the air when you exhale. Then the cycle starts again (figure 4-29).

At rest, most people exchange a few pints of air with each breath. When you are active, your breathing rate

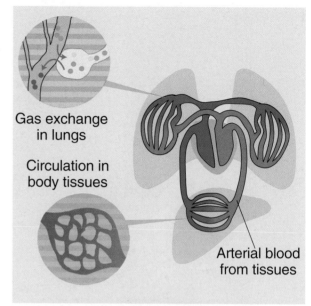

Gas exchange in lungs

Circulation in body tissues

Arterial blood from tissues

FIGURE 4-29. YOUR BLOODSTREAM CIRCULATES OXYGEN TO YOUR TISSUES AND REMOVES CARBON DIOXIDE.

increases. This is your body's response to the increased production of CO_2 created by activity. The harder you exercise, the more air you breathe. Because the cylinders you use for diving hold only a finite amount of air, you can see how exertion uses up your air supply faster than when you are relaxed.

How Carbon Dioxide Controls Your Breathing

Actually, your breathing rate is not controlled by the amount of oxygen, but by the amount of carbon dioxide, in your bloodstream. Based on input from chemical receptors in parts of your body, your brain senses the carbon dioxide level in your blood and then increases or decreases the muscular activity that controls breathing. The more carbon dioxide you have in your blood, the more you want to breathe.

How to Breathe Under Water

Because pressure and density are different under water than on land, you must modify your breathing to accommodate these differences. Generally, for maximum efficiency, your breathing should be slightly slower than normal and deeper than you usually breathe (figure 4-30).

FIGURE 4-30. YOUR BREATHING SHOULD BE SLOWER THAN NORMAL AND DEEPER THAN YOU USUALLY BREATHE.

Shallow Breathing

One mistake that divers make is to breathe too shallowly. If you breathe too shallowly, you do not exchange enough air with each breath. Only a small amount of carbon dioxide is eliminated when you breathe out. If you have too much carbon dioxide in your lungs, your body will not allow much carbon dioxide to pass out of your bloodstream and into your lungs. The increased level of carbon dioxide in your blood will stimulate your desire to breathe. This need to breathe will get worse if you continue breathing shallowly. You will feel as if you cannot get enough air. The simple solution to this problem is stop your activity and concentrate on breathing slowly and deeply. Be especially sure to **exhale** fully with each breathing cycle.

Hyperventilation

You can also get into trouble if you deliberately breathe deeply and rapidly. This type of breathing is called *hyperventilation* and has the effect of lowering your body's carbon dioxide level. Deliberate hyperventilation can be hazardous when you follow it with a breath-hold skin dive.

If you hold your breath after excessive hyperventilation, your body will continue using oxygen, but your carbon dioxide level will not reach the point where your brain senses it is time to breathe. Therefore, you can pass out from a lack of oxygen before you ever feel the need to breathe. This is called shallow water blackout.

Moderate hyperventilation can extend your breath-holding time without a high level of risk, but only if you take a few breaths. You should only take a maximum of three or four deep breaths before any breath-hold dive.

Skip Breathing

Skip breathing is a dangerous technique some divers use because, incorrectly, they think it will extend the amount of time their cylinder of air will last under water. When a diver skip breathes, they hold each breath for an extended period of time rather than breathing normally. Underwater photographers will skip breathe to minimize the interference of bubbles. You have already read about the extreme danger of lung overexpansion injuries if you hold your breath (*Lung Overexpansion Injuries*, page 112). The additional danger in skip breathing is the buildup of carbon dioxide in the body. If the carbon dioxide builds up, the diver is unable to breathe enough air for comfort in any situation that calls for them to exert themselves under water. They feel as if they are suffocating. Divers who skip breathe can also develop painful headaches.

Air Starvation

You should also avoid overexertion under water. Regulators have a limit as to how much air they can give you. Basically, you are breathing through a restriction like a straw. Should you try to work hard under water, the carbon dioxide level will build up in your body, even if you are breathing deeply because of the added effort of breathing through a restriction. When this happens, you feel starved for air, and you feel that your regulator is not supplying you with the amount of air you need. If you do not take prompt action to resolve the situation, you will begin to have feelings of anxiety and possibly panic. The action to take is to **stop** what you are doing, **rest**, and **breathe slowly and deeply** until you recover, being sure to exhale fully with each breath.

By taking it easy under water and learning your limits of exertion at various depths, you can avoid overexertion. You must learn to breathe slowly and deeply whenever you use scuba gear.

What Happens When You Inhale Water

Any time you are in the water, whether you are free diving, on scuba, or swimming, the possibility exists that you will get a mouthful of water when you least expect it. This commonly happens to swimmers, and sometimes happens to divers.

Even a few drops of water can cause you to cough or choke. Keep your regulator in your mouth and choke or cough right through the mouthpiece. You can also sneeze through your regulator.

You can almost eliminate choking as a problem if you always inhale cautiously when taking your first breath after clearing your regulator or snorkel. If you do inhale a little water, cough and swallow repeatedly. Do not ascend when coughing or choking. Coughing and choking or your response to it can close your airway and ascending could cause a lung overexpansion injury.

Verify What You Have Learned

Review the following questions about your lungs and breathing:

24. Lung expansion injuries are caused by

_____ or

_____.

25. Lung volume should be kept as

_____ as possible during your ascent from a dive.

26. The stimulus to breathe is the amount of

_____ in your blood.

27. When you are breathing on scuba, you should breathe _____ and

_____.

28. If you should choke, cough, or sneeze while diving, you should

_____.

INDIRECT EFFECTS OF PRESSURE

The primary effects of pressure are physical changes that are easy to see and experience. Other, more subtle, effects from pressure are just as important to your safety under water. These *indirect* effects of pressure impact divers by means of the gases in the air we breathe while diving.

Ingassing and Offgassing

When you breathe in and out, the air you breathe is 78% nitrogen. Nitrogen is a metabolically inert gas, which means that your body does not use it. However, nitrogen is absorbed and dissolved in your bloodstream and tissues. The pressure of nitrogen is balanced between the air and your body. This state is called *equilibrium*.

Under increased pressure, the air you breathe is denser and the *partial pressure* of nitrogen you inhale with each breath is increased. Therefore, the pressure of nitrogen in the air you are breathing is greater than the pressure of nitrogen in your body. Your body *ingasses* nitrogen until the partial pressure of nitrogen in the air you breathe is equal to the pressure of nitrogen in your body.

When you ascend, the pressure decreases, and the partial pressure of nitrogen decreases. Now the pressure of nitrogen in your body is greater than the partial pressure of nitrogen in the air you are breathing. To compensate, your body *offgasses* nitrogen until the nitrogen is balanced between the air and your body.

Decompression Sickness

A problem called *decompression sickness (DCS)* can occur if you absorb a great deal of nitrogen and then ascend too quickly. It takes time for nitrogen to enter your body and it takes time for the nitrogen to leave your body. When you ascend your body begins to eliminate nitrogen. If too much is still present after you surface, the excess nitrogen forms bubbles in your body (figure 4-31). There are different types of DCS. Each type has its own symptoms.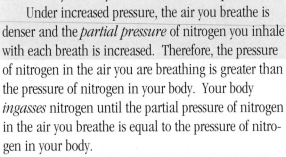

When bubbles form in your blood, they can create microscopic clots that impair your circulation. When a

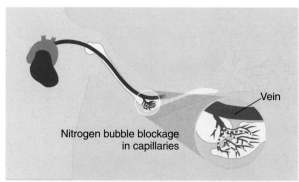

FIGURE 4-31. A PROBLEM CALLED DECOMPRESSION SICKNESS (DCS) CAN OCCUR IF YOU ABSORB A GREAT DEAL OF NITROGEN AND THEN ASCEND TOO QUICKLY.

Nitrogen bubble blockage in capillaries

Vein

FIGURE 4-32. IF YOU DO SUFFER DCS, YOU WILL NEED TO BE TREATED IN A HYPERBARIC CHAMBER LIKE THIS ONE.

bubble forms in your tissues, your body reacts to the bubble as if it were a foreign body. Symptoms of DCS can range from a skin rash, extreme fatigue, coughing, and painful joints to paralysis and unconsciousness.

You can and must prevent DCS when you dive. During your NAUI Scuba Diver certification course, you will learn to use the NAUI Dive Tables. These tables give you time limits for your diving depths. Staying within the time limits is the first step in preventing DCS. The second step to preventing DCS is to always ascend at a rate no faster than 9 meters (30 feet) per minute when you are using the NAUI Dive Tables to plan your dives. This gives your body a chance to offgas some slight amount of nitrogen as you ascend and to avoid the rapid pressure change that could cause bubble formation. The third step to preventing DCS is to always perform a precautionary decompression stop at 4.5 meters (15 feet) for 3 to 5 minutes.

You can also use a dive computer instead of the NAUI Dive Tables to help avoid DCS. Remember that there is always a slight risk that you can suffer DCS even if you follow your NAUI Dive Tables or use your dive computer correctly.

If you do suffer DCS, you will need to be treated in a *recompression chamber* or *hyperbaric chamber* as soon as possible (figure 4-32). The chamber is pressurized to cause the nitrogen bubbles to go back into solution. Then, the pressure in the chamber is released slowly, so the nitrogen can move from your tissues to your bloodstream, and out with each of your exhalations.

If you have any signs or symptoms of DCS, you must seek medical attention immediately. You should never go back under water to try to relieve the symptoms.

Nitrogen Narcosis

Nitrogen under pressure can also produce an effect on your body called *nitrogen narcosis* or *"rapture of the deep"* (figure 4-33). At depths approaching 24 meters (80 feet), nitrogen can be *intoxicating*. The narcotic effect of nitrogen produces impaired thought and judgment, and it reduces a diver's physical ability. The danger exists that a diver would be unable to function well enough to ensure their safety. The effects vary by individual and by day.

The prevention to this problem is simple: avoid deep dives. The symptoms of nitrogen narcosis increase in intensity with depth. Recovery is as simple as ascending to a shallower depth where nitrogen has no effect. The symptoms leave as rapidly as they occur and there are no after effects.

Oxygen Toxicity

Oxygen is essential to sustain life, but breathing pure oxygen at depths below about 7.5 meters (25 feet) can be deadly. Oxygen becomes toxic at about that depth and, depending on individual sensitivity, can cause convulsions that can lead to drowning. Scuba

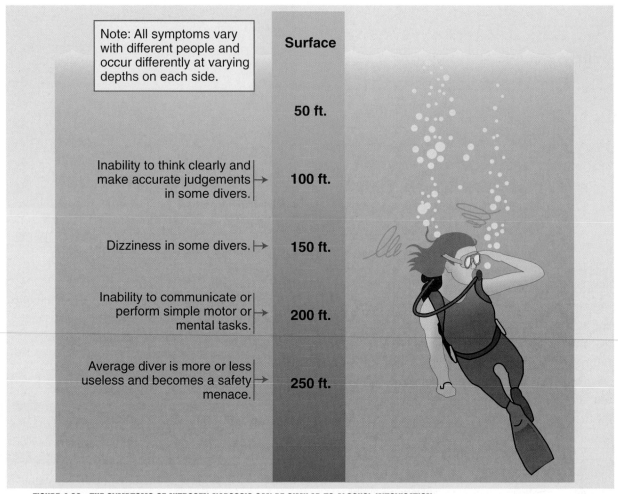

Note: All symptoms vary with different people and occur differently at varying depths on each side.

Surface

50 ft.

Inability to think clearly and make accurate judgements in some divers. → 100 ft.

Dizziness in some divers. → 150 ft.

Inability to communicate or perform simple motor or mental tasks. → 200 ft.

Average diver is more or less useless and becomes a safety menace. → 250 ft.

FIGURE 4-33. THE SYMPTOMS OF NITROGEN NARCOSIS CAN BE SIMILAR TO ALCOHOL INTOXICATION.

tanks must never be filled with pure oxygen. The percentage of oxygen in regular air is not toxic until well below to the sport-diving limit of 40 meters (130 feet).

Some divers receive specialized training in the use of special gas mixtures that have a percentage of oxygen and nitrogen different from the percentages in regular air. These mixtures are referred to as nitrox or enriched air (figure 4-34). Nitrox has other benefits, but because it has a higher percentage of oxygen than air, maximum dive depths are actually reduced. Using these gases requires special training. Ask your instructor about the NAUI Enriched Air Nitrox specialty courses in your area if you are interested in learning about diving with these gases.

Carbon Monoxide Toxicity

Carbon monoxide is a gas formed by the incomplete combustion usually of a petroleum product such as gasoline or oil. This gas is potentially dangerous even in small concentrations, especially when it is breathed under pressure. Carbon monoxide itself is colorless, odorless, and tasteless but air that has been contaminated with it might taste and smell oily or foul.

Divers can encounter problems with carbon monoxide if exhaust fumes from a gasoline- or diesel-powered engine contaminate their air supply. This occurs when the intake for the compressor is placed too close to the exhaust for any engine, including the engine that drives the compressor. In this situation, gases from the engine exhaust are compressed along with the air. In addition,

FIGURE 4-34. NITROX IS AN ACCEPTABLE GAS TO USE FOR DIVING IF YOU HAVE BEEN TRAINED TO USE IT.

FIGURE 4-35. ALWAYS HAVE YOUR TANKS FILLED AT A PROFES-SIONAL DIVING CENTER OR STORE.

a compressor that has been lubricated with the wrong oil or that overheats can produce carbon monoxide. Truck or automobile exhaust fumes are another potential source of carbon monoxide. Keep the compressor intake as high and as far away from potential carbon monoxide sources as possible.

Once carbon monoxide is inhaled, it interferes with the blood's ability to carry oxygen to the tissues. Symptoms of carbon monoxide poisoning include nausea, blue lips and nail beds, confusion, headache, and unconsciousness. Fresh air is helpful, but pure oxygen and immediate medical attention are needed for proper treatment.

If the air in your tank has an odor or taste, do not use it. Notify the facility that filled the tank as soon as possible so they can investigate the problem. You can avoid carbon monoxide poisoning by always having your tanks filled at a professional dive facility where the compressor is properly set up and maintained (figure 4-35).

People who smoke expose themselves to increased levels of carbon monoxide. This is another reason divers should not smoke.

Verify What You Have Learned

Review the following questions about the indirect effects of pressure:

29. How can you prevent oxygen toxicity?

_____

30. How can you prevent carbon monoxide toxicity?

_____

31. How can you prevent DCS?

_____

_____

_____

32. How can you prevent nitrogen narcosis?

_____

33. If your buddy has symptoms of nitrogen narcosis, what should you do?

_____

THERMAL EFFECTS OF DIVING

When the water temperature is colder than your skin temperature, you should wear some type of insulation while diving. You lose heat under water in several ways:

- The water conducts heat away from your body rapidly.
- Each time you take a breath under water, you breathe in cool, compressed air that you must warm to your body temperature.
- Each time you exhale under water, you lose the heat energy you used to warm the air you inhaled.

Diving Science

Humidity and Temperature

Humidity is the amount of water vapor in the air. The higher the temperature of the air, the more water vapor it can hold. If the air containing the water vapor is cooled, the water vapor in the air condenses.

When you enter the water and descend, the air inside your mask cools. This causes the water vapor in the air to condense, which fogs the lenses in your mask (figure 4-36). This is known as *condensation*.

When water condenses on the lens of a mask, it forms beads of water. If you use a defogging solution you reduce the *surface tension* of the water in the mask. When the surface tension is reduced, any moisture that does condense spreads out in a thin film instead of forming drops that can block your vision.

The air inside your scuba cylinder also warms and cools. In extremely cold water, condensation can cause scuba regulators to freeze and freeflow unless a cold-water diver takes special precautions with their regulator.

Normally, the air in scuba cylinders has had almost all of the water removed from it as the air is compressed into the cylinder. This is necessary to keep moisture out of your cylinder to prevent corrosion. Because the air you are breathing is so dry, your body must heat and humidify it as you breathe in. Having to humidify the air causes *dehydration*, which is the loss of body fluids.

FIGURE 4-36. YOUR MASK FOGS WHEN THE WATER VAPOR IN THE AIR IN YOUR MASK CONDENSES.

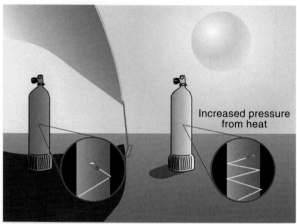

Increased pressure from heat

FIGURE 4-37. WHEN THE TEMPERATURE OF A SCUBA CYLINDER RISES, THE GAS MOLECULES INSIDE THE CYLINDER ALSO BECOME MORE ACTIVE. THIS CAUSES THE PRESSURE INSIDE THE CYLINDER TO RISE.

You must drink plenty of fluids before, between, and after dives to replace the lost fluids. Dehydration decreases your ability to exercise at full capacity and makes you more susceptible to decompression sickness.

Anything you drink before diving must be non-alcoholic and should not contain *caffeine*. Caffeine is a *diuretic*, which means it will cause you to urinate and lose additional fluids. You should drink decaffeinated coffee, caffeine-free soft or sport drinks, decaffeinated tea, juices, and water.

Scuba Cylinders and Temperature

When a container filled with a gas is heated, the gas molecules inside the container become more active. If the container is flexible, the container will expand. If the container is not flexible (for example, a scuba cylinder), the pressure inside the container will rise (figure 4-37).

Cylinders should be kept from extreme heat after they are filled. If the cylinder is subjected to changes in temperature once it is full, the pressure inside can vary by several bar (several hundred psi). The pressure will increase or decrease by approximately 0.6 bar for each change of 1°C (5 psi for each change of 1°F) even though no air has been added or lost.

This change occurs because the molecules of air speed or slow their activity as the temperature rises or falls, respectively. Because of this change, it is not a good idea to store scuba cylinders in car trunks, which can reach temperatures of over 50°C (122°F). There is little danger from the pressure increase because of heat, but if a cylinder becomes hot enough, it will rupture the burst disk in the valve. Also, if the cylinder repeatedly expands and contracts from the changes in temperature, it will stress the metal and shorten the useful life of the scuba cylinder. It is better to store cylinders with only 7 to 14 bar (100 to 200 psi) of air and fill them just before use than to store them full.

The metal alloys from which aluminum cylinders are made will crystallize if subjected to relatively low heat. They should not be placed near fires. If smoke stains are found during the annual visual cylinder inspection, the cylinder cannot be approved for use.

Verify What You Have Learned

Review the following questions about the thermal effects of diving:

34. You lose most heat under water primarily from water _____ and some from warming _____.

35. Water vapor in air condenses to a liquid when _____.

36. You can prevent a mask from fogging under water by lowering the _____ of the water.

37. You must drink plenty of fluids when diving to _____.

38. True or False. If the temperature surrounding a rigid container full of gas increases, the pressure of the gas increases.

CHAPTER

5

Decompression, Dive Tables, and Dive Computers

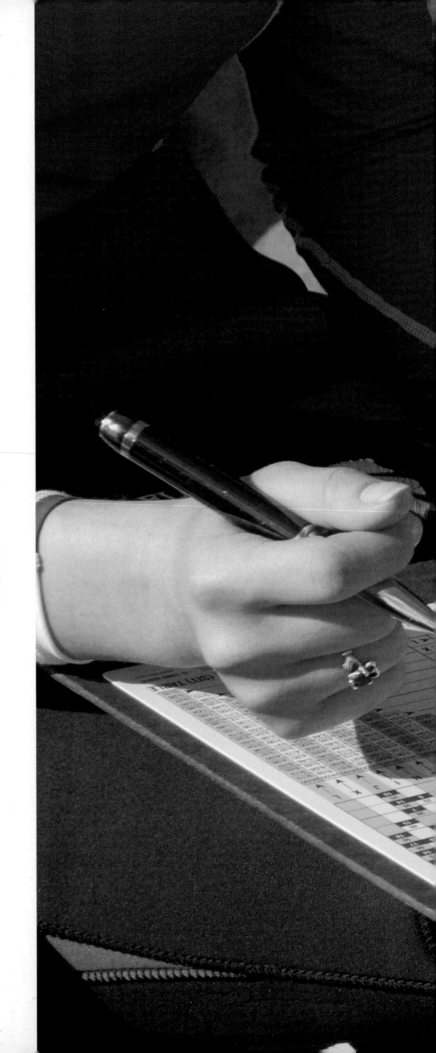

LEARNING GOALS

In this chapter you will:

- Learn about ingassing and offgassing nitrogen and how it affects the amount of time you can spend underwater.
- Understand the concept of residual nitrogen.
- Learn about dive table terms and rules.
- Learn how to use the NAUI Dive Tables to plan your dives and find your Letter Group designation after each dive.
- Be introduced to the NAUI Dive Planning Worksheet and how to use it to keep track of the information from your dives and the NAUI Dive Tables.
- Learn about precautionary and mandatory decompression stops and how important they are in minimizing the risk of decompression sickness.
- Be introduced to the NAUI Dive Time Calculator and how to use it.
- Be introduced to dive computers and their benefits.

Your depth, and the number and depth of dives you have made in a series are two major factors that determine the length of time you can stay under water. This chapter explains the use of the NAUI Dive Tables, the NAUI Dive Time Calculator, and dive computers. You plan your dives with the correct time and depth limits by using either version of the NAUI Dive Tables or a dive computer.

NITROGEN AND DIVING

The gases in the air you breathe dissolve into your body's tissues according to the partial pressure of each gas in the air. Air is 78% nitrogen, 20.9% oxygen, and 1.1% other gases. Your body uses part of the oxygen you inhale with each breath. Your tissues use the oxygen for the chemical processes that keep you alive, converting it to carbon dioxide and other waste products. However, the nitrogen that dissolves in your tissues during your dive is the gas you must be concerned about when you plan your dives.

Ingassing Nitrogen

When you breathe in and out, the air you breathe is 78% nitrogen. Nitrogen is a metabolically inert gas, which means that your body does not use it. However, nitrogen does absorb into your bloodstream and tissues as oxygen does. The pressure of nitrogen is balanced between the air and your body. This state is called *equilibrium*.

Under increased pressure, the *partial pressure* of nitrogen you inhale with each breath is increased. Therefore, the pressure of nitrogen in the air you are breathing is greater than the pressure of nitrogen in your body. Your body *ingasses* nitrogen until the pressure of nitrogen in your body equals the pressure of nitrogen in the air you breathe.

If the new pressure is constant, ingassing occurs rapidly at first and then slows until your body reaches equilibrium many hours later. You do not experience any negative effects when ingassing occurs at moderate depths.

The different tissues of your body (fat, muscle, bone, and so on) absorb nitrogen at different rates when you are under water. Your muscle absorbs nitrogen quickly, but fat absorbs nitrogen slowly. There are different ingassing rates for each type of tissue. Calculating the cumulative effects of the ingassing rates for each type of tissue requires complex mathematics. Dive tables, dive computers, and dive time calculators consider all these varying rates and eliminate the need for you to make complex calculations.

Offgassing Nitrogen

After you spend time under water, the increased partial pressure of nitrogen has caused your body to absorb a quantity of nitrogen from the air you breathe on scuba. This quantity has been added to the quantity found in your body at sea level. When you ascend, and the ambient pressure decreases, the partial pressure of nitrogen decreases. The pressure of nitrogen in your body is now greater than the partial pressure of nitrogen in the air you are breathing. Your body will offgas nitrogen until the nitrogen is balanced between your body and the air.

FIGURE 5-1. THIS BOTTLE OF SODA WAS SEALED UNDER PRESSURE. WHEN THE BOTTLE IS OPENED, BUBBLES FORM BECAUSE OF THE SUDDEN DROP IN PRESSURE INSIDE THE BOTTLE.

The excess nitrogen passes from your body tissues into your blood. The nitrogen then passes from your blood to your lungs, where you exhale the nitrogen. This process occurs rapidly during the first few minutes after your ascent, but it takes many hours for your body's nitrogen level to return to normal.

If you reduce the pressure on your body gradually, and the reduction in pressure from the depth of your dive to the surface is not too rapid for the amount of nitrogen you have absorbed, offgassing occurs without a problem. However, if the change in pressure is sudden, the nitrogen in your tissues can come out of solution so rapidly that bubbles form in your body. These bubbles can damage tissues and cause a painful condition known as *decompression sickness (DCS)* or classically, as the *bends*.

A bottle of soda can illustrate the principle of DCS. Carbon dioxide is dissolved in the soda under pressure and it remains in solution until opening the bottle reduces the pressure. The rapid drop in pressure causes the carbon dioxide to form bubbles in the liquid and the

soda foams (figure 5-1). If you open the bottle slowly, reduced bubbling occurs.

You must control the two factors that affect in-and offgassing: time and pressure. You do this by controlling your dive time and depth. To do this, you rely on the information provided by dive tables, dive time calculators, and dive computers.

You must also consider factors that can increase your chances of suffering DCS in situations where it might not normally occur. These factors include dehydration, fatigue, injuries, hard work during or shortly after a dive, effects of drugs or alcohol, obesity, or advanced age. In any case, you must be fit for diving and dive conservatively.

Bubbles form in the human body if pressure is reduced beyond a specific point. If you dive deeper than approximately 6 meters (20 feet) and then ascend, the pressure change might be sufficient for bubbles to form if you have absorbed enough nitrogen. If you dive to depths of 6 meters (20 feet) or less, DCS is not likely to occur unless you go to altitude after diving, which reduces the pressure outside your body and can create a sufficient pressure differential to cause bubbling.

For depths of 6.4 meters (21 feet) or deeper, time limits called *dive time limits* or *no-decompression limits* have been established. The time spent at a given depth is not to exceed these limits, or you could experience DCS during or after your ascent from the dive. If you take special precautions, involving offgassing in a series of planned decompression stops during ascent; you lessen your risk of DCS.

The United States Navy has established time limits for various depths based on research and field experience of military divers. Recreational diving uses shorter time limits than those in the US Navy tables (figure 5-2). Research and analysis by many experts determined that shorter dive time limits would reduce the risk of DCS during recreational diving. Reduced time limits have been incorporated into the NAUI Dive Tables and NAUI Dive Time Calculator. Most dive computers also use shorter time limits than the US Navy tables for a single dive at a constant depth.

Any dive you make puts you at risk for DCS. However, diving within the limits set by the dive tables

Decompression, Dive Tables, and Dive Computers

125

Decompression, Dive Tables, and Dive Computers

DIVE LIMITS		
DEPTH	**NAUI LIMIT**	**U.S.N. LIMIT**
0-20' (0-6m)	No Limit	No Limit
21-40' (6.4-12m)	130 mins.	200 mins.
41-50' (12.5-15m)	80 mins.	100 mins.
51-60' (15.5-18m)	55 mins.	60 mins.
61-70' (18.6-21m)	45 mins.	50 mins.
71-80' (21.6-24m)	35 mins.	40 mins.
81-90' (25-27m)	25 mins.	30 mins.
91-100' (27.6-30m)	22 mins.	25 mins.

FIGURE 5-2. RECREATIONAL DIVING USES SHORTER DIVE TIME LIMITS THAN THE US NAVY TABLES.

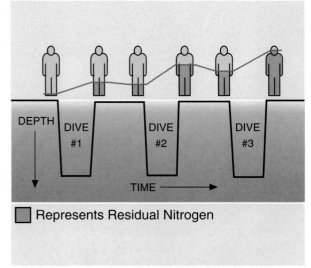

Represents Residual Nitrogen

FIGURE 5-3. RESIDUAL NITROGEN IS THE NITROGEN THAT STAYS IN YOUR BODY FROM DIVES MADE IN THE PREVIOUS 24 HOURS.

lessens the risk. Divers who use time limits in excess of the recommended limits (for example, technical divers) recognize and accept the increased risk that is associated with these longer dive times and the need for special decompression procedures.

Deeper diving requires experience, planning, and training. As a certified entry-level NAUI Scuba Diver, you should not dive to depths deeper than 18 meters (60 feet). As a certified NAUI Advanced Scuba Diver, you should not dive to depths deeper than 30 meters (100 feet). The maximum recommended depth for all recreational divers is 40 meters (130 feet).

You do not need to memorize the dive time limits. They are included in your NAUI Dive Tables or your NAUI Dive Time Calculator. Note that the dive time decreases as the depth increases. If you are using a dive computer, the limits will probably be different from the limits presented in this textbook.

Nitrogen offgassing occurs at different rates among your various body tissues. The rate of offgassing for different tissues is the basis for the non-linear variation in time limits for different depths. You should be familiar with this concept because it does form the basis for the calculations performed by dive computers and the time limits established by dive tables and dive computers. When you take the NAUI Master Scuba Diver course, you will learn various principles and theories behind dive tables.

Residual Nitrogen

To properly use dive tables, dive time calculators, and dive computers, you must understand the concept of residual nitrogen. In reality, it takes hours to fully absorb nitrogen into your body or fully eliminate nitrogen from your body. If you dive and absorb nitrogen at depth, ascend to the surface, and then make another dive within 24 hours of the first dive, you will still have nitrogen in your body from the first dive (figure 5-3). This is called *residual nitrogen*.

Your body will absorb nitrogen from the second dive in addition to the nitrogen remaining from the first dive. You must always take the nitrogen remaining in your system from any previous series of dives into account when planning your next dive. This residual nitrogen reduces your time limits for any given depth on your next dive.

Verify What You Have Learned

Review the following questions about ingassing and outgassing nitrogen:

1. When you go under pressure, your body _____ nitrogen until it reaches a state of _____.
2. Bubbles form during offgassing when you _____.
3. You can dive to _____ meters (_____ feet) without a dive time limit.
4. Residual nitrogen is the nitrogen _____.

DIVE TABLE OVERVIEW

The NAUI Dive Tables use a Letter Group designation to express the amount of residual nitrogen in your body. The letters range in sequence from A to L. The letter A represents a small amount of nitrogen and the amount of nitrogen increases as the letters progress towards L. When you dive, a Letter Group from the tables designates the amount of nitrogen you have absorbed during the dive. As you spend time on the surface between dives, you are assigned to "lower" Letter Groups as you offgas nitrogen.

When you start a dive again to a given depth, your Letter Group at that time determines the time representing the residual nitrogen in your body. The tables show you how to subtract this time from the normal dive time limits, which results in a shorter time limit for your repetitive dive. You must add your residual nitrogen time to the time you actually spent diving to determine your total nitrogen time at the end of the dive. You use the total time to determine a new end-of-dive Letter Group.

The NAUI dive time calculator is based on the NAUI dive tables, but it eliminates the calculations required to determine Letter Groups when you make more than one dive. The dive time calculator also reduces the errors that are often made when reading dive tables. It is easy to learn how to use a dive time calculator, but you should do this only after you are familiar with the procedures for planning dive time limits using the dive tables. A dive time calculator might not always be available, but dive tables usually are (figure 5-4).

A variety of dive tables, dive time calculators, and dive computers exist. The information they provide varies and some are more conservative than others. Numbers and Letter Groups are not always interchangeable between tables. Always use the type of table, calculator, or computer with which you are familiar. If your dive buddy is using a different type, you should agree to use the most conservative dive planning information.

Dive Table Terms

Different dive tables and dive computers might use terms different from the ones used in the NAUI Dive Tables (figure 5-5). Also, the same term might have a different meaning.

The following terms apply to the NAUI Dive Tables:

- *Dive Schedule*. This is an abbreviated statement giving the depth and time of the dive. It is expressed as depth/time (for example, 21 meters/40 minutes or 70 feet/40 minutes). It is also called a dive profile, especially when it is one dive in a sequence of dives.
- *Maximum Dive Time* (MDT). This is the time you can spend at a given depth without having to do a required decompression stop during ascent. This time is also known as the *Maximum Allowable Dive Time* or *no-decompression limit*.
- *Decompression Stop*. This is a point in a dive where you stop at a specified depth for a specified

FIGURE 5-4. DIVE TABLES ARE USED TO PLAN YOUR DIVE.

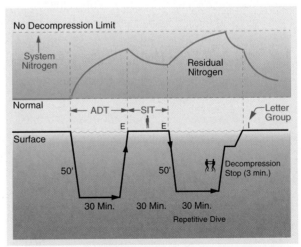

FIGURE 5-5. THE DIVE TABLE TERMS FOR THE NAUI DIVE TABLES MIGHT HAVE DIFFERENT MEANINGS WITH OTHER DIVE TABLES.

time during ascent to allow nitrogen offgassing before continuing your ascent or surfacing.

– *Precautionary Decompression Stop.* This is a stop at five meters (15 feet) for three minutes as a safety precaution when you have not exceeded the Maximum Dive Time. You should perform such a stop at the end of every dive. It is also known as a *Safety Stop*.

– *Required Decompression Stop.* This is the amount of time specified by the NAUI Dive Tables, that you must spend at five meters (15 feet) whenever you exceed the Maximum Dive Time. Other tables specify additional stop depths for deeper or longer dives.

- *Actual Dive Time (ADT).* This is the elapsed time from the moment you begin your descent from the surface until the time you return to the surface. Time spent at your Safety Stop does not need to be included in the Actual Dive Time when determining your Letter Group.

- *Residual Nitrogen.* This is the excess nitrogen remaining in your body from any dive or dives made before you have completely offgassed.

- *Letter Group Designation.* This letter symbol identifies the amount of residual nitrogen you have in your system. The closer the letter is to the beginning of the alphabet, the less residual nitrogen you have in your body.

- *Surface Interval Time (SIT).* This is the time spent on the surface between dives. During this time, your body is eliminating excess nitrogen. Your Letter Group will change and move closer to the beginning of the alphabet, depending on how long you are on the surface.

- *Repetitive Dive.* This is any dive that you make before you have completely offgassed from any previous dive or dives.

- *Residual Nitrogen Time (RNT).* This is the amount of time you must consider as already having been spent at a given depth for a planned repetitive dive. This time is based on the residual nitrogen remaining in your body from a previous dive or dives.

- *Adjusted Maximum Dive Time (AMDT).* This is the Maximum Dive Time minus the Residual Nitrogen Time for a repetitive dive to a given depth.

- *Total Nitrogen Time (TNT).* This is the sum of your Residual Nitrogen Time and your Actual Dive Time following a repetitive dive. You use this total to obtain your new Letter Group at the end of the dive.

Dive Table Rules

You must understand the following NAUI Dive Table rules completely. Similar rules will apply to any new set of dive tables or dive computer that you might use to calculate your dive times.

- Ascend no faster than 9 meters (30 feet) per minute. This is 0.3 meters (1 foot) every two seconds. You need a timing device and a depth gauge (or a dive computer) to measure your rate of ascent. This rate will seem quite slow to you.

- Use the exact or the next greater number listed in the table for your depth. If you exceed a number in the table, use the next greater number. The depths in the table range from 12 meters (40 feet) to 40 meters (130 feet) and increase in increments of 3 meters (10 feet). For example, you round a dive to 13 meters (43 feet) up to a 15-meter (50-foot) dive.

- Use the exact or the next greater number listed in the table for your time. If you exceed a number in the table, use the next greater number. The times range from 5 minutes to 130 minutes. For example, you round a dive to 15 meters (50 feet) for 41 minutes up to 50 minutes.

- Use the deepest depth you reached during your dive to determine the dive schedule for your dive. For example, if you do a dive to 18 meters (60 feet), but spend most of the time at 12 meters (40 feet), you must consider the dive to be an 18 meter (60 foot) dive.

- Always make your deepest dive first when making a series of dives. Plan each of your repetitive dives to a shallower depth than your previous dive. This might allow you to offgas nitrogen on

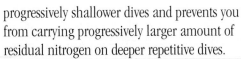

progressively shallower dives and prevents you from carrying progressively larger amount of residual nitrogen on deeper repetitive dives.

- Consider any dive shallower than 12 meters (40 feet) to be a 12-meter (40-foot) dive when planning your dives.
- Surface Interval Time (SIT) must be at least 10 minutes between dives. If your SIT is less than 10 minutes, you must consider your second dive as a continuation of the first dive. NAUI recommends a SIT of at least one hour between dives.
- Use the next greater dive time if your dive is particularly cold or strenuous. For example, if you do a dive to 18 meters (60 feet) for 22 minutes, the 22 minutes rounds to 25 minutes. However, if you become chilled during the dive, round the time again to 30 minutes.
- Avoid dives that take you right to the no-decompression limit for any given depth and time combination. If you accidentally overstay your bottom time or use an incorrect ascent rate on such a dive, you could be in a required decompression situation or suffer DCS. Always allow yourself enough time to make a slow, comfortable ascent with plenty of air.

Verify What You Have Learned

Review the following questions about Dive Table Rules:

5. When you use the NAUI Dive Tables, you ascend from all dives at a maximum rate of _____ meters (_____ feet) per minute.

6. You should allow a minimum of _____ minutes between dives and NAUI recommends a SIT of _____.

7. Arrange the following dives into the preferred sequence:
   - _____ 9 meters (30 feet)/40 minutes
   - _____ 18 meters (60 feet)/30 minutes
   - _____ 15 meters (50 feet)/20 minutes

8. A dive of up to 8 meters (26 feet) for 40 minutes should be considered as a dive schedule of _____ when planning a repetitive dive.

DIVE TABLE ORGANIZATION

The NAUI Dive Tables are composed of three tables:
- Table 1 – End-Of-Dive Letter Group
- Table 2 – Surface Interval Time (SIT) Table
- Table 3 – Repetitive Dive Timetable

The NAUI Dive Tables are based on the US Navy Decompression Tables and have been designed specifically for recreational diving (figure 5-6). The tables are designed to flow from one to the other in a continuous loop (figure 5-7).

When you are using the tables, be sure to use a ruler or a straight-edged object to read the numbers across and work your way from table to table. If you try using a finger to trace your path through the tables, you might slide into another row and read the table incorrectly, especially if you are on a rocking boat.

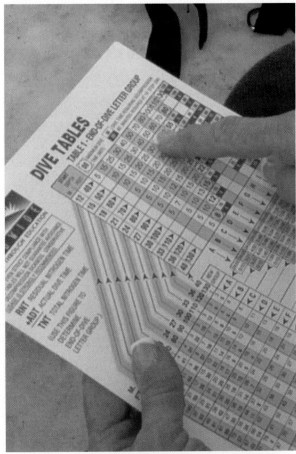

FIGURE 5-6. THE NAUI DIVE TABLES HAVE BEEN DESIGNED FOR RECREATIONAL DIVING AND ARE EASY TO USE.

Decompression, Dive Tables, and Dive Computers

Decompression, Dive Tables, and Dive Computers

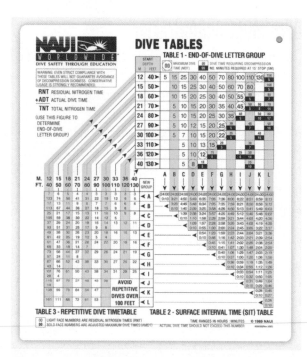

FIGURE 5-7. THE NAUI DIVE TABLES ARE DESIGNED TO FLOW FROM ONE TABLE TO THE NEXT IN A CONTINUOUS LOOP.

TABLE 1 - END-OF-DIVE LETTER GROUP

START DEPTH M	FEET	00 = MAXIMUM DIVE TIME (MDT) / 00 = DIVE TIME REQUIRING DECOMPRESSION, NO. MINUTES REQUIRED AT 15' STOP (5M)											
		A	**B**	**C**	**D**	**E**	**F**	**G**	**H**	**I**	**J**	**K**	**L**
12	40►	5	15	25	30	40	50	70	80	100	110	(130)	150/5
15	50►		10	15	25	30	40	50	60	70	(80)	100/5	
18	60►		10	15	20	25	30	40	50	(55)	80/5	80/7	
21	70►	5	10	15	20	30	35	40	(45)	50/5	60/8	70/14	
24	80►	5	10	15	20	25	30	(35)	40/6	50/10	60/17		
27	90►	5	10	12	15	20	(25)	30/5	40/7	50/18			
30	100►	5	7	10	15	20	(22)	25/5	40/15				
33	110►	5	10	13	(15)	20/5		30/7					
36	120►	5	10	(12)	15/5			25/6	30/14				
40	130►	5	(8)	10/5				25/10					

A B C D E F G H I J K L

FIGURE 5-8. TABLE 1 — END-OF-DIVE LETTER GROUP.

Table 1 — End-Of-Dive Letter Group

Table 1 — End-Of-Dive Letter Group gives you a Letter Group designation at the end of your dive (figure 5-8). This table also gives you the Maximum Dive Time (MDT) information for depths from 12 meters to 40 meters (40 feet to 130 feet). The MDTs are the red, circled numbers.

The table is arranged with the depths in columns on the left side of the table and the times for each depth in rows across the table. To find your Letter Group, use the following steps:

1. Take the deepest depth you reached during your dive and round it to the next greater depth found in Table 1. For example, if the deepest part of your dive was to 23 meters (75.5 feet), round the number to 24 meters (80 feet).
2. Locate the row corresponding to your deepest depth.
3. Follow the row across until you find the column containing the total time of your dive. You might have to round the total time of your dive to the next greater time found on the table. For example, if the total time for your dive to 23 meters (75.5 feet) was 26 minutes, you must round the time to 30 minutes.
4. Follow the column containing the total time of your dive down until you reach a letter. This is your Letter Group designation for your dive. For example, the Letter Group for the dive to 23 meters (75.5 feet) for 26 minutes, which is rounded to 24 meters (80 feet) for 30 minutes, is G.

Verify What You Have Learned

Review the following questions about Table 1:

9. If you do a dive to 18 meters (60 feet) for 42 minutes, your Letter Group is _____.
10. If you do a dive to 12 meters (40 feet) for 88 minutes, your Letter Group is _____.
11. If you do a dive to 36 meters (120 feet) for 9 minutes, your Letter Group is _____.

Table 2 - Surface Interval Time (SIT) Table

The longer you stay on the surface between dives, the more excess nitrogen you eliminate. Table 2 — Surface Interval Time (SIT) Table gives you credit for eliminating nitrogen by changing your Letter Group (figure 5-9). Table 2 consists of blocks containing two numbers. The numbers are expressed as hours and minutes.

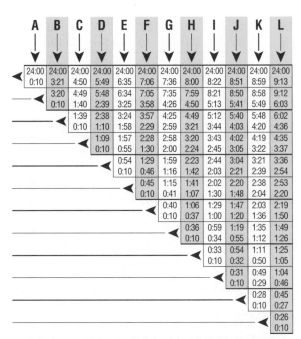

FIGURE 5-9. TABLE 2 — SURFACE INTERVAL TIME (SIT) TABLE.

The lower number in the block is the minimum Surface Interval Time (SIT) for a particular group and the upper number is maximum SIT for a particular group.

To find your new Letter Group based on your SIT, use the following steps:

1. Look across the top row of the table until you come to the Letter Group designation you had at the end of your previous dive. For example, you had a Letter Group of G.

2. Go down the column until you find the block into which your SIT fits. For example, you were out of the water for three hours. The block into which three hours fits is the one which starts at 2:59 and ends at 4:25.

3. Move left across the row containing your corresponding block until you come to another letter. For example, if you had a Letter Group of G and were out of the water for three hours, you would have a new Letter Group of C.

Note that the maximum time in this table is 24 hours. All excess nitrogen is considered eliminated after you have been on the surface for 24 hours. Therefore, a dive after 24 hours on the surface is not considered a repetitive dive.

Verify What You Have Learned

Review the following questions about Table 2:

12. If you have a Letter Group of I and your SIT is 2 hours and 36 minutes, your new Letter Group is _____.

13. If you have a Letter Group of C and your SIT is 3 hours, your new Letter Group is _____.

14. If you have a Letter Group of G and your SIT is 42 minutes, your new Letter Group is _____.

Table 3 - Repetitive Dive Timetable

Table 3 — Repetitive Dive Timetable provides your Adjusted Maximum Dive Time (AMDT) for your next dive and your Residual Nitrogen Time (RNT) based on your current Letter Group (figure 5-10). You use this table twice for each repetitive dive. First, you use the table to find your AMDT when planning your dive. Next, you use the table to find your RNT after you complete your dive. You add the RNT to your Actual Dive Time (ADT) to find your Total Nitrogen Time (TNT).

The table is arranged with the depths from 12 meters to 40 meters (40 feet to 130 feet) in columns across the table and the Letter Groups in rows down the table. Each block of the table contains two numbers. The upper number is the RNT corresponding to each depth and Letter Group. The lower, red number is the AMDT for each depth and Letter Group.

Use the following steps to find your AMDT when planning a repetitive dive:

1. Find your new Letter Group, based on your SIT, in the column on the right side of the table. For example, you have a new Letter Group of C.

2. Search along the row corresponding to your Letter Group until you come to the column corresponding to the depth to which you want to dive. For example, you want to dive to 15 meters (50 feet).

3. Look at the lower number to find your AMDT. For example, with a Letter Group of C, you can dive to 15 meters (50 feet) for a maximum of 59 minutes.

Use the following steps to find your TNT at the end of your repetitive dive:

1. Find your new Letter Group, based on your SIT, in the column on the right side of the table. For example, you have a new Letter Group of C.
2. Move along the row corresponding to your Letter Group until you come to the column corresponding to your deepest depth during the dive. For example, you went to 14 meters (47 feet), which rounds to 15 meters (50 feet).
3. Read the upper number in the block. This is your RNT. For example, the RNT for a dive to 15 meters (50 feet) for Letter Group C is 21 minutes.
4. Add the RNT to your ADT to find your TNT. For example, if your ADT was 35 minutes, you must add your RNT of 21 minutes from step 3 to get a TNT of 56 minutes.

Note that the AMDTs and RNTs in each block add up to the circled MDT for each corresponding depth in Table 1.

Verify What You Have Learned

Review the following questions about Table 3:

15. If you have a new Letter Group of D and you want to dive to 18 meters (60 feet), your AMDT is _____ minutes.
16. If you have a new Letter Group of B and you want to dive to 27 meters (90 feet), your AMDT is _____ minutes.
17. True or False. If you have a new Letter Group of G, you can dive to 24 meters (80 feet) for 32 minutes.
18. If you have a new Letter Group of E and you dive to 17 meters (57 feet), your RNT is _____ minutes.
19. If you have a new Letter Group of G and you dive to 11 meters (37 feet), your RNT is _____ minutes.
20. If you have a new Letter Group of C and you dive to 20 meters (67 feet) for 22 minutes, your TNT is _____ minutes.
21. If you have a new Letter Group of D and you dive to 16.2 meters (54 feet) for 18 minutes, your TNT is _____ minutes.

| M. | 12 | 15 | 18 | 21 | 24 | 27 | 30 | 33 | 36 | 40 | NEW |
FT.	40	50	60	70	80	90	100	110	120	130	GROUP
	7	6	5	4	4	3	3	3	3	3	◄ A
	123	74	50	41	31	22	19	12	9	5	
	17	13	11	9	8	7	7	6	6	6	◄ B
	113	67	44	36	27	18	15	9	6		
	25	21	17	15	13	11	10	10	9	8	◄ C
	105	59	38	30	22	14	12	5			
	37	29	24	20	18	16	14	13	12	11	◄ D
	93	51	31	25	17	9	8				
	49	38	30	26	23	20	18	16	15	13	◄ E
	81	42	25	19	12	5	4				
	61	47	36	31	28	24	22	20	18	16	◄ F
	69	33	19	14	7						
	73	56	44	37	32	29	26	24	21	19	◄ G
	57	24	11	8							
	87	66	52	43	38	33	30	27	25	22	◄ H
	43	14									
	101	76	61	50	43	38	34	31	28	25	◄ I
	29	4									
	116	87	70	57	48	43	38	AVOID			◄ J
	14							REPETITIVE			
	138	99	79	64	54	47		DIVES OVER			◄ K
	161	111	88	72	61	53		30 METERS (100')			◄ L

FIGURE 5-10. TABLE 3 — REPETITIVE DIVE TIMETABLE.

DIVE PLANNING WORKSHEET

You must systematically keep track of your depth, dive time, surface interval, Letter Group designations, and other information when you work with the NAUI Dive Tables or NAUI Dive Time Calculator. There is a NAUI Dive Planning Worksheet (figure 5-11) on the back of your NAUI Dive Tables. This section explains how to use the worksheet, which is very useful for helping prevent errors. This method of calculating your dive times is called the *profile method*.

You can write on the NAUI worksheet on your NAUI Dive Tables with a pencil and erase it or scour it clean without damaging the tables. You should use the worksheet on each dive, so take a pencil with you when you go diving and write your dive information directly on the NAUI worksheet. Your NAUI Dive Tables are also waterproof so you can record information on them in the water or refer to the planning information while you are on your dive.

In this section, you will see how to use the NAUI Dive Planning Worksheet and your NAUI Dive Tables to make or plan two dives in one day.

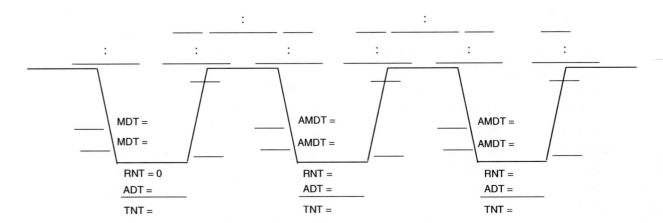

FIGURE 5-11. THE NAUI DIVE PLANNING WORKSHEET PROVIDES AN EASY WAY TO KEEP TRACK OF YOUR DIVES.

Planning Your Dive

To plan your dive with your NAUI Dive Planning Worksheet (figure 5-12), use the following steps:

1. Write your planned depth on the top line of the left side of the first profile. For example, plan a dive to 21 meters (70 feet).
2. Write your planned depth plus three meters (10 feet) on the lower line to the left side of the first profile. For example, your planned depth plus 3 meters (10 feet) is 24 meters (80 feet).
3. Look at Table 1 and find the MDT for your planned depth. For example, the MDT for 21 meters (70 feet) is 45 minutes.
4. Record the MDT next to your planned depth on the first profile.
5. Find the MDT for your planned depth plus 3 meters (10 feet). For example, the MDT for 24 meters (80 feet) is 35 minutes.
6. Record the MDT next to your planned depth plus 3 meters (10 feet) on the first profile.

At this point, you have finished planning your dive with regard to depth and time limits. Now it's time to dive your plan.

Finding Your Letter Group

The next step using your NAUI Dive Planning Worksheet is to record the information from your first dive and find your Letter Group designation (figure 5-13).

Use the following steps to find your Letter Group:

1. In the time slot at the upper left corner of the first profile, record the time that you started your descent. For example, your first dive started at 9:45 a.m.
2. On the line to the lower right side of the first profile, record your deepest depth. For example, you went to 20 meters (66 feet).
3. In the time slot at the upper right corner of the first profile, record the time you completed your ascent. For example, you surfaced at 10:20 a.m.

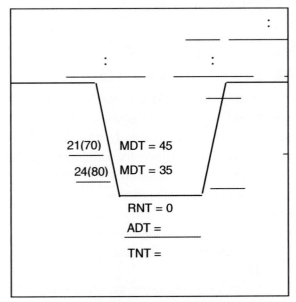

FIGURE 5-12. THIS PROFILE HAS BEEN COMPLETED FOR A DIVE PLANNED TO 21 METERS (70 FEET).

Decompression, Dive Tables, and Dive Computers

133

4. At the bottom of the first profile (next to ADT), record your ADT. Remember to subtract your three minute precautionary decompression stop, which is considered neutral time. For example, your total dive time was 35 minutes – subtracting the three minute precautionary stop gives you an ADT of 32 minutes.

5. Add your ADT to the RNT to get your TNT. For example, because this was your first dive of a trip, your RNT is 0 (zero), so your TNT is 32 minutes plus 0 minutes for a total of 32 minutes.

6. On Table 1, find the row corresponding to your deepest depth and follow the row across to the block containing the time corresponding to your TNT. For example, your depth was 20 meters (66 feet), which rounds up to 21 meters (70 feet) and you follow the row over to 32 minutes, which rounds up to the 35 minute block.

7. Trace the column containing the appropriate time down until you reach a letter. This is your Letter Group. For example, for a dive to 21 meters (70 feet) for 35 minutes, your Letter Group is G.

8. Record the Letter Group on the line above the time you completed your dive.

This completes the dive profile for your first dive.

Recording Your Surface Interval and Finding Your New Letter Group

Once you have completed your first dive, you must spend at least 10 minutes on the surface to avoid counting two dives as one. The length of your Surface Interval Time (SIT) will determine what your new Letter Group will be for planning your next dive (figure 5-14).

Use the following steps to find your new Letter Group after you have completed your SIT:

1. Record your SIT in the time slot to the right of your Letter Group. For example, your SIT is 2 hours.

2. Find your Letter Group in the row of letters between Table 1 and Table 2. For example, you had a Letter Group of G.

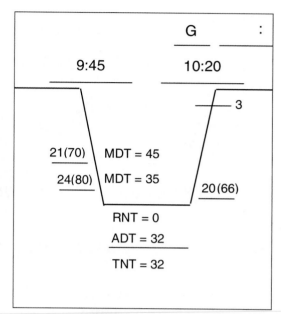

FIGURE 5-13. THIS PROFILE IS COMPLETE FOR A DIVE TO 20 METERS (66 FEET) FOR 32 MINUTES.

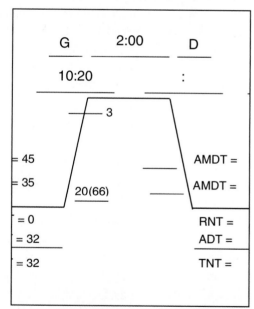

FIGURE 5-14. YOU RECORD YOUR SURFACE INTERVAL TIME BETWEEN YOUR LETTER GROUP FROM YOUR PREVIOUS DIVE AND YOUR NEW LETTER GROUP.

3. Look down the column until you find the block into which your SIT fits. For example, you are on the surface for 2 hours. The block into which 2 hours fits is the one that ranges from 2:00 to 2:58.

4. Move across the row containing your corresponding block to the left until you come to another letter. For example, you had a Letter Group of G and you have been on the surface for 2 hours, so your new Letter Group is D.

5. Record the new Letter Group to the right of your SIT.

Once you have determined your new Letter Group, you are ready to plan a repetitive dive.

Planning Your Repetitive Dive

When planning repetitive dives, you use the NAUI Dive Planning Worksheet as you did for the first dive (figure 5-15). However, you must use Table 3 to find your AMDT when planning your dive.

Use the following steps to plan a repetitive dive:

1. Write your planned depth on the top line to the left of the second profile. For example, plan a dive to 15 meters (50 feet).

2. Write your planned depth plus three meters (10 feet) on the lower line to the left of the second profile. For example, your planned depth plus three meters (10 feet) is 18 meters (60 feet).

3. Look at Table 3 and find the AMDT for your

planned depth. For example, the AMDT for 15 meters (50 feet) for Letter Group D is 51 minutes.

4. Record the AMDT next to your planned depth on the second profile.

5. Find the AMDT for your planned depth plus 3 meters (10 feet). For example, the AMDT for 18 meters (60 feet) is 31 minutes for Letter Group D.

6. Record the AMDT next to your planned depth plus 3 meters (10 feet) on the second profile.

At this time, you have finished planning your repetitive dive regarding depth and time limits. Now it's again time to dive your plan.

Recording Your Repetitive Dive

Recording your repetitive dive is similar to recording your first dive. However, this time you have residual nitrogen in your body and you must consider that before you find your new Letter Group (figure 5-16). Use the following steps to record your repetitive dive and find your new Letter Group:

1. In the time slot at the upper left corner of the second profile, record the time that you started your descent. For example, your second dive started at 12:35 p.m.

2. On the line to the right side of the second profile, record your deepest depth. For example, you went to 16 meters (52.5 feet).

3. In the time slot at the upper right corner of the first profile, record the time you completed your ascent. For example, you surfaced at 1:05 p.m.

4. Record your ADT at the bottom of the second profile (next to ADT). Remember to subtract your 3 minute precautionary decompression stop, which is considered neutral time. For example, your total dive time was 30 minutes – subtracting the 3-minute precautionary stop gives you an ADT of 27 minutes.

5. Find your RNT for your depth and Letter Group on Table 3. For example, you had a Letter Group of D and you went to 16 meters (52.5 feet), which gives you an RNT of 24 minutes.

6. Record the RNT at the bottom of the second profile (next to RNT).

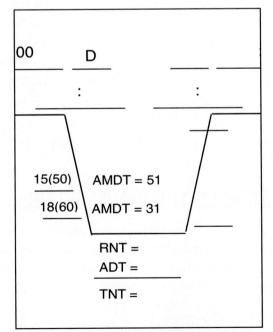

FIGURE 5-15. THE DIVE PLAN FOR THE SECOND DIVE TO 15 METERS (50 FEET) HAS BEEN COMPLETED ON THIS WORKSHEET.

135

Decompression, Dive Tables, and Dive Computers

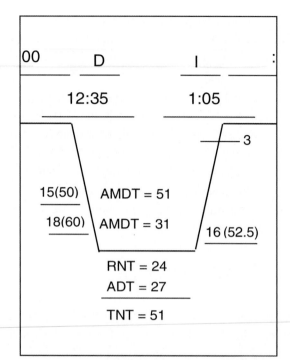

00   D   I

12:35   1:05

3

15(50)   AMDT = 51

18(60)   AMDT = 31   16 (52.5)

RNT = 24

ADT = 27

TNT = 51

FIGURE 5-16. THIS PROFILE IS COMPLETE FOR A REPETITIVE DIVE TO 16 METERS (52.5 FEET) FOR 30 MINUTES.

7. Add your ADT to your RNT to get your TNT. For example, your ADT is 27 minutes, plus an RNT of 24 minutes, gives you a TNT of 51 minutes.

8. Go back to Table 1 and find the row corresponding to your deepest depth. Follow the row across to the block containing the time corresponding to your TNT. For example, your depth was 16 meters (52.5 feet), which rounds up to 18 meters (60 feet) and your TNT was 51 minutes, which rounds up to the 55 minute block.

9. Look down the column containing the appropriate time until you reach a letter. This is your Letter Group. For example, for a dive to 18 meters (60 feet) for 55 minutes, your Letter Group is I.

10. Record the Letter Group on the line above the time you completed your second dive.

This completes the dive profile for your second dive. Use the same steps to plan and perform a third dive.

Do not rely on your memory to keep track of dive times, maximum depths, or *surface intervals*. You must record this information, and the NAUI Dive

Planning Worksheet provides a convenient way to record your data. Get into the habit of recording your dives on the worksheet, and it will become easy to keep track of your diving. This will also make it easier to complete your logbook at the end of the day.

Verify What You Have Learned

Review the following problems using the NAUI Dive Planning Worksheet and your NAUI Dive Tables:

22. Your first dive of the day was to 20 meters (66 feet). You descended at 9:40, surfaced at 10:19, and completed a three-minute precautionary decompression stop(ADT=36). Your second dive was to 14 meters (46 feet). You descended at 12:32, surfaced at 1:13, and completed a three-minute precautionary decompression stop(ADT=38). Your third dive was to 12 meters (40 feet). You descended at 2:43, surfaced at 3:26, and completed a three-minute precautionary decompression stop(ADT=40).

23. Your first dive of the first day of your trip was to 24 meters (80 feet). You descended at 8:35, surfaced at 8:58, and completed a three-minute precautionary decompression stop(ADT=20). Your SIT was two hours and 46 minutes. Your second dive was to 16 meters (52.5 feet) for 36 minutes including your precautionary decompression stop(ADT=33). You surfaced at 12:20. Your third dive was to 10 meters (33 feet). You descended at 3:10, surfaced at 4:10, and completed a three-minute precautionary decompression stop(ADT=57).

MAXIMIZING YOUR UNDERWATER TIME

There are times when you are making repetitive dives that you will either not be able to dive to the depth you would like or for the length of time you would like. You can maximize your underwater time and depth to which you want to dive by adjusting your SIT, your depth, or your ADT. In this section, you will see how the three factors interact and how working with them will get you the depth or time you want.

Limiting Your Dive Time

The first way to keep within the Maximum Dive Time is easy – limit your ADT. Your first dive of the day must not exceed the MDT for the depth of that dive, and your repetitive dives must not exceed the AMDT for your planned depth. This can be restrictive.

Suppose you want to make three 25 minute dives to a depth of 18 meters (60 feet). You want to spend an hour on the surface between each dive. Your first dive is to 18 meters (60 feet) for 25 minutes so your Letter Group is E. After a SIT of 1 hour, your new Letter Group is D.

With a Letter Group of D, your AMDT for a dive to 18 meters (60 feet) is 31 minutes. If your ADT for the second dive to 18 meters (60 feet) is 25 minutes, your RNT is 24, and your TNT is 49. Your Letter Group following this dive is H.

After another hour of SIT, your new Letter Group is G. According to Table 3, the maximum time you can spend at 18 meters (60 feet) is 11 minutes. You can see that making three back-to-back dives to depths of 18 meters (60 feet) or more can be quite limiting if you want to spend the maximum amount of time in the water.

Planning Your Surface Intervals

Planning your surface intervals carefully is a good way to control your residual nitrogen and your AMDT for repetitive dives. The longer you remain on the surface between dives, the less nitrogen remains in your body, and the longer you can stay under water on your next dive. You must be able to determine how long a surface interval is required to carry out a planned dive without nearing the no-decompression limits.

Surface intervals must be at least 10 minutes in length. NAUI recommends that you spend at least an hour on the surface between dives. Choosing to spend more than an hour on the surface between dives gives you more time to offgas nitrogen and will give you more time under water on your next dive.

If you use the same example from the previous section, you have a Letter Group of H after your second dive of the day. For your third dive, you want to go to 18

meters (60 feet) for at least 25 minutes. If you look at the 18-meter (60-foot) column on Table 3, you see that you must have a Letter Group of E to be able to spend a maximum of 25 minutes at 18 meters (60 feet).

To find out how long you must stay on the surface to change from a Letter Group of H to a Letter Group of E, follow the E row from Table 3 back to Table 2. At the same time, follow the H column down from Table 1. Find the block where the E row and H column intersect. It should have a minimum time of 1:42 and a maximum time of 2:23. By spending one hour and 42 minutes on the surface between your second and third dives, you can dive to 18 meters (60 feet) for 25 minutes.

Limiting Your Depth

Your third option in dive planning is to increase your bottom time by limiting your depth. If you were not able to extend your surface interval between the second and third dives in the previous example and you did not want to make a dive shorter than 25 minutes, you could dive to a shallower depth and spend more time there.

If you have a Letter Group of G following a one hour SIT and you know you want to spend at least 25 minutes on your dive, follow the G row in Table 3 until you find a column that has an AMDT of at least 25 minutes. In this example, the depth of 12 meters (40 feet) has an AMDT of 57 minutes. Therefore, by diving six meters (20 feet) shallower, you can make a 25 minute dive. These examples show how you can use the dive tables to your advantage.

SPECIAL RULES

There are a number of special rules and procedures you must also learn to handle special situations. These situations include decompression, cold or strenuous diving, flying after diving, and altitude diving.

Decompression Diving

Intentionally exceeding the Maximum Dive Time is unwise, unsafe, and discouraged. As you will learn in advanced or specialty training for deep diving, you must meet many requirements to carry out decompression dives properly. In normal recreational diving decompression dives are still discouraged, even if you meet all the requirements. Diving is only a sport — why risk injury?

Some divers engage in *technical diving*, an extremely advanced recreational diving activity. Technical diving can involve planned decompression dives. You must have special equipment and training as well as extensive diving experience to participate. In addition, this type of diving is much more hazardous than other recreational diving. Technical divers accept the fact that risk of DCS or other problems is much greater.

Precautionary Decompression Stops

You should stop at 5 meters (15 feet) for 3 minutes at the end of each dive for a *precautionary decompression stop* or *safety stop*. Taking this action is recommended to help prevent DCS and to maintain control of your ascent near the surface.

Time spent decompressing is considered *neutral time*. It does not count as part of your ADT. For example, if you dive to 21 meters (70 feet) for 45 minutes, you should stop at 5 meters (15 feet) for an additional 3 minutes. However, you determine your Letter Group using the dive schedule of 21 meters/45 minutes (70 feet/45 minutes). You can also include the 3 minutes as part of your ADT as an extra precaution.

You document your precautionary decompression stop on your NAUI Dive Planning Worksheet next to a short horizontal line drawn through the ascent line of the dive profile.

Required Decompression

If you accidentally exceed a Maximum Dive Time or Adjusted Maximum Dive Time, you must decompress by stages. You must stop at 5 meters (15 feet) during your ascent and stay there for a specified time to allow your body to offgas nitrogen. You must keep your physical activity to a minimum during your decompression stop.

FIGURE 5-17. IT IS USEFUL TO HAVE A MEANS TO HELP MAINTAIN A CONSTANT DEPTH DURING YOUR DECOMPRESSION STOP.

It is useful to have a means of support to maintain a constant depth during your stop. An ascent line, a decompression bar suspended from a boat, or the contour of the bottom in shallow water are all examples of support (figure 5-17). Without something to grasp, it is difficult to remain at one depth in shallow water. Swimming and hovering decompression are possible, but not easy, and the activity might offset the benefit of offgassing nitrogen.

Table 1 gives you required decompression times for each depth. To the right of the Maximum Dive Times for each depth are split squares containing two sets of numbers. The top number represents dive time. The lower number represents the decompression time required for that dive time. The decompression time is the length of time you must spend at 5 meters (15 feet) to help avoid DCS. For example, if your TNT on a 24-meter (80-foot) dive was 45 minutes, you would have to perform a 10-minute decompression stop.

Time spent decompressing is considered *neutral time*. It does not count as part of your ADT. You document your required decompression stop on your NAUI Dive Planning Worksheet next to a short horizontal line drawn through the ascent line of the dive profile.

Omitted Decompression

If you surface and discover you omitted a required

decompression stop, take the following steps:

1. Discontinue diving for 24 hours no matter how well you feel.
2. Breathe 100% oxygen, if available. If only a small, portable unit is available, breathe the oxygen until the cylinder is depleted.
3. Drink plenty of fluids.
4. Rest.
5. Watch for symptoms of DCS.

If you suspect that you have DCS, you must seek medical help. If there is an operational chamber nearby, go there. Otherwise, have medical help call Divers Alert Network (DAN) at (919) 684-9111, which is their 24-hour emergency line. They will advise you of the procedure to follow to obtain chamber treatment. **Never go back into the water to try to make up for the omitted decompression stop.**

Cold or Strenuous Dives

If you get cold, do strenuous physical work during or after a dive, or both, use the next greater time for your dive schedule. For example, a dive to 18 meters (60 feet) with a TNT of 40 minutes would become a 50 minute dive.

Flying after Diving

If you decrease pressure below one ATM by going to an altitude above sea level after diving, you increase your risk of suffering DCS. Commercial planes pressurize their cabins to an altitude equivalent to about 2400 meters (8000 feet) or 0.75 ATM or less.

If you only do one no-decompression dive, you can fly after waiting 12 hours. If you do more than one no-decompression dive in a day, or do multiple days of diving, you should wait longer. The current recommendation is to wait 24 hours after the completion of your last dive. If you make dives that require a decompression stop, or you omit a required decompression stop, wait more than 24 hours before flying.

Altitude Diving

Atmospheric pressure decreases with altitude, which

means that the rate of change in pressure is greater when you descend into water at altitude. To account for this difference, you need to use altitude conversion tables or the NAUI Altitude Tables and follow special procedures.

Before you dive at altitudes above 300 meters (1000 feet), you must be trained in special altitude diving procedures. Your table depths, maximum rate of ascent, and the depths for decompression stops change with altitude. Your depth gauge will also give incorrect data.

If altitude diving is common in your area, your instructor might provide additional information as part of your course, and also might recommend that you participate in a high-altitude specialty-training program before you receive your NAUI Scuba Diver certification.

High-altitude training is beyond the scope of this textbook. Do not attempt high-altitude diving without first completing an appropriate high-altitude training program.

USING THE NAUI DIVE TIME CALCULATOR

The NAUI Dive Tables are the basis for the NAUI Dive Time Calculator, which eliminates some calculations required with the tables (figure 5-18). Once you are familiar with the NAUI Dive Tables, learning how to use the NAUI Dive Time Calculator is easy.

General Organization

NAUI Dive Tables 1 and 3 are combined on the baseplate. Letter Group designations appear around the circumference, and ADTs in minutes appear in the window. End-of-Dive Letter Groups appear to the right of the ADT numbers in the disk window. Dive Table 2 is printed on the disk.

Using the Calculator

To plan your first dive of the day, use the following steps:

1. Find the **No Group** section on the baseplate.
2. Align the depth arrow on the edge of the disk with the planned depth of your dive. The Maximum Dive Time for that dive appears as the

FIGURE 5-18. THE NAUI DIVE TIME CALCULATOR ELIMINATES SOME CALCULATIONS REQUIRED BY THE NAUI DIVE TABLES.

largest number in the window. For example, a **No Group** diver who plans a dive to 18 meters (60 feet) would have a Maximum Dive Time of 55 minutes.

To find your Letter Group at the completion of your dive, use the following steps:

1. Find the **No Group** section on the baseplate.
2. Align the depth arrow on the edge of the disk with the deepest depth of your dive.
3. Read the bottom times from the center of the disk outward and find the first time that you do not exceed.
4. Look to the right of the window to see your End-Of-Dive Letter Group. For example, if you do a dive to 18 meters (60 feet) and your ADT is 23 minutes, the first time you do not exceed is 25 minutes. The End-Of-Dive Letter Group next to the 25 is E.

To plan a repetitive dive, use the following steps:

1. Use Dive Table 2 on the disk to find your new Letter Group after your SIT.
2. Find your new Letter Group on the circumference of the baseplate and align the depth arrow on the disk with the planned depth of your repetitive dive. For example, if you have a Letter Group of E and do a 1 hour SIT, your new Letter Group is D. If you want to return to 18 meters (60 feet), align your arrow with the **18 meters (60 feet)** depth in the **D Group** section. The longest time

limit in the window is 31 minutes.

To find your End-Of-Dive Letter Group for a repetitive dive, use the following steps:

1. Find your new Letter Group on the circumference of the baseplate and align the depth arrow on the disk with the deepest depth of your repetitive dive. For example, align your arrow with the **18 meters (60 feet)** depth in the **D Group** section.
2. Read the bottom times from the center of the disk outward and find the first time that you do not exceed. For example, if you do a repetitive dive to 18 meters (60 feet) with a Letter Group of D and your ADT is 23 minutes, the first time you do not exceed is 26 minutes.
3. Look to the right of the window to see your End-Of-Dive Letter Group. For example, the End-Of-Dive Letter Group next to the 26 is H.

The calculator design eliminates the AMDT. It also eliminates adding the ADT to the RNT to obtain a TNT. However, the answers are the same as those obtained from the dive schedules using the NAUI Dive Tables.

Dive Planning with the Calculator

You can use the NAUI Dive Time Calculator to achieve the same three methods of dive planning as you can using the NAUI Dive Tables:

- Limit your bottom time to the maximum number indicated for a given depth and group.
- Extend your surface interval to move to a group letter earlier in the alphabet.
- Dive to a shallower depth.

For example, you are a diver with a Letter Group of F and you want to dive for 25 minutes. You move the window back and forth and find that you can dive to 18 meters (60 feet) for 19 minutes or to 15 meters (50 feet) for 33 minutes. To avoid exceeding the Maximum Dive Time, you know you can dive no deeper than 15 meters (50 feet) and stay no longer than 33 minutes.

You want to dive to 18 meters (60 feet) for 25 minutes, but cannot because you are a diver in Letter Group F. You need to determine the Letter Group that will allow you to make the dive. You also need to determine the minimum surface interval that would allow you to achieve that Letter Group. To determine the group that will allow you to make the dive, align the depth arrow with 18 meters (60 feet) in group F. Work back, one Letter Group at a time, realigning the depth arrow with 18 meters (60 feet) for each group, until you find a Maximum Dive Time of 25 minutes or longer. In this example, the first Letter Group allowing a Maximum Dive Time of 25 minutes is E.

In some instances, the words **DO NOT DIVE** appear in the calculator window. This means that you have too much residual nitrogen to permit a dive at the depth selected for a particular Letter Group. You will have to extend your surface interval to dive at that depth, or dive at a shallower depth.

Required decompression information is handled differently using the NAUI Dive Time Calculator than with the NAUI Dive Tables. A separate Decompression Timetable is provided. To use this table, use the following steps:

1. Look in the first column corresponding to the depth of your dive.
2. Look in the second column for your depth for the first time that equals or exceeds your ADT in excess of the Dive Time limit for your depth. For example, you can dive to 24 meters (80 feet) for a MDT of 35 minutes. If your ADT was 38 minutes, your excess time is 3 minutes. The first time that equals or exceeds your excess time in column two is 5 minutes.
3. Decompress at 5 meters (15 feet) for the time indicated in column three.

As you can see, using the NAUI Dive Time Calculator is even easier than using the NAUI Dive Tables.

SAMPLE PROBLEMS

Use the NAUI Dive Tables or the NAUI Dive Time Calculator to solve the following dive profiles:

1. Your first dive of the day is planned for a depth of 18 meters (60 feet), begins at 9:30 a.m., and lasts for 23 minutes. The actual depth of the dive is 16.7 meters (55 feet). You make a precautionary decompression stop at 5 meters (15 feet) for 3 minutes, you surface at 9:56 a.m. and remain out of the water until 10:40 a.m. Your next dive is to a depth of 15 meters (50 feet) for 23 minutes. You make a precautionary decompression stop at 5 meters (15 feet) for 3 minutes. You surface at 11:06 a.m. and have a SIT of 1 hour and 50 minutes. At 12:56 p.m., you begin your third dive to a planned depth of 12 meters (40 feet), but you end up reaching a depth of 13.7 meters (45 feet) with an ADT of 30 minutes. You make a precautionary decompression stop at 5 meters (15 feet) for 3 minutes and you surface from the third dive at 1:29 p.m. What is your final Letter Group?

2. Your first dive of the day begins at 8:00 a.m. and is to a depth of 18 meters (60 feet) for 31 minutes. You make a precautionary decompression stop at 5 meters (15 feet) for 3 minutes. You surface at 8:34 a.m. Your SIT is 1 hour and 31 minutes. The second dive begins at 10:05 a.m., is to a depth of 16.8 meters (55 feet), and lasts for 24 minutes. You make a precautionary decompression stop at 5 meters (15 feet) for 3 minutes and surface at 10:32 a.m. Your third dive, which begins at 12:36 p.m., is to 15 meters (50 feet) for 31 minutes. What time do you surface from this dive and what is your Letter Group?

3. Your first dive is to 18 meters (60 feet) for 30 minutes followed by a 30-minute SIT. The second dive is to 15 meters (50 feet) for 30 minutes. What is your Letter Group after the second dive?

4. Your first dive is to 17 meters (56 feet) for 31 minutes and it is followed by a 1 hour SIT. The second dive is to 16 meters (52.5 feet). What is the AMDT for the second dive? What is your Letter Group if you reach the AMDT?

5. After the second dive in problem 4, how long a SIT is required to make a 25-minute dive to 15 meters (50 feet) without exceeding the AMDT? What is your Letter Group following the third dive if your ADT is 25 minutes?

USING DIVE COMPUTERS

There are three ways to determine how long you can dive and then ascend within the dive time limits. We have already discussed two. The third and easiest way is to use a dive computer (figure 5-19). This is also the most expensive way to monitor your bottom times, but it is used by more divers every day.

Different body tissues absorb and release nitrogen at different rates. Mathematical *models* (programs) considering *theoretical tissues* have been developed to estimate ingassing and outgassing from various tissues. Dive computers with these mathematical models continuously sample depth and time and calculate the amount of nitrogen in each tissue model for any given moment. The computer uses this information to determine the time limits for the current depth and displays it for the diver. Remember that both dive tables and dive computers are only theoretical models of what happens in the human body. No presently available method of calculating your excess nitrogen accurately accounts for your individual age, body type, level of fitness, fatigue, drug or alcohol use, and so on.

Dive tables provide time limits in increments of 3 meters (10 feet) of depth and assume that you spend the entire dive at the deepest depth. This is one disadvantage to the use of the tables as compared to a dive computer. A dive computer might calculate both ingassing and offgassing in increments as little as 0.3 meters (1 foot) for the depth at which you are diving. The computer constantly recalculates as your depth changes during your dive.

A dive computer does not count all of your dive time as having occurred at your deepest depth. When you spend part of your dive in water shallower than your maximum depth, a dive computer considers this. The computer calculates only the amount of nitrogen that its mathematical model predicts you ingas or offgas at each depth. A dive computer allows a dive with time spent at shallower depths (called a *multilevel* dive profile) to have longer dive time limits. Also, there is a lesser penalty for residual nitrogen than when you use the fixed-calculation dive tables.

A dive computer is an electronic device that can

FIGURE 5-19. THERE ARE MANY DIFFERENT TYPES OF DIVE COMPUTERS.

fail without warning. Most dive computers are highly reliable, but you must always consider this possibility. When a dive computer fails, your only option is to surface at the rate of ascent specified by the manufacturer and make a 3- to 5-minute precautionary decompression stop at 5 meters (15 feet). Then you must stop diving for the period recommended by the manufacturer. You must do this because there is usually no way to recalculate your previous dive or dives using tables. Also, you cannot start with a *fresh* computer when you have residual nitrogen in your system.

There are dive tables available that you can use to compute multilevel dives. The manual planning and execution of these dives is complex and not recommended for recreational diving. If you want to receive credit for reduced nitrogen absorption during multilevel dives, use a dive computer. However, using a dive computer increases the need for understanding and being able to work the dive tables.

Dive Computer Terms

You must be familiar with the terms associated with dive computers. A *ceiling* is the shallowest depth to which you can ascend without risk of forming bubbles in your body (figure 5-20). You must not pass or *violate*

FIGURE 5-20. THE CEILING DISPLAY INDICATES THAT YOU MUST MAKE A DECOMPRESSION STOP.

this ceiling. If your computer displays a ceiling, you have entered a decompression situation. To help avoid suffering DCS, you should use your computer to prevent a ceiling from being established.

Scrolling occurs when your computer continuously flashes the Maximum Dive Times in sequence for progressively deeper depths. This feature is an aid for dive planning and for chamber treatment, should you develop DCS. Scrolling can also show your current dive profile history.

Displays

Although many different dive computers are available, many share the same functions. The layouts of the display screens differ among computers, but they all display much of the same information.

Many dive computers will also interface with a personal computer so that you can download and visually

display, or even log, your dives on your computer.

This section describes a typical dive computer and explains the most common screens and functions. Your computer might be different and not function in the same way. It might also use the same terms with different meanings. You must read and understand the manual that is supplied with your computer.

Initialization

When a dive computer is first turned on, it must *initialize* itself. This is a process where the operating program is checked and loaded into the computer's memory. When this happens, the computer typically runs through a self-diagnostic test and checks all of its functions. The computer display fills during this sequence to ensure that the entire display is working (figure 5-21). Also, any alarms that the computer has will display or sound.

You can turn on all computers manually to check their operation. Some computers must be turned on

FIGURE 5-21. A DIVE COMPUTER DISPLAY WILL LIGHT UP COMPLETELY DURING INITIALIZATION.

FIGURE 5-22. WHEN A COMPUTER IS IN DIVE MODE, IT WILL DISPLAY DATA SUCH AS YOUR CURRENT DEPTH, MAXIMUM DEPTH, WATER TEMPERATURE, ACTUAL DIVE TIME, AND THE TIME YOU HAVE LEFT AT YOUR CURRENT DEPTH.

FIGURE 5-23. AN AIR-INTEGRATED COMPUTER WILL SHOW YOU THE AMOUNT OF AIR LEFT IN YOUR CYLINDER AS WELL AS THE AMOUNT OF AIR TIME YOU HAVE LEFT.

with a switch before you enter the water. Other computers turn on automatically when you enter the water.

You must initialize your computer to check its operation before you begin your dive. If you must turn your computer on with a switch, do not turn it on at depth, or after you have started your descent, because your dive will not be recorded accurately. You can damage some computers by turning them on at depth.

Scrolling

All computers can scroll before diving (after they are initialized) and between dives. Between dives, the computer accounts for your residual nitrogen and the time you have been on the surface. It shows your Allowable Maximum Dive Time for your next dive for each depth programmed in the computer. This is called scrolling.

Some computers will scroll continuously while you are on the surface. Once they have scrolled through the

maximum dive depths that they are able to calculate they show your last dive or series of dives. Other computers will scroll only if put in *Planning* mode. Read your dive computer's manual to learn how to make your computer scroll.

Dive Mode

When a computer is in dive mode, it will display data such as your current depth, maximum depth, water temperature, actual dive time, and the time you have left at your current depth (figure 5-22). Some computers will also show a graphic representation of the nitrogen in your body or in various theoretical tissues.

An air-integrated computer will show the air pressure in your cylinder. It might also indicate how much time you have left at your current depth based on your air consumption (figure 5-23). Some dive computers will compare your remaining air time with your remaining dive time and display whichever is the shorter, limiting factor.

As your bottom time lessens and you approach

FIGURE 5-24. ALL DIVE COMPUTERS WILL GIVE YOU A WARNING SIGNAL WHEN YOU EXCEED THE ASCENT RATE.

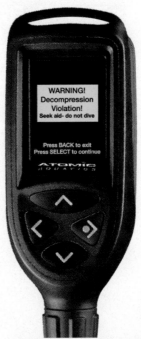

FIGURE 5-25. YOU SHOULD NEVER SEE THIS WARNING ON YOUR COMPUTER. IF YOU DO, BEGIN YOUR ASCENT IMMEDIATELY AND FOLLOW YOUR COMPUTER'S INSTRUCTIONS.

decompression status, some computers give you a visual warning message such as "**GO UP**." When this occurs, you must begin your ascent immediately, but at the proper rate.

Most computers require that you use an extremely slow ascent rate. Some models have different ascent rates for different depth ranges. All dive computers give a warning signal when you exceed the ascent rate (figure 5-24). Some computers warn you with a flashing screen stating something similar to "**SLOW**" or will warn you with a flashing red light. Other models warn with a beep or a synthesized voice.

No matter what the signal, you must slow down or possibly stop your ascent until your computer tells you to ascend. Any time you violate your computer's ascent rate, you increase your risk of DCS. Always monitor your computer carefully during ascent.

If you are ever foolish enough to exceed your computer's maximum depth range, your computer will warn you with a message such as "**OUT OF RANGE**" (figure 5-25). If this occurs, you must begin your ascent immediately. Your computer will give you the information

you need to complete your decompression and ascent. The computer might also prevent you from using the computer for 24 hours. You should plan your dives and then dive your plan so that you never see a message such as "**OUT OF RANGE**."

Decompression

You should never see the ceiling display. When your dive computer displays a *ceiling*, it means that you have an obligation to decompress. The ceiling depth is the depth of your first decompression stop. You must not ascend above the depth of that ceiling. You can be 0.3 or 0.6 meters (1 or 2 feet) deeper, but you must not be shallower.

If you require more than one decompression stop, your computer will display another ceiling at a shallower depth than the first stop. You must complete this stop, as well as any others, until your computer displays a zero ceiling or no ceiling at all.

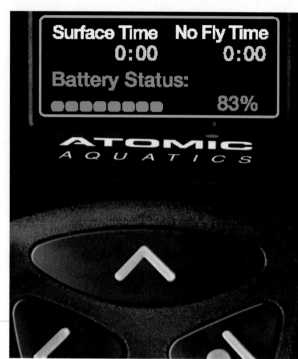

FIGURE 5-26. A DIVE COMPUTER WILL TELL YOU HOW MANY HOURS YOU MUST WAIT BEFORE YOU CAN FLY AFTER DIVING.

FIGURE 5-27. THE LOG MODE SHOWS YOU THE INFORMATION FROM YOUR PREVIOUS DIVES.

Decompression, Dive Tables, and Dive Computers

Planning Repetitive Dives

During your surface interval, your computer will give you credit for offgassing. If you monitor your display as it is scrolling, you will see that the maximum time allowed at any depth increases as you stay out of the water. A surface interval of at least one hour is still recommended even if you are using a computer.

When you are rested and ready to do a repetitive dive, look for the depth of your planned dive as the computer is scrolling and see how long the computer will allow you to stay at that depth.

Safe to Fly Indicators

Most computers will tell you when it is safe to fly based on their mathematical model. The computer might show an icon of an airplane or the words "**TIME TO FLY**" with hours and minutes listed beside it (figure 5-26). The computer is telling you how long you must wait before it is safe to fly. When you no longer see an airplane or the words "**TIME TO FLY**," it is safe to fly.

NAUI and most medical diving authorities recommend that you be conservative when flying after diving, especially if you have been on a multiday diving trip. You should plan your trip so that you have at least 24 hours on the surface before you need to fly.

Logging Your Dives

Even if you use a computer, you still need to log your dives. Some computers will allow you to download the information so you can keep your dive log on your personal computer. Others only hold a few dives in their memory so you should get in the habit of transferring the information to your paper logbook once per day.

On most computers, you can call up the *Log* mode manually by pressing a series of buttons or contacts on the computer (figure 5-27). The contacts usually require that your fingers are moist and you must touch multiple contacts at one time to complete an electric contact. Once you are in *Log* mode, the computer will show you the stored dives, starting with your most recent dive and moving backward through the stored dives.

Dive Computer Rules

You must obey the following rules when using a dive computer:

- A buddy team cannot share one computer; each diver must have their own computer. A dive computer used by one diver cannot be used by another diver on a subsequent dive until the time required by the computer for complete offgassing has expired.
- Read your computer manual carefully and use the computer in compliance with the manufacturer's instructions. Completing a Dive Computer Specialty course is recommended.
- If your dive computer fails at any time during your dive, you must end the dive and ascend to the surface at the ascent rate required by your computer's failure instructions. Do not forget to perform a 3-minute precautionary decompression stop before surfacing.
- If you have been diving on tables and want to start diving with a computer, you must wait 24 hours after your last dive before using a computer.
- If your computer must be turned on manually, do not turn it off until it indicates that offgassing is complete.

- Use the ascent rate specified for your make and model of dive computer. Most computers specify ascent rates that are slower than those for dive tables.
- A three to five minute precautionary decompression stop at 5 meters (15 feet) is recommended for all dives made with a dive computer, even if the computer does not display a ceiling.
- Plan repetitive dives deep to progressively shallower.
- Plan multilevel dives to start at the deepest depth, followed by progressively shallower depths.
- Do not make repetitive dives in one day to depths greater than 30 meters (100 feet).

Verify What You Have Learned

Review the following questions about dive computers:

24. A ceiling display indicates the depth to which you can _____.
25. The maximum recommended depth for a repetitive dive using a dive computer is _____ meters (_____ feet).
26. A computer goes through an _____ when you first turn it on.
27. _____ occurs when a computer reads out each allowable depth and maximum dive time when you are on the surface.
28. If you ascend above the ceiling indicated on your dive computer, you risk

    _____

    .
29. Two ways a computer can warn you that you have exceeded your ascent rate are _____ and _____.

CONCLUSION

By working with the NAUI Dive Tables and the NAUI Dive Time Calculator, you will soon feel comfortable with their use. Your instructor will help you with any difficulties you might have. Remember that you must plan and record your dives to help prevent DCS.

Computer diving is easier than diving with manual calculations, but you must remember how to use your dive tables in case a computer is not available. Dive computers are in common use, and there will probably be a time when divers no longer use dive tables. However, to be a versatile, as well as knowledgeable diver, you must understand the dive tables and the principles of dive computers.

Be sure to read the manual for your dive computer so you are completely familiar with its operation. Be sure to take the manual with you on your dive trips for handy reference.

Computers and dive tables will not eliminate the risk of DCS. Always make a precautionary decompression stop at the end of every dive and be conservative in the use of your dive computer or dive tables.

CHAPTER

6

Dive Planning and Recording

LEARNING GOALS

In this chapter you will:

- Learn about the steps to long range and short range planning.
- Be introduced to the steps to follow to safely conduct your dive.
- Learn why it is important to plan your dive and dive your plan.
- Be introduced to the importance of recording each dive you do.

To further reduce the risks in diving, it is essential that you plan and prepare your dives in advance. Also, the best way for you to get the most enjoyment out of diving is to plan your dives. For our purposes, *planning* is all of the arrangements you make for a dive, from the time you decide to go diving until your planned dives are complete.

Planning is divided into sections:

- Long range planning.
- Short range planning.
- Preparing to dive.
- Conducting your dive.
- Post-dive review.

You need to know the steps of planning so you can enjoy the best kind of dive. Planning ensures you have all the equipment you need in good working order, that you know what to expect at the dive site, and helps you avoid any last minute rush. In some cases, being able to go diving is possible only because you have made reservations in advance. When you, your equipment, and your buddy are well prepared for a dive, you will have the best possible chance of having a pleasurable experience, which is the goal of recreational diving.

LONG-RANGE PLANNING

Your long-range planning begins many months ahead of a major dive trip. For a day of diving at a local site, your long-range planning also begins well before your dive. If you wait until the night or even the week before a dive to start planning, it may be too late to pull everything together to have a successful dive.

Your first step is to plan the objective of your dive. For example, you might want to practice your navigation skills or try out a new underwater camera. Your objective might also be to see a new area of the world and the diving it has to offer.

Your second step is to select your location. Your location could be anywhere in the world, and take from a few minutes to a number of days to reach. You should also discuss an alternate location in case conditions are unacceptable at your primary location. Remember to investigate whether the location is a marine preserve, whether boat traffic or fishermen are present, and so on.

If the dive site is unfamiliar to you, you must research it. Books are available that provide information on popular locations, but you should also find a contact person in the area to obtain local knowledge about the proposed site. Sources include dive resorts, dive stores, dive clubs, dive instructors and dive masters. The more you can learn in advance, the better prepared you will be.

FIGURE 6-1. PRE DIVE OBSERVATIONS ARE AN IMPORTANT COMPONENT OF DIVE PLANNING.

FIGURE 6-2. ONE OF THE BEST WAYS TO MAINTAIN FITNESS FOR DIVING IS TO SWIM REGULARLY WITH MASK, SNORKEL, AND FINS.

If possible, you should also look at the dive site in advance (figure 6-1). This will show you a great deal about the site's accessibility, parking, fees, conditions, facilities, and entry and exit points. You might also find divers who can point things out and explain the best procedures for the location. Do not forget to investigate the emergency services in the area. Also, remember that conditions on your dive day can be radically different.

Your third step is to determine the date and time of your dive or dive trip. Be aware of any conflicting activities that might affect the date you want to dive, including plans you have made for the night before the dive. It is unwise and unsafe to dive the morning after attending a late night party you had forgotten was planned when you scheduled your dive. You should not consume alcohol within 12 hours of a planned dive. It is even better if you do not consume alcohol within 24 hours of a planned dive. You must not be hung over and you must be well rested.

If you are diving from shore, the time of day for your dive is also a consideration. Local winds might be light in the morning and strong in the afternoon, or vice versa. You might want to schedule your dive during high tide, because visibility is usually better at this time.

Your fourth step is to make travel arrangements. This could be anything from deciding whether you or your buddy will drive to the dive site to making airline, hotel, and boat reservations.

Your fifth step is to determine your equipment needs. For example, if the water temperature is different

from the water temperature where you normally dive, you might need to obtain a different type of diving suit. Different diving suits will change the amount of weight you need to wear to ensure that you have good buoyancy control during your dive.

Check to see if your buoyancy compensator or regulator needs annual servicing. If so, make sure you have any item in need of service checked at your local NAUI Pro Center well in advance of the trip.

Your sixth step is to determine whether you need to take a NAUI Refresher Scuba Experience before your trip. If you have not been diving in six months or more, a refresher is a good way to brush up on your knowledge and water skills. Check with your local NAUI Pro Center or the instructor who trained you on the availability of a NAUI Refresher Scuba Experience. You must also be fit to dive. Regular exercise helps to develop stamina. One of the best ways to maintain fitness for diving is to swim regularly with mask, snorkel, and fins (figure 6-2).

It is vital to prepare a "to-do" list for arranging your dive. Keep it handy so you can add to it as thoughts occur. NAUI Pro Centers have checklists available on a slate if you prefer not to make your own. Use this list to develop a checklist that will be helpful when planning future dives and dive trips. Do not rely on your memory. See Appendix C for a sample checklist.

Verify What You Have Learned

Review the following questions about long-range planning:

1. The six steps to long range planning are:
   a. _____
   b. _____
   c. _____
   d. _____
   e. _____
   f. _____
2. You should start planning a major dive trip _____ in advance of the trip.
3. You should start planning a day of diving at a local site _____ in advance of the dive.

Dive Planning and Recording

SHORT-RANGE PLANNING

Short-range planning starts about a week before your dive. You need to inventory your gear and inspect it to be sure it is in good condition and ready for use. Make any repairs you are qualified to make, such as replacing cracked straps on your fins or mask.

Avoid waiting until the last minute to buy items you will need for your trip. Determine what you need, write it down, and get it in advance. Typical items include air fills for your scuba cylinders, extra batteries for your dive light or camera, sunscreen, seasickness medication, fishing licenses, light sticks for night diving, and defogger for your mask. Your list should also include spare parts for your diving equipment. Having an extra mask strap or tank valve O-ring can save time and frustration at the dive site. As you pack your gear, check it against a list to ensure you have everything you need.

One or two days before your trip check the weather trends, water conditions, tides, and the long-range weather forecast. Your NAUI instructor will advise you about available sources of this type of information. If you know in advance that the weather might be bad on the day you plan to dive, you might be able to avoid wasting a trip.

Always be sure to leave a copy of your plans with someone. Be sure to include the following in your plans:
- Your destination and dive sites.
- Contact telephone number.
- The date and time you expect to arrive back home.

This way, assistance can be summoned to look for you if you are unusually late in returning home. Do not forget to notify the person holding the plans if you are going to be intentionally late.

Planning a dive might seem like a lot of trouble, but it becomes easy and fun to do after a few times. You will enjoy talking diving with your buddy and others from whom you obtain information. You will feel better from being prepared. To be comfortable with your dive, you must arrive at the dive site feeling that you have done everything possible to ensure success.

Verify What You Have Learned

Review the following questions about short-range planning:

4. Some typical items you might need to buy for your trip include _____, _____, _____, and _____.

5. You should leave a copy of your plans with someone at home so _____.

6. Check the _____, _____, _____, and _____ a few days before your trip.

PREPARING TO DIVE

Once you have completed all your long- and short-range preparations, it should be easy to complete the last-minute details of preparing for a dive. The day or evening before your scheduled dive, gather all your equipment and personal articles in one place.

Pack your gear into two bags: one for your dive gear and one for personal items. Your personal items include your towel, extra dry clothing such as a jacket, snacks, a camera, and so on.

Pack your dive gear in reverse order of its use. Put your fins, mask (in a crush-proof box), and snorkel on the bottom, and your buoyancy compensator and regulator on top, as those are usually assembled on your cylinder first. Do not pack your weight belt with your dive gear. The weights will make your bag too heavy and could damage it, or other items. The easiest way to carry your belt is to wear it.

Be sure to get a good night's rest and avoid drinking alcohol at least 12 hours before diving. It is even better if you can avoid drinking alcohol for 24 hours. You must be well rested, in good health, and have a good feeling about the dive.

Verify What You Have Learned

Review the following questions about preparing to dive:

7. One item that should go towards the bottom of your dive bag is _____.

8. One item that should go towards the top of your dive bag is _____.

9. You should abstain from drinking alcohol at least _____ hours before diving.

CONDUCTING YOUR DIVE

When you and your buddy arrive at your selected site, you must agree on how you will conduct your dive before you enter the water. The acronym, **SEABAG**, is an easy way to remember the series of steps that you follow to plan a dive and check each other's equipment. SEABAG stands for:

- **S**ite survey
- **E**mergency plan and information
- **A**ctivity
- **B**uoyancy
- **A**ir
- **G**ear and go

See Chapter 3 for the steps for buoyancy, air, and gear and go. The steps for site survey, emergency, and activity are covered in this section. A checklist for the steps is included in Appendix C.

Site Survey

Before you even suit up, evaluate the conditions at the site to determine if they are acceptable for your planned activity. If the conditions are bad, travel to an alternate location or do not dive. Never be afraid to say that you do not feel good about diving in poor conditions. The purpose of a dive is enjoyment, and there is no fun if the conditions are bad.

Once you decide you can dive, you must determine which buddy will be the leader of the team. This person is in charge of the decision-making during the dive,

including when to change course, when to begin the return leg, and when to surface. Partners can always make suggestions, but both must agree that most decisions be made by the dive leader. The leader does not necessarily need to be the most experienced or qualified member of the team. The person who is most familiar with the area should lead on the first dive, and the other buddy can lead on subsequent dives, or the pair can alternate.

Emergency Plan

You must discuss contingency plans, emergency procedures, and accident management. Agree on what to do if one of you runs out of air under water. Agree on what to do if you get separated under water. One suggested plan for a lost buddy is fully explained in Chapter 3 – Buddy System.

Agree on how to summon help if you need it. Discuss the steps you will take if an accident or emergency should occur. Make sure you have the information about local emergency contacts available and that you know the location of the nearest phone. Take some time to be prepared for emergencies, because little time will be available if one occurs. Accidents can happen any time you are diving. You must be prepared for them.

Activity

There are many things you can do while diving, but you should select only one activity as the purpose of any one planned dive (figure 6-3). It is unwise, and can be unsafe, to try and combine activities on a single dive. If you try to spear fish and take photographs on one dive, you are not likely to do either very well. It also helps if you and your buddy have similar interests.

You must agree on the activity and objective of your dive. Discuss what you want to do, how you will accomplish the activity, and any special signals you will be using. You must also review your standard hand signals. Communicate as much as possible before the dive, because it is more difficult after you are under water.

You must decide on your entry and exit points and your dive pattern. You must both understand the course you will follow and agree on it (figure 6-4).

Set your limits for depth, time, and air supply. Decide on your depth and time limits according to your dive tables or dive computer. Decide at what point you will turn around and start toward your exit point.

Verify What You Have Learned

Review the following questions about conducting your dive:

10. SEA stands for _____,
    _____, and
    _____.

11. The first decision you should make when you reach your dive site is _____
    _____.

12. The dive leader is responsible for
    _____, _____,
    and _____.

13. You should wait at the surface for your buddy for _____ minutes before signaling for help.

14. You should verify that the telephone closest to your dive site is _____ before you start your dive.

15. Your activity planning should include setting your limits for _____,
    _____, and _____.

FIGURE 6-3. WHEN YOU DIVE, CONCENTRATE ON ONLY ONE ACTIVITY. FOR EXAMPLE, UNDERWATER PHOTOGRAPHY TAKES GREAT CONCENTRATION TO DO WELL.

DIVING YOUR PLAN

You must carry out the plan you have made for your dive. You must not abandon the dive plan midway through the dive. If something occurs that must cause you to deviate from your plan, surface or even exit long enough to make new plans, rather than to try and change them under water. You and your dive buddy must be in accord when you dive. This is difficult to do even when you agree on your plan before the dive. If one team member varies from the plan, confusion results.

Plan ahead when you dive. Remind one another of your depth and time limits, and follow your plan throughout the dive. Accomplishing what you set out to do and ending a dive exactly where you planned is very rewarding. Consider dive planning and the ability to execute your plan as a challenge (figure 6-5). This will add to your enjoyment of the dive and reduce any risks.

When you are prepared for a dive, many benefits result, and these benefits are worth the time you take to properly plan and prepare. As you work with others to coordinate your dive, that work will become first easy, then fun. You will find yourself enjoying the preparations involved for the dive as well as the dive itself.

Verify What You Have Learned

Review the following questions about diving your plan:

16. If one team member varies from the predetermined dive plan, _____ results.

17. Dive planning and the ability to execute your plan with the desired results is a _____ and is _____ when you achieve your goal.

CONTINGENCY PLANNING

Contingency planning is an important part of dive planning. For each step of your plan, you need to have a contingency plan. When you choose your site, also choose an alternate site or an alternate activity for the day in case conditions are not right for diving.

When you are checking your equipment and packing for your dive, consider taking extra gear along if you have it. If you have a group going on a trip, the members of the trip might be able to bring along an extra regulator, buoyancy compensator, fins, mask, and snorkel among them. It is much easier to switch to another piece of gear than to fix a piece of gear in the field.

When you are planning the direction of your dive, be sure to consider an alternate route or alternate exit point to be used if conditions change while you are on your dive. Be sure to consider what you will do if your buddy has a problem under water.

FIGURE 6-4. AS A TEAM, YOU MUST DECIDE AND AGREE ON YOUR ENTRY AND EXIT POINTS AND YOUR DIVE PATTERN.

Verify What You Have Learned

Review the following questions about contingency planning:

18. When you choose your site, you should also choose an _____ or an _____.

19. When you plan the route of your dive, you should also consider _____.

RECORDING YOUR DIVE

After each dive, you should record information from your dive in your logbook (figure 6-6). There are spaces on your logbook pages in which you record:

- The number of your dive.
- The date.
- The water visibility.
- Your starting air pressure.
- Your ending air pressure.
- Your deepest depth.

On the right side of the NAUI Logbook pages are three boxes for recording your diving hours. Use these to keep a running total of your *dive time*. The number in the Start box is the same as the number in the Total box from your previous dive. The number in the Dive Time box is the number of minutes from your current dive. Add the number of minutes from your current dive

FIGURE 6-5. ALWAYS PLAN YOUR DIVE AND THEN DIVE YOUR PLAN.

to your total from the Start box and put the new total in the Total box.

Underneath the boxes are lines to record:

- The location of your dive.
- The name of your buddy.
- Remarks about the dive.

Your remarks about the dive can include information such as the diving suit and the amount of weight you were wearing, the cylinder size, whether you liked the site, what you saw, and so on.

The bottom of the page has a blank area for you to record your dive profile information from your NAUI Dive Planning Worksheet on the back of your NAUI Dive Tables. The bottom also has space for an instructor to sign if the dive was a training dive. On a dive trip, many divers ask the dive operator to stamp or sign this area.

Get into the good habit of recording the information from your dives at the end of each diving day or after each dive. The information will be fresh in your mind and easy to record. If you wait until the end of a trip to record the information, there is a good chance you will forget some important information.

Verify What You Have Learned

Review the following questions about recording your dive:

20. List three pieces of information you record in the boxes at the top of each page of your logbook:

    _____

    _____

    _____

21. In the NAUI Logbook, the purpose of the Hours box is so you can _____.

22. Remarks about your dive can include information such as _____ and _____.

FIGURE 6-6. YOU MUST RECORD YOUR DIVES IN YOUR LOGBOOK.

Dive Planning and Recording

Notes

CHAPTER
7

Problem
Solving

LEARNING GOALS

In this chapter you will:

- Learn the general method for resolving problems under water.
- Be introduced to situations that can occur under water and how you can prevent them from occurring or resolve them if you do encounter them.
- Learn how to assist another diver if they are having a problem.
- Be introduced to the steps you need to take to rescue another diver at the surface and underwater.
- Learn about first aid for aquatic injuries.
- Be introduced to the importance of safe diving practices.

Diving always entails some degree of risk. Even if you do everything right, there is still a slight but real possibility that you might be injured, while under water. Fortunately, diving accidents are rare, and you can avoid them by solving small problems early – before they become big problems.

DIVING SITUATIONS

Some situations can occur as you dive that will bother you. You can deal with most of these situations if you stop to analyze and cope with them calmly. As long as you have air to breathe, you can deal with almost anything. Keep this thought in mind, and you will soon view everyday dive problems as the minor annoyance they are.

General Method of Resolving a Problem

There are three steps to solving a problem under water:
1. Stop your activity.
2. Get firm control of yourself and analyze the situation.
3. Take action based on your analysis.

Remembering and following these three steps will help you deal with any situation in a calm manner and can prevent a situation from getting worse.

Heat Loss

Water conducts heat quite efficiently and it can absorb a great deal of heat with very little change in its own temperature. When you are immersed in water without proper thermal protection, heat is rapidly drawn from your body. This process is called *conduction*.

You also lose heat under water every time you take a breath and exhale, as your body warms the air you inhale. You can lose a significant amount of your body heat this way. This effect increases with depth, because the density of the air you are breathing increases with increased pressure. The temperature of the water can also drop as you dive deeper.

The deeper you dive, the greater the pressure that works to compress your wetsuit. The more your wetsuit compresses, the less insulation you have. This is unfortunate, because as you dive deeper, the water usually gets colder. This is another good reason to limit your diving to shallower depths. Diving is more fun, and safer, when you are warm.

If your body loses enough heat, you can develop a medical condition known as *hypothermia*. In Greek, *hypo* means low and *therm* means heat or temperature. The symptoms of heat loss include:

- Loss of muscle strength.
- Muscle cramps.
- Numbness in your arms and legs or inability to use your fingers or hands.
- Increased breathing rate with no increase in your activity.
- Shivering.
- Fatigue.
- Loss of ability to think clearly.

If you ignore the symptoms, your body continues to lose heat, and you will develop a serious medical emergency. Heart irregularities, unconsciousness, and even death can occur.

If you become cold while diving, you must rewarm yourself. End your dive and get out of the water. Get into warm, dry clothing as soon as possible. Layers of clothing or blankets also help to trap warmth near your body. Warm drinks will help, but avoid any with caffeine or alcohol. A warm, not hot, bath might also help.

Hot baths are not recommended after deep dives, because they might increase the possibility of decompression sickness (DCS) or cause other problems as cold blood diverts from your extremities. Hot baths for severe cases of heat loss must be avoided. Medical attention is necessary.

There are many defenses against heat loss in the water. Some of these are natural, but some require deliberate action on your part. Your body's first defense is to reduce the circulation of blood to your arms and legs. This conserves heat in the core of your body where the vital organs are located. Once your *core temperature* (the internal temperature of your body) lowers sufficiently, you begin to shiver.

Shivering indicates chilling. Normally, the purpose of shivering is to produce heat, but shivering when you are under water cannot help with your heat loss and might make it worse. You must take shivering as a signal to end your diving activities until you recover.

If you eat a well-balanced meal at least two hours before diving, your body will generate heat and your body will have fuel to dive. Your activity level while you dive also affects how much heat your body generates. Kicking at a moderate pace will help generate some heat. Just remember that heavy exercise is difficult under water as it requires you to use large amounts of air that quickly depletes your air supply.

Your best defense in cold water is to wear the right amount of insulation for your needs. If you get cold while diving, you need to wear more insulation. If you are already wearing a full wetsuit with hood, boots, and gloves and are cold, you might need to switch to a dry suit to keep warm. If you are wearing a dry suit and are still cold, you might need more insulation or a different type of underwear beneath your suit. It is especially important to cover your high heat loss areas, including your head, hands, torso, groin, and neck. With the proper insulation, you can stay warm in almost any diving environment.

You must learn to recognize heat loss as a potentially serious diving problem. You should stop diving when you become chilled. Rewarm yourself completely before you dive again. If you wear the right amount of insulation, dive wisely, recognize the symptoms of

heat loss, and respond appropriately, you can avoid heat loss problems.

Overheating

Most people tend to think about problems associated with staying warm in cold water rather than with overheating. Problems with overheating usually occur on the surface as you are preparing to dive, but can occur while diving in warmer waters.

A diving suit protects you against heat loss in the water, and it also does so when you are on the surface. This can lead to serious problems due to overheating before, during, and after the dive.

Your body's first reaction to overheating (*hyperthermia*) is to perspire. This can lower your body temperature as the moisture evaporates from your skin. Unfortunately, this does not work when you are covered head to toe by a dry suit, wetsuit, or other insulating garments.

If you overheat and do not act to cool your body, you will experience some or all of the following symptoms of heat exhaustion:

- Pale, clammy skin.
- A feeling of weakness and fatigue.
- Headache.
- Nausea and possibly vomiting.

You should take action immediately to lower your body temperature. If you are in a wetsuit, get into the water for a quick cool-off dip. If you cannot do this, get out of your exposure suit and get wet to start cooling down. If you are not nauseous, you can drink cool water to rehydrate your body. Be sure to stay out of the sun and rest until the symptoms go away.

If you do not take these actions, and your body temperature continues to increase, your self-cooling responses will shut down. This leads to an extremely serious, life-threatening condition known as *heat stroke*. The skin of a heat stroke victim is dry and hot to the touch. You must get medical assistance immediately.

 To prevent overheating, pace yourself when donning your exposure suit. Be sure to stay out of the sun. If necessary, get the suit wet and keep it wet while you are donning the suit and then enter the water quickly after you have finished suiting up.

Problem Solving

Cramps

Cold, exertion, incorrect kicking with fins, restricted circulation, or some combination of these factors can lead to cramps, which usually occur in the legs. The best way to deal with this problem is to prevent cramps before they occur. Avoid becoming chilled or exhausted, and avoid wearing protective clothing that is too tight.

If you experience a cramp, stretch the cramped muscle and massage it (figure 7-1). For cramps in your calf or foot, pull on the tip of your fin gently as you straighten your leg. This stretches the muscles that are responsible for the cramp. Stretch your muscle gently or you can injure the muscle or tendons.

Once you have relieved a cramp, rest and recover, and then continue your dive at a slower pace. You can also use a different kick to help keep a leg cramp from recurring.

FIGURE 7-2. REMAIN CALM IF YOU BECOME ENTANGLED, DETERMINE WHERE YOU ARE CAUGHT, AND WORK SLOWLY AND DELIBERATELY TO FREE YOURSELF.

Entanglements

Entanglements typically occur with underwater plants, fishing line, or fish nets (figure 7-2). You should have a knife available so you can cut yourself free, but that is seldom your first reaction to an entanglement. First, stop your activity and get control. Second, determine where you are caught and what object has caught you. Remain calm.

You might be able to free yourself by pulling the plant, line, or net clear of you and your gear, or by getting your buddy to help you. Sometimes you can reverse your direction to get free. Remember that you have buoyancy control and the ability to move up and down to free yourself. Avoid turning around, because this will usually make an entanglement worse.

One of the most likely points of entanglement is your cylinder valve and the first stage of your regulator. Unfortunately, you cannot see this area, so you should signal your dive buddy to help you. If your buddy is not close to you for some reason, you can remove your scuba unit, free the entanglement, and put the unit back on.

FIGURE 7-1. YOU CAN RELIEVE A CRAMP BY GENTLY STRETCHING THE AFFECTED MUSCLE.

If none of these actions clears you of the entanglement, you might have to use a knife to cut yourself free. Use caution and work slowly and deliberately. Panic is your worst enemy in this situation, not the entanglement.

Disorientation and Vertigo

Disorientation, not knowing where you are or literally which way is up, can occur for several reasons when you dive. *Sensory* deprivation, where you cannot see anything in the water around you, can occur during poor visibility or night diving. Sensory deprivation can cause dizziness or vertigo (figure 7-3). Ear problems, a ruptured eardrum, or trouble equalizing when you descend or ascend, can also cause vertigo.

To help overcome disorientation, you must overcome the dizziness and then determine which way is up. To overcome dizziness, hold onto a solid object or hug yourself until the dizziness passes. Do not close your eyes. To know which way is up, look at your bubbles. Air always rises.

You should postpone night or limited visibility diving until you acquire confidence through dives with good visibility.

If you have an ear problem that might not allow you to equalize your middle ear pressure, you might experience vertigo. Vertigo sometimes occurs during ascent, when one ear equalizes more rapidly than the other. The dizziness will pass in a few moments. Do not get excited if you do experience vertigo.

Problems with disorientation are rarely severe. Your most likely problem is not knowing your position under water relative to where you want to go. Develop the ability to know where you are through natural and compass navigation and you are not likely to experience the nuisance of disorientation.

Equipment Difficulties

Equipment difficulties include gear that is or becomes improperly adjusted, undone, or lost while diving. It also includes gear that malfunctions. Any good diver can handle these difficulties, so you will want to learn how to handle them as well. Your instructor will

FIGURE 7-3. PROBLEMS WITH DISORIENTATION ARE RARELY SERIOUS, BUT IT CAN INVOLVE VERTIGO.

help you develop this skill by giving you typical equipment problems to solve as your training progresses.

You can adjust almost every piece of equipment while in the water. If you must make an adjustment, first think about what you need to do, then work slowly and deliberately to make the adjustment. If you become excited and find yourself working hard, stop your activity, breathe slowly and deeply, recover, think, and start again slowly. Working with your gear in the water is good practice to keep many of your diving skills sharp.

You could lose your mask, snorkel, fins, or weight belt under water. Each piece of equipment is needed for diving, but you must be able to either recover the lost item and continue your dive or be able to reach the surface and exit the water without the missing item. Practice swimming without items of equipment to develop the techniques for handling this type of difficulty.

Occasionally, the power-inflator mechanism on your buoyancy compensator (BC) can stick in the open position, which causes the BC to inflate. If this happens, you must vent the excess air and disconnect the power-inflator hose (figure 7-4). If you do not vent the

Problem Solving

FIGURE 7-4. IF YOUR POWER-INFLATOR MECHANISM STICKS IN THE OPEN POSITION, AND YOU CANNOT DISCONNECT IT, ASCEND TO THE SURFACE.

air immediately, you can experience an uncontrolled ascent, which could lead to a lung overexpansion injury or DCS. If your disconnected power-inflator hose itself continues to free-flow, you should ascend immediately at a normal rate, as your air supply will be quickly exhausted.

One way to slow a buoyant ascent is by flaring. To flare your body, get yourself face up and parallel to the surface. Spread your arms and legs out and away from your body and hold the blades of your fins parallel to the surface. Doing this will create as much surface area and drag as possible to slow your ascent.

Regulators do not usually fail in a closed position in which they will not deliver any air. Usually, any malfunction causes a free-flow. If either does happen, or your regulator second stage floods because of a leaking exhaust valve, you must treat the situation as an out-of-air situation. Follow the procedures outlined in Chapter 3 for handling out-of-air problems.

Seasickness

Seasickness is an unpleasant occurrence that no one enjoys. Seasickness results when the signals from your inner ear and the signals from your eyes to your brain do not match.

If you start to feel nauseous while on the boat, do the following to help prevent seasickness:
1. Avoid eating greasy foods.
2. Stay out of the cabin or any enclosed space on the boat.
3. Settle yourself in a spot midway between the *bow* (front) and *stern* (back) of the boat and between the *starboard* (right) and *port* (left) sides. This is the boat's midpoint. The boat is most stable at its midpoint.
4. Look at the horizon.

If you must vomit, go to the *lee* (downwind) side of the boat to be ill. Never use the boat's *head* (bathroom).

Many divers who get mildly seasick find that they usually feel better once they are under water. You must not dive if you are actively vomiting or extremely nauseated, though, because of the danger of inhaling vomit through your regulator. This can cause you to choke and the vomit can injure your lungs, or cause lung infections.

If you know you get seasick and can avoid it by using medication, it might be permissible to do so. If you do take medication for seasickness, it must not produce adverse side affects (such as drowsiness or dizziness) that could put you in danger under water. You must test the medication for its effects on you well in advance of your day of diving. Be aware that the effects might be radically different when under pressure so you must be alert to the effect of the medication under pressure as well.

If you wait until the boat is moving to take medication, it is too late. For best results, you should usually start taking seasickness medication the night before your trip. Follow the dosage instructions of the manufacturer.

Choking and Coughing

It is possible to inhale a little water when you breathe through a regulator under water and start to choke. You should try to prevent this from occurring by using the following steps:
1. Raise your tongue to the roof of your mouth to form a barrier to keep drops of water from going through your mouth and into your throat.

2. Make your first breath after clearing a snorkel or regulator shallow and cautious.

If you must cough, keep the regulator or snorkel in your mouth. Keeping the mouthpiece in place will help you not breathe in any more water, which will make the situation worse. Swallow several times in quick succession to aid in your recovery. Trust your regulator. You can cough or sneeze into it and through it.

You can temporarily choke if water enters the windpipe leading to your lungs. If this happens, it might be difficult or impossible to breathe without considerable effort for a few moments. Deliberately relax your body and wait for your airway to relax before you resume normal breathing.

Air Starvation

Any time you find yourself feeling starved for air, either below or on the surface, or if you feel that the regulator is not delivering enough air, stop what you are doing, and relax (figure 7-5). Concentrate on breathing slowly and deeply until you regain control of your breathing and the feeling of air starvation will pass. Be sure to exhale completely!

If your cylinder valve is not fully open, it is possible that the valve could be restricting your flow of air. If your submersible pressure gauge needle dips with each inhalation, this is a sure sign of restricted air flow. It is also the reason you should watch the SPG as you check regulator function during dive preparations. Open the valve yourself if you can reach behind you, or have your buddy open it if you cannot.

Summary

Being able to solve minor problems without stress shows that you are a good, skilled diver. By the time you complete your training, you should feel capable of preventing or handling any problem described here. This feeling of confidence will make you much more relaxed so you can fully enjoy diving.

FIGURE 7-5. IF YOU FEEL STARVED FOR AIR UNDER WATER, STOP WHAT YOU ARE DOING AND RELAX.

Verify What You Have Learned

Review the following diving situations and identify at least one correct action you can take to prevent the problem:

1. Chilling.
2. Overheating.
3. Muscle cramps.
4. Entanglement.
5. Vertigo.
6. Stuck power-inflator mechanism.
7. Seasickness.
8. Coughing.
9. Air starvation.

ASSISTING OTHER DIVERS

As a diver, you have two responsibilities to your buddy. First, you must help to keep problems from occurring. Second, you must help your buddy overcome any problems that do occur.

Problem Solving

As you have learned in the preceding chapters, diving problems can be classified as either minor incidents or emergencies. This section describes how to help a buddy overcome minor problems. The situations described here are rare and should be prevented before they ever occur. However, you need to know what to do in case they ever do occur.

 Most diving problems occur at the surface rather than under water (figure 7-6). If your buddy is in distress at the surface, there are three actions you must take to assist your buddy:

1. Help your buddy establish buoyancy.
2. Get your buddy to relax, breathe deeply, and rest.
3. Provide assistance as needed.

Give your buddy assurance and encouragement, and if possible, help your buddy recover and overcome the difficulty without your direct interference. Establish positive buoyancy for yourself and remember to control your own level of exertion. Your main task is to remain close to your buddy and give optimistic encouragement and advice.

FIGURE 7-6. A DIVER IN DISTRESS AT THE SURFACE USUALLY HAS THEIR MASK DISCARDED AND THEY WAVE THEIR ARMS OR FLAIL IN THE WATER.

FIGURE 7-7. A FLOAT IS A GOOD WAY TO PROVIDE BUOYANCY FOR A BUDDY IN DISTRESS.

Establishing Buoyancy

You can help your buddy establish buoyancy in several ways. If you instruct your buddy to inflate their buoyancy compensator (BC) or drop their weight belt and they respond appropriately, this is the best way to help them establish buoyancy and personal control. If they do not respond to your instructions, you can extend a surface float to them for them to hang onto (figure 7-7). It might be necessary to help them inflate their BC or drop their weights.

Resting and Breathing

Once your buddy has flotation, you must get your buddy to rest and breathe deeply. Make sure they also remember to exhale completely. Have your buddy discard any items they are carrying in their hands or have them give the items to you. Then you can discard the items if necessary.

Providing Assistance

Try to get your buddy to solve their own problem. If this is not possible, or your directions are not followed, you will have to provide direct assistance. The best assist is one done casually – even unnoticed. Your help might consist of working out a cramp, solving an equipment problem, or assisting your buddy to the exit point.

If you must help your buddy through the water, you can use various swimming assists and tows. You can push your buddy through the water using the do-si-do position. Have your buddy lie flat in the water with their face up. Put your arm over and under your buddy's upper arm, grasp the top of the BC behind their neck, and push them along. This assist provides control and allows good eye and voice communication between the two of you.

Another push is the biceps push. It is similar to the do-si-do, but you place your left hand on their bicep instead. This push also enables you to have good eye contact and voice communication.

You can also push your buddy through the water using the fin push. Have your buddy lie flat in the water with their legs straight and their face up. Place their feet against your shoulders. Place your hands under their legs and grasp their legs behind the knee or on the calf. With this position, you can easily push your buddy through the water.

Never allow a diver to swim to shore or a boat alone. You and your buddy should practice swimming assists from time to time, because you must learn how to function as both the diver needing assistance and the diver providing assistance.

Verify What You Have Learned

Review the following questions about assisting other divers:

10. Your two responsibilities to your buddy are

_____ and

_____.

11. Most diving problems occur at the

_____.

12. The three steps to assisting your buddy in distress are _____,

_____, and

_____.

RESCUES

Divers usually can avoid trouble under water. If not, they can frequently overcome their problems either independently or with help from their buddy. Most emergencies in the water are preventable, and many usually occur because divers violate safety rules.

As a diver, you must know the fundamentals of making a full rescue of an incapacitated diver, even though it is unlikely that you will ever need to apply what you have learned. If you need to rescue someone, you will know how to proceed. Further training in diver rescue techniques is available in the NAUI Scuba Rescue Diver course. This training is recommended for every diver.

A diving emergency occurs when a diver is unconscious or otherwise helpless and, possibly, not breathing. Possible causes include drowning, a lung overexpansion injury, head injury, or drugs in the diver's system. These injuries are rare, but you must be able to help if another diver is unable to care for themselves. If you discover a diver in the water who appears to be unconscious, you must get them to the shore or boat as quickly as possible where CPR can be performed, if necessary, and medical assistance can be obtained.

At the Surface

If a diver is apparently unconscious at the surface, use the following steps to perform a rescue:

1. Establish positive buoyancy for yourself.
2. Make contact with the victim to see whether they are unconscious or able to respond.
3. Pull the victim to a face-up position and establish buoyancy for the victim. You can accomplish this by inflating the victim's BC or dropping their weight belt.
4. Yell and signal for help.
5. Remove your mask.
6. Remove the victim's mask.
7. Look, listen, and feel to see if the victim is breathing.
8. Start artificial respiration if the victim is not breathing and the shore or boat is more than about

50 meters or 50 yards away. See *In-Water Artificial Respiration* later on this page for the procedure.

9. Continue rescue breathing as you transport the victim to your exit point. Your instructor will train you in the do-si-do transport that can be used to accomplish this.

You need both training and practice to become proficient at in-water artificial respiration and rescue. Only the basic steps are learned in your NAUI Scuba Diver certification course. The NAUI Scuba Rescue Diver course teaches you further techniques, including how to remove a victim's equipment as well as your own as you transport the victim. Their equipment and your own must be removed before you can get the victim out of the water.

FIGURE 7-8. WHEN YOU LOCATE AN UNCONSCIOUS DIVER UNDER WATER, YOUR PRIMARY CONCERN IS GETTING THAT DIVER TO THE SURFACE.

Underwater

If you find an apparently unconscious victim under water, your primary concern is getting them to the surface. Use the following steps when rescuing a diver under water:

1. Make contact with the victim to see whether they are unconscious.

2. Pull the victim to a face-up position and check their mask. If there is any water in the mask and the diver is not breathing, remove the mask so air increasing in volume from decreased pressure will not force water down the victim's windpipe.

3. If the diver is breathing, hold their regulator in their mouth while you swim them to the surface (figure 7-8).

4. If the diver is not breathing, leave the regulator alone.

5. You may need to ditch the victim's weight belt to make the victim buoyant. This will allow you to swim the victim to the surface without exerting yourself.

6. While ascending with the victim, control your ascent to the surface by venting air from the victim's BC. However, if they start to rise too quickly, and you cannot control their ascent, let them go and control your own ascent to the surface. You cannot allow them to make you a second victim.

7. If need be, establish buoyancy for the victim when you reach the surface. You can accomplish this by inflating the victim's BC or removing the weight belt, if this has not already been done.

8. Signal for help.

9. Place the victim in the do-si-do transport position.

10. Remove your mask.

11. Remove the victim's mask and regulator if still in place.

12. Look, listen, and feel to see if the victim is breathing.

13. Start artificial respiration if the victim is not breathing and you are more than 50 meters or 50 yards away from the exit point. See *In-Water Artificial Respiration* for the procedure.

14. Continue rescue breathing as you transport the victim to your exit point.

In-Water Artificial Respiration

Use the following procedure to administer in-water artificial respiration:

1. Place the victim in the do-si-do transport position.

2. Use your outside hand to gently tilt the victim's head back and open the airway.

3. Check the victim's mouth to be sure no obstructions are present.

FIGURE 7-9. BECOMING PROFICIENT IN ADMINISTERING IN-WATER ARTIFICIAL RESPIRATION REQUIRES ADDITIONAL TRAINING AND PRACTICE.

4. Check to see if the victim is breathing by using the following method:
   - Look to see if their chest is rising and falling. This might be difficult to see, depending on the dive gear the victim is wearing.
   - Listen to hear air escaping from their nose or mouth.
   - Feel whether air is hitting your cheek and lips when you hold them close to their mouth.
5. If the victim is not breathing, pinch their nose, rotate their face toward you, and give them five full breaths.
6. Give them another breath every 5 seconds. Your NAUI instructor will show you how to count seconds.
7. Continue giving the victim one breath every five seconds or 12 breaths per minute.

Take care to prevent water from entering the victim's mouth and being blown into the lungs. You must keep water out of the victim's lungs. Unless the distance to the shore or boat is short, maintain rescue breathing as you transport the victim (figure 7-9). It is most important to get them to the exit point where full CPR can begin, if needed, and other care can be obtained.

Learn to pace yourself so you will not become too exhausted to be of any assistance. By the end of your NAUI Scuba Diver certification course, you will be able to perform the basic steps of in-water respiration, but additional training and practice are required to become proficient. Additional training in first aid, CPR, lifesaving, oxygen administration, and diver rescue are helpful and strongly recommended.

Verify What You Have Learned

Review the following questions about rescues:

13. A diving emergency occurs when a diver is

_____
_____.

14. Four types of recommended emergency training are _____,

_____,

_____, and

_____.

15. The first action you should take when assisting an unconscious diver at the surface is

_____.

16. Your primary concern when you find an unconscious diver on the bottom is to

_____.

17. The two most important points for providing in-water artificial respiration are

_____ and

_____.

18. The most important thing to do for a non-breathing diver in the water is to

_____
_____.

EMERGENCIES AND FIRST AID

To be a qualified dive buddy, you must be able to assist or rescue your buddy, render proper first aid, and manage an emergency. While few diving accidents are life threatening, injuries and fatalities do occur, just as in most physical activities. You must be prepared to cope with injuries ranging from cuts and bruises to wounds from aquatic animals to respiratory and cardiac arrest. You might be the only person available to offer immediate assistance.

Be Prepared

To prepare yourself to handle emergencies, you need training, emergency equipment, emergency contact information and plans, and the determination to act. The first rule of first aid is to "*Do no harm.*" The best way to follow this rule is to keep your training in first aid, CPR, and diving rescue techniques current. Practicing with your buddy several times a year is a good way to keep your emergency skills sharp.

Emergency equipment can be extensive. At a minimum, you should have a first aid kit available. A suggested contents list is in Appendix C. Other useful equipment includes an oxygen unit (if you are trained in its use), a cloth or space blanket, and a supply of clean fresh water. You must have emergency equipment ready at your dive site. Replace any equipment or supplies immediately after you use them.

Oxygen is extremely valuable for treating serious diving injuries such as air embolism, DCS, and near drowning cases. Very few areas prohibit the use of oxygen equipment by non-medically trained personnel. Most areas accept training in oxygen administration by a recognized agency such as NAUI. Check with your instructor about the laws in your area. Dive boats are usually equipped with emergency oxygen systems (figure 7-10). First aid at the dive site is more effective if you can administer oxygen.

You must also know how to call for help. In most areas, you need to know who to call for medical attention or medical evacuation and transport. Always be sure to know the number for summoning the local emergency service.

Divers Alert Network (DAN) is a worldwide emergency network that can help provide consultation, information on hyperbaric chambers and diving physicians, transportation, and treatment through a single, 24-hour emergency telephone number: (919) 684-9111. DAN's headquarters in the United States is in North Carolina. DAN also has emergency numbers established throughout the world to assist you with a diving emergency.

Ask your NAUI instructor for the appropriate number to use in your area. Write your local emergency numbers, as well as the telephone number for DAN, on

FIGURE 7-10. HAVING AN OXYGEN UNIT AT YOUR DIVE SITE AND BEING PROPERLY TRAINED IN ITS OPERATION ARE VITAL WHEN TREATING DIVING EMERGENCIES SUCH AS AIR EMBOLISM AND DCS.

a card, and include them in your first-aid kit.

The last requirement for preparation is being determined to act appropriately in an emergency. Rather than become involved, most people tend to stand by and watch as an accident occurs. You must decide in advance that you will act if you are present at the scene of a diving accident and if you are trained and competent to deal with the situation. Be sure not to interfere with professional assistance, but be ready to help if needed and capable.

Basic First Aid

First aid includes the following:
1. Survey the accident scene to determine if it's safe to render aid.
2. A quick examination of the victim to determine the seriousness of the injury.
3. Immediate treatment for life-threatening emergencies such as cessation (stopping) of breathing or arterial bleeding.
4. Treatment for less serious injuries and shock.
5. Arrangements for medical care and transport.

There are five major categories of injuries for which you should be prepared to administer first aid:

Problem Solving

FIGURE 7-11. IN ADDITION TO ADMINISTERING OXYGEN FOR A DIVING EMERGENCY, YOU MUST ALSO TREAT FOR SHOCK, MONITOR THE VICTIM, AND OBTAIN THEIR TRANSPORT TO MEDICAL ATTENTION.

- Severe bleeding.
- Respiratory failure.
- Heart failure.
- Shock.
- Serious diving accidents such as lung overexpansion injuries and DCS.

Emergency training in first aid will teach you how to properly respond in the first four areas.

First aid for air embolism and DCS also includes lying the victim down and maintaining their respiration and circulation. You must also treat for shock, administer oxygen if available, constantly monitor the victim, and transport the victim to the nearest appropriate medical facility or operational recompression chamber (figure 7-11).

NAUI recommends that you take the NAUI Scuba Rescue Diver course, in which you can learn and practice accident management. See your instructor for more information about this important course.

CPR and Oxygen Administration

You should have training in first aid and artificial respiration. Everyone, diver or not, should be prepared to administer first aid and especially cardiopulmonary resuscitation (CPR). If you have not taken courses to acquire these skills or refreshed your knowledge for one or two years, you should complete one of the programs available through various agencies. As a diver, you should also complete training in oxygen administration through a NAUI instructor.

Aquatic Life Injuries

General first aid training does not cover treatment of injuries from aquatic life, although most of the general procedures also apply to this specialty area. General guidelines are presented here. Your instructor will give you specific treatments for injuries from aquatic life in your area.

Prevention

Aggressive animal behavior under water is rare. Any injury you might receive from an aquatic animal will almost always result from a defensive action on the part of the creature, but it will hurt anyway! Remember that nearly all animals will attack if they feel cornered or threatened. Avoid potential problems with aquatic life in your area by learning how to identify hazardous creatures and how to avoid them.

Remember that when you are diving, you are entering the home of these creatures. Respect the creatures and their home, and they will leave you alone. If you act aggressively towards any marine life, they will attack to protect themselves. Some are very territorial, and will attack if you approach their home.

Treatment

Injuries from aquatic life are classified in one or more of the following categories:
- Punctures
- Stings
- Bites and lacerations
- Amputations

Sea urchins, spiny fish, or stingrays can cause puncture wounds. If possible, remove any material in the wound. Toxins might have been injected and must be treated by soaking the wounded area in water as hot as the victim can tolerate for at least 20 minutes. Some divers

Problem Solving

might be hypersensitive to wounds from marine animals. Get the victim to medical attention as soon as possible.

Jellyfish or coral can cause stings. Remove the stinging materials and apply a neutralizing agent. Your instructor will tell you the correct procedure for neutralizing stings caused by creatures in your local area. Medical attention is required if the injury is serious or the victim shows signs or symptoms of an allergic reaction.

Almost any aquatic animal can bite. First aid can range from simple, antiseptic cleaning of the wound to control of serious bleeding. Medical attention is necessary if the wound is serious, significant blood loss occurs, or the victim shows signs or symptoms of an allergic reaction.

Injuries from aquatic life are as varied as the diving environment. You must know what wounds are likely to occur in a given area as well as the first aid for them. Even more important, learn how to avoid being wounded.

Verify What You Have Learned

Review the following questions about emergencies and first aid:

19. Four requirements for being prepared to handle a diving emergency are

_____,
_____,
_____, and
_____.

20. To ensure that your skills will be adequate in an emergency, you should

_____ and
_____.

21. Four recommended items of equipment for emergencies are

_____,
_____,
_____, and
_____.

22. _____ is a worldwide network of hyperbaric chambers and diving physicians who provide consultation for transportation and treatment of diving accidents.

SAFETY IN SUMMARY

Diving safety is primarily a matter of knowing the rules, following them, and being prepared. Being aware of safe diving practices, both generally and locally, and following them will do more than anything else to ensure your safety. If something unexpected does occur, being prepared to deal with the situation can make it simply something easily dealt with rather than a serious problem.

Diving safety primarily involves attitude. *Safety* occurs when a diver respects the environment and wants to be properly prepared for diving. For divers who are prepared for emergencies and follow the buddy system as well as other good diving practices, safety is simply a byproduct of that attitude.

You should abide by the NAUI Recommended Diving Practices, summarized in Appendix B. By applying these principles, you will see for yourself that the saying "*Diving safety is no accident*" is not merely a play on words.

RESPONSIBLE SCUBA DIVING PRACTICES

You must be trained for what you plan to do or might have to do in diving, and you must resist the temptation to teach others unless you become certified as a NAUI instructor. Your training should continue with advanced, specialty, and refresher courses to keep your knowledge and skills current and progressing.

Only dive when you are feeling well- mentally and physically. Annual physical examinations are important. Do not dive under the influence of drugs, including prior indulgence in alcohol. Keep yourself in good physical condition, know your limits, dive within them, and maintain a reserve of energy and air as margins of safety. If you grow cold, tired, ill, or low on air while diving, exit the water immediately.

You must properly maintain your equipment according to the manufacturer's recommendations and check it before each dive. Have it serviced professionally as the manufacturer recommends, and use all recommended equipment when diving. Be properly weighted, and particularly avoid diving with excess ballast. Never loan your equipment to anyone not certified to dive.

Know the location where you will dive. Respect the environment, and avoid dangerous sites and poor diving conditions. Fly the diver down flag to warn boaters of your presence, and then dive near that flag. Exercise moderation with depth and time limits.

Take the time to properly plan your dive, and follow your plan. Know the rules of the buddy system and abide by them for your own enjoyment and security. Dive regularly, or renew your skills after a period of inactivity before diving again. Log your dives to remember the details and experiences.

If you follow the Recommended Diving Practices presented to you by your NAUI instructor from the outset of your training, they will soon become part of your routine and you will perform them with little effort. Make this your goal, and you will set yourself on a good course to avoid the hazards of diving. Safety is an attitude, and this is reflected in the NAUI motto *"Dive Safety Through Education."*

Problem Solving

CHAPTER

8

Diving Environment

Diving Environment

LEARNING GOALS

In this chapter you will:
- Learn about the physical characteristics of dive sites.
- Be introduced to the types of water movement and how it can affect your dive.
- Learn about the different categories of marine life and how to avoid situations with them.
- Be introduced to the positive impacts you can have on the underwater environment.
- Learn about some of the popular diving areas throughout the world.

Underwater conditions vary from one part of the world to another. Visibility, water temperature, waves, currents, and other factors are all different in each dive area. These differences influence the way you dress for a dive and the techniques you use.

No matter where you dive, you will discover special requirements pertaining to diving in that area. Before you go diving someplace you have never been before, you must learn about the environmental conditions that could affect your diving and know how the local divers deal with them.

You must also consider other environmental and physical variations, such as the season of the year, the weather, dive-site characteristics, and shore conditions. The continental United States is a good example of a country with some of the most varied diving conditions in the world.

The underwater environments of the United States include diverse areas, such as:
- Oil rigs off Louisiana and California.
- Tropical waters off the coast of Florida.
- Cold waters in the Great Lakes, New England, and Alaska.
- Kelp forests off the coast of California.

These environments are extremely different, and each requires certain specific skills, techniques, and equipment.

This chapter examines ways dive site characteristics and shore conditions affect your diving techniques in different areas. It considers variations in temperature,

visibility, and aquatic life. It also addresses conservation and ways you can help preserve the underwater environment. Your instructor will supplement this material by explaining the ways local conditions affect diving near your home.

PHYSICAL CHARACTERISTICS OF A SITE

A variety of characteristics determine the type of site and bottom conditions. The characteristics of the site will dictate how you enter and exit the water as well as how you dive.

Types of Sites

Divers will dive almost anywhere there is water, but they are frequently attracted to interesting underwater formations. These formations can be man-made, such as an artificial reef, oil rig, breakwater, jetty, or shipwreck (figure 8-1). Man-made sites can be as fascinating as any natural underwater formation. In particular, many divers find shipwrecks to be among the most exciting dive sites (figure 8-2).

FIGURE 8-1. DIVING SITES VARY WIDELY. OIL RIGS ARE ONE EXAMPLE OF A MAN-MADE SITE THAT PROVIDES GOOD DIVING.

FIGURE 8-2. SHIPWRECKS ARE ALSO POPULAR DIVE SITES.

FIGURE 8-4. DIVING INSIDE WRECKS ALSO REQUIRES SPECIAL TRAINING AND EQUIPMENT.

FIGURE 8-3. CAVE DIVING REQUIRES SPECIAL TRAINING AND EQUIPMENT.

Natural dive sites include submarine canyons with sheer drop-offs, lakes, rivers, and coral and rock reefs. Natural sites have the benefit of marine growth that might be thousands of years old. Specially trained divers also enjoy the thrill of exploring underwater caves and caverns or diving beneath the ice of frozen lakes.

While there are many types of fascinating places to explore under water, many of them require special training beyond the NAUI Scuba Diver certification course.

Any diving environment that does not allow direct vertical access to the surface is called an *overhead environment*. Overhead environments include caves, the interiors of wrecks, and waters beneath the ice or heavy kelp (figures 8-3, 8-4, and 8-5). These environments are highly specialized. They require additional special equipment and training no matter how much experience a diver might have diving under other conditions. Even instructors need special training for these types of environments.

ENTRIES AND EXITS

The easiest diving is usually from boats, and in many situations, boat diving offers some of the best diving available. Beach diving is a popular alternative for many divers and can be extremely enjoyable. Beach diving is generally more strenuous than boat diving, but both present varied and unique diving situations (figure 8-6).

Diving Environment

FIGURE 8-5. DIVING UNDER ICE PRESENTS UNIQUE CHALLENGES TO EVEN EXPERIENCED DIVERS.

FIGURE 8-6. BEACH DIVING CAN BE EXTREMELY ENJOYABLE, BUT TENDS TO TAKE MORE ENERGY.

FIGURE 8-7. ROCK ENTRIES CAN BE HAZARDOUS. YOU MUST PLAN THE ENTRY BEFORE ATTEMPTING IT.

One of the most challenging aspects of beach diving can be getting to the water's edge. Beach access can be difficult in areas with steep cliffs and rugged shores. To dive in some of the more remote areas along coastlines, you might need to walk or climb over rugged terrain, covering considerable distances either wearing or carrying your gear. This can be exhausting and hazardous. To dive under these conditions, you must know your capabilities and limitations and plan for them. When diving in these areas, also make sure that you have the energy to safely return to your starting point after the dive.

As you enter the water, shoreline conditions can create other problems. The shape of the bottom can affect currents and wave action. The bottom might slope gradually, drop off suddenly, or have scattered holes and rocks. The composition of the bottom will affect the way you enter the water (figure 8-7).

Whenever you dive in a new area, you need an orientation to the dive site. You need to know what to look for and what to avoid, as well as any diving techniques that might be unique to that area. This can be learned by diving in new areas with a NAUI Instructor, NAUI

Divemaster, or other experienced local divers (figure 8-8). Always seek information about new dive sites from experienced divers. As you gain experience and participate in advanced courses, you will be able to explore new areas confidently and without supervision.

Bottom Conditions

The bottom composition of a site also affects your diving. This is true whether you dive in a quarry, lake, river, or ocean.

Diving Environment

FIGURE 8-8. ALWAYS GET AN ORIENTATION TO A NEW AREA FROM AN EXPERIENCED DIVER WHO KNOWS THE AREA.

FIGURE 8-9. ROCKY AREAS HIDE MANY MARINE CREATURES.

Usually, you can expect the underwater terrain at the dive site to be an extension of the shoreline. If the shore is rocky and rugged, you will probably find similar underwater conditions. A wide, sandy beach usually indicates a vast expanse of sand offshore. There are exceptions, so it helps to check with other divers regarding an unfamiliar site. Some information about bottom conditions is also available on navigation charts used for boating.

In most cases, the greater vertical relief (wall) there is to a dive site and the more aquatic plants present, the greater the amount of marine life in the area (figure 8-9). Flat stretches of bottom tend to be lacking in readily visible life compared with kelp forests and coral reefs. Divers tend to seek areas with plenty of marine life to be seen, which makes diving more interesting.

You find many different bottom compositions under water. These include mud, silt, clay, sand, pebbles, rocks, and coral.

Mud and silt bottoms are easily stirred up. This can reduce visibility to zero because of suspended sediment. Sand bottoms have better visibility, but these tend to be underwater deserts visually, because most of the life is in and under the sand, or flees at your approach. Rocky

bottoms provide a good base for marine plants and provide many holes and crevices that aquatic animals use as homes.

Aquatic plants do not grow well in tropical waters, but coral thrives in these waters and provides excellent diving. Barnacles, rocks, and underwater formations might have sharp edges, so you must have good buoyancy control to prevent cuts and scratches when diving in areas with these features.

Varying bottom compositions require different diving techniques. You must learn one technique for a beach entry on a sandy bottom that provides good footing and another for a muddy bottom, which can pose an entirely different set of challenges. Mud can also be very slippery when you are entering or exiting the water. Once you have entered the water, you will find that you must move carefully to avoid stirring up a muddy or silty bottom.

Sandy bottoms do not cloud the water as easily as muddy or silty bottoms. Coral and rock reefs usually provide the best visibility as well as many interesting things to see. Once you begin diving in open water, you will better appreciate the ways bottom composition is one of the many elements that affect your dive.

Verify What You Have Learned

Review the following questions about the physical characteristics of a site:

1. Who is best qualified to give you an orientation to a new area?

   _____

2. Two types of overhead environments that require special training are _____ and _____.

3. Two types of man-made dive sites are _____ and _____.

4. Two types of natural dive sites are _____ and _____.

5. The bottom of a dive site can be composed of _____, _____, or _____.

6. The underwater environment is usually an extension of the _____.

WATER CONDITIONS

Water temperature and visibility are probably the two most important factors in determining the ease and comfort of your dive. Diving in warm, clear water is relatively simple, because you must wear only a minimal amount of insulation and it is always easy to see where you are. Diving in colder, darker water is more difficult because you must wear more insulation to be comfortable and it is not always possible to tell exactly where things are under water beyond the range of your vision.

VISIBILITY

A major factor affecting all dives is the underwater visibility, which can range from zero to well over 30 meters (100 feet). Diving in water where the visibility is severely restricted can be hazardous, and zero-visibility diving requires special equipment, training, and procedures.

FIGURE 8-10. A BUDDY LINE IS ONE WAY OF MAINTAINING CONTACT IN WATER WITH POOR VISIBILITY.

If you arrive at a site and find that you cannot see anything under water, you should postpone the dive until a day when the visibility is better. Zero-visibility diving is a necessary part of search-and-recovery diving training, but it is not fun or safe when you are just learning to dive.

The locale, seasons, weather, water movement, composition of the bottom, and other factors affect underwater visibility. For example, in California visibility is usually best during the calm fall months, and worst during the winter rains and storms. In the Sea of Cortez, in Mexico, there is good visibility in the summer months and poor visibility in the winter months. Tidal changes also affect visibility. See *Tides* on page 183 for information about tides.

Several problems relate to poor visibility. The most common is disorientation. With limited visibility, you can become disoriented and dizzy from a lack of visual references while you are submerged. You can avoid this by not diving in poor visibility until you have been trained in the proper techniques. Entanglement in fishing line and other debris can also be a serious problem in low-visibility conditions.

There are special techniques for diving in limited visibility. Divers can hold hands to stay together or use a buddy line (figure 8-10). A buddy line is a short length of rope up to 2 meters (6 feet) in length, with a loop at each end. Each diver in the buddy team holds one end of the line to maintain contact. Limited-visibility diving is a specialty area. Your instructor will cover any special techniques that relate to visibility where you will be diving.

In extremely clear water, estimating distances can be difficult (figure 8-11). The surface, your boat, and other things appear closer than they are. When this happens, it is easy to exceed your planned depth, because some objects will be deeper and further away than they appear, as well. Under these conditions, it is important to monitor your depth gauge even more frequently than normal.

Whether visibility is good or poor, you can see why you and your buddy must stay close together under water. In poor visibility, it is easy to become separated and lose track of one another. If you are unable to find your buddy within one minute under these conditions, you must surface, using the standard technique to search for a lost buddy. In good visibility, it is easy to get too far apart, which means you will be unable to help if your dive buddy needs assistance. Begin developing good diving habits from the very first time you go under water. If you want to be considered a good buddy, learn to stay within touching distance of your buddy without getting in their way.

TEMPERATURE

Water temperature can range from freezing to over 30°C (86°F). Diving in water colder than about 26°C (79°F) normally requires that you wear some type of diving suit, depending on the duration of your dive, your activity level during the dive, and your individual physiology. As a rule, the colder the water, the more insulation you will need to wear. Almost all diving requires some type of insulation because the water temperature will be colder than your body's skin temperature.

Even if you usually dive in reasonably warm water, you will need to prevent getting chilled because of the water's capacity to conduct and absorb heat, you will chill rapidly if you do not wear adequate protection. Water temperature is always a major factor to consider when planning a dive. In most cases, the deeper you dive, the colder the water temperature.

In freshwater lakes, a phenomenon known as a *thermocline* will appear in the summertime (figure 8-12). This is a thin zone of radical change in water temperature between the warm surface and cold bottom layers.

FIGURE 8-11. CORAL REEFS USUALLY HAVE EXCELLENT VISIBILITY THAT CAN BE GREATER THAN 30 METERS (100 FEET).

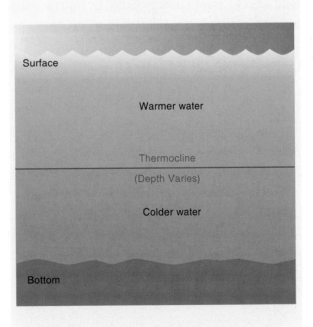

FIGURE 8-12. A THERMOCLINE IS A DISTINCT, THIN ZONE OF RADICAL CHANGE IN WATER TEMPERATURE BETWEEN SURFACE AND BOTTOM LAYERS OF A LAKE.

Diving Environment

The two layers of water can vary in temperature as much as 10°C (18°F). They remain distinctly separated and do not mix. If your diving suit is appropriate for only the surface water temperature, you might find that this drastic temperature change at depth would force an early end to your dive. Thermoclines are commonly found in many lakes, but they also occur in the ocean.

Freshwater lakes also experience changes in water temperature throughout the year. During the fall, as the surface water cools, the wind mixes it with the deeper water and eliminates the thermocline. During the winter, the surface temperature of a freshwater lake can drop to near freezing and a reverse thermocline develops, with the colder water as the top layer, and warmer water as the lower layer. During the spring, as the surface water warms, the wind mixes it with the deeper water and eliminates the reverse thermocline.

You must obtain information about the water temperature at the depths to which you plan to dive before entering the water. This information is usually available from local instructors, divemasters, or dive stores. You must select suitable thermal protection for both the water temperature and your individual physiological needs.

Verify What You Have Learned

Review the following questions about water conditions:

7. A thermocline is a

_____

_____.

8. _____, _____,

_____, and _____ can

affect visibility.

9. Diving in water with no visibility can cause

_____.

MOVING WATER AND ITS EFFECTS

Water is heavy. If you think about the weight of a sealed can of water and how it would feel to have one dropped on your foot, you can imagine the enormous potential energy contained in a large amount of moving water. It is useless to fight against strong water movement, such as a strong current, because you cannot effectively swim against it. It is possible to use the movement of the water to assist you in diving, and this is something you will learn during your NAUI Scuba Diver certification course.

You must understand what sets water into motion, how the water moves, and how to function effectively in moving water. This understanding will help you plan ahead to cope with the movement of water and use it to your advantage.

Waves and Surf

As wind blows across the water, it transfers its energy to the water. The water starts to push into peaks and valleys to become waves. In the open ocean, these waves are called swells. With increasing wind, or as the wind blows for a longer time, larger swells form. Unless the swells are quite large and the wind blows hard, waves usually do not break in the open ocean.

The energy of the waves — but not the water itself — can travel across thousands of miles of ocean. As waves enter shallow water and are affected by the bottom, they break and form surf. The larger the waves, the larger the surf.

The *surf zone* is the area where waves are breaking as the water gets shallower closer to shore (figure 8-13). In coastal areas where beach diving is popular, divers must go through the surf zone to enter the water. Chapter 3 provides an introduction to surf entries. Your instructor will cover these entries in detail if they are common in your diving area.

Surge is the underwater back-and-forth movement of water you will experience when diving in areas close to a shore with wave action. When you are in shallow water close to shore and there are large waves, you will feel the effects of surge. As the waves move over you toward the shore, the surge will tend to push your body first away from and then toward the shore.

FIGURE 8-13. SURF FORMS WHEN WAVES BREAK CLOSE TO SHORE.

In most areas with large waves, surf, and heavy surge, visibility will be poor. Different beach conditions require different entry-and-exit techniques, so always get an orientation to any new diving area from a NAUI Instructor or a NAUI Divemaster.

Tides

 Tides cause water movement in many areas. Tides are caused by the gravitational attraction between the Earth, the Moon, and the Sun. In different areas of the world, the water level change between low tide and high tide can range from less than 0.3 meters (1 foot) to 12 meters (40 feet). Usually, the difference between low and high tide is only a few feet of water.

The change in the water level at a dive site due to the tide can cause problems while you are on your dive if you do not plan for it. For example, when the tide is in, or high, the water extends further onto the beach, covering rocks that are just outside the waves. This makes it easy to enter the water, because you can swim over the rocks. When the tide is out, or low, the water recedes, uncovering any rocks. If this happens while you are in the water, you might be forced to climb back over the rocks to return to the beach. This can be much more difficult and dangerous than swimming over them. You avoid this by timing your dive properly.

Tides can also affect your diving if you are using a small boat that is docked or launched at a marina. As the tide goes out, floating dock and launch ramps can become quite steep. Launch ramps in particular can be extremely slippery, because the marine plants that grow on them are exposed at low tide.

 Water movement because of tides can also affect underwater visibility. The best diving visibility is usually during high tide. There are exceptions, and you will learn more about local tides from your instructor as part of your open water training.

Currents

A *current* is the movement of water in a particular direction. Currents are like rivers or streams within the ocean. Winds, tides, gravity, and the Earth's rotation cause currents in the oceans. Rivers have a generally constant current flow due to gravity.

You must consider currents when you plan a dive, because attempting to swim against a strong current can exhaust you very quickly. Usually, you begin a dive into the current, no matter how slight it is. If your entry and exit points are the same, you can use the current to help you return to your exit point at the end of your dive.

If you are diving from an anchored boat, a trail line 30 meters (100 feet) long with a buoy at the end should be extended behind the boat (figure 8-14). This way, if you accidentally end your dive downcurrent from the boat, you will usually be able to grab the line and pull yourself back to the boat. In the NAUI Advanced Scuba Diver course, you can learn how to *drift dive*. When you drift dive, you use the current to move you along, planning your exit downcurrent of your entry point.

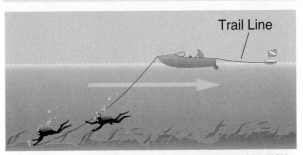

Trail Line

FIGURE 8-14. BE SURE TO USE A TRAIL LINE WHEN YOU DIVE FROM A BOAT IN AN AREA THAT MIGHT HAVE A CURRENT.

Currents can be separated into three categories:
- Standing
- Tidal
- Transitory

Standing currents are regular, steady currents that do not change very much, if at all. In many parts of the world, longshore currents normally flow in one direction along the coast. This is a good example of a standing current. The Gulf Stream in the Atlantic Ocean flows from the Caribbean north toward Nova Scotia and then around to Europe. This is an open-ocean standing current. Rivers and streams are also examples of standing currents. You must be aware of the speed and direction of any standing current present where you plan to dive and account for it in your dive plan.

Tidal currents are caused by tides. When these currents pass through restricted areas, they can be quite strong, even strong enough to sweep you away no matter how hard you swim. Most divers cannot swim any faster than 1.8 kilometers per hour (1 knot) for longer than a few minutes. Many tidal currents are 3.7 kilometers per hour (2 knots) to 9 kilometers per hour (5 knots) or faster. In areas with strong tidal currents, you must consult tide and current tables, which are readily available, to help plan your dives for *slack-water* periods only (a time when there is no tidal current).

Transitory currents are currents that suddenly appear and disappear. A good example of a transitory current is a rip current caused by surf (figure 8-15).

FIGURE 8-15. YOU CAN EASILY IDENTIFY RIP CURRENTS ONCE YOU KNOW WHAT THEY LOOK LIKE.

Rip currents occur near the shore and form when wave or wind action pushes water up onto the shore and the water then funnels back out to sea through a narrow passage. This passage or restriction can be a narrow opening in a reef, sandbar, or other large formation otherwise channeling the return of water to the ocean. The offshore flow of a rip current is narrow and can be quite strong.

If you find yourself being carried away from shore or you are unable to make progress when trying to return to the beach, you might be in a rip current. You can escape these currents by swimming across the rip current, usually parallel to the shore. Once you are out of the current, you can then turn towards shore and swim in. The rip current might empty into a longshore current. If you try to swim out of the rip current and into the longshore current, the longshore current will push you back into the rip current. If this happens, swim out of the rip current in the other direction.

With experience, you will be able to easily identify rip currents. If they occur in your area, your instructor will familiarize you with them and the areas in which they appear.

You can also use currents to carry you to your planned exit point, which adds to the ease and enjoyment of your dive. When you take the NAUI Advanced Scuba Diver course, you will learn how to use currents to make ocean diving easier and more exciting. As a new diver, you must learn more about local currents and how to recognize them before you attempt to make unsupervised dives. The best way to accomplish this is by training with a NAUI instructor who has experience in your local area.

Even with experience, advanced divers should ask local divers about local current and diving conditions when they plan on diving at a new site. If you travel to a new area where conditions differ from those where you trained, get a local orientation. For example, if all of your diving has been in freshwater lakes, you will need an orientation to dive in the ocean, and vice versa. Or, if you learned in Florida but want to dive in the kelp forests of California, you also need an orientation.

Verify What You Have Learned

Review the following questions about the movement of water:

10. Three causes of water movement are

_____, _____,
and _____.

11. To escape from a rip current, you must swim _____ the current.

12. You always begin a dive from an anchored boat _____ the current.

13. Tides are caused by the _____ of the _____ and

_____.

MARINE LIFE

The many different types of life in the underwater world make diving interesting. There are thousands of animals and plants to interest and amaze you. There is beauty and color that surpasses anything you can imagine. It is natural to be concerned about dangerous animals and plants, given the overblown portrayal of dangerous marine life you have seen in movies and television. As you will learn, these dramatic portrayals are usually gross exaggerations of the dangers posed by these creatures. Most divers look forward to encounters with underwater life.

There are potentially dangerous animals and plants under water, just as there are potentially dangerous plants and animals on land. You probably know how to avoid attracting or agitating bears or snakes when you go camping, and how to handle aggressive dogs in your own neighborhood. By reading, or through training and experience, you have learned how to recognize and avoid dangerous animals so you can go hiking, camping, or walking around your neighborhood without fear.

Going under water is similar to going hiking or camping. Some aquatic animals can be just as harmful as a snake or bear, but as you learn more about them, you will be able to encounter them, with confidence. The most dangerous creature you are likely to meet under water is another diver.

Aggressive animal behavior is rare under water. Any injury you might receive from an aquatic animal almost certainly would result from a defensive action on the part of the creature. Remember that nearly all animals will attack if they feel cornered or threatened, or their territory is invaded.

You might injure yourself by accidentally encountering an animal or disturbing it. Avoid potential problems with hazardous marine life by learning to identify such creatures that exist in your area. Each region has its own hazardous animals. Identification and avoidance are your keys to safety. A good rule is to touch nothing – you might kill or injure creatures that are harmless to you, as well as provoke others.

During your NAUI Scuba Diver certification course, your instructor will teach you about animals in your area. You must obtain similar information about the marine life in each area that you visit. Learning what marine life lives in a given area is one of the reasons for getting a formal orientation for diving in a new region.

Some creatures can bite, some can stick you, some sting, some can scrape you, and some can even deliver an electric shock.

Animals That Bite

Most divers are concerned about encountering larger, more aggressive animals that can bite, such as sharks (figure 8-16) and killer whales. Seeing these animals while diving is rare.

FIGURE 8-16. OBSERVING SHARKS IN THE WILD CAN BE A RARE AND A THRILLING EXPERIENCE.

Diving Environment

FIGURE 8-17. BARRACUDAS LOOK MEAN, BUT ARE ONLY CURIOUS. HOWEVER, THEY STILL NEED TO BE TREATED WITH RESPECT.

FIGURE 8-18. EELS LOOK MENACING BUT WILL USUALLY ONLY BITE IF YOU REACH NEAR OR INTO THEIR HOLES.

Your chance of seeing a large shark that could injure you is much lower than having a traffic accident on your way to the dive site. Because shark attacks occur so infrequently, the media portrays them much more dramatically than traffic accidents. Many divers pay substantial amounts of money to go on diving trips specifically to see sharks, because sighting one on an ordinary dive is so rare.

Barracuda are large, curious fish with a menacing appearance (figure 8-17). These fish occasionally attack divers if they feel cornered. They can cause a painful bite, but there has never been a recorded case of a barracuda injury killing a diver. Barracudas will follow divers for long periods. Bright, shiny objects, such as jewelry, attract them. In most cases, barracuda will turn away if you swim directly towards them.

Eels are long, snakelike fish that live in rocks and crevices (figure 8-18). They have a menacing appearance and long sharp teeth. They breathe by opening and closing their mouths to flow water over their gills and might look as if they are readying to bite you. Unless you stick your hand near or in a hole containing an eel, they will not normally attack you.

Freshwater also contains hazards, such as alligators in the southeastern United States, crocodiles in Africa and Central America, muskrats, snakes, and even snapping turtles. It is rare for a diver to have a negative encounter with these animals. In most cases, they avoid divers.

Animals With Barbs

In salt water, the most common form of hazardous marine life is probably the sea urchin (figure 8-19). These are small creatures covered with sharp spines. They are found in almost every ocean. Sea urchins are extremely slow-moving creatures and they do not attack divers. Divers are injured when they bump into or step on these creatures and impale themselves on the spines. You can usually avoid this type of injury through good buoyancy control.

Stingrays are one example of marine life with an external body spine that can cause injury (figure 8-20). Most fish with defensive spines such as these introduce a toxin into the wound they make when they respond to a threat. Like most of the other fish with spines, stingrays are docile creatures that spend much of their time lying on the bottom. They will attack only when they are provoked, usually because a diver has stepped on them. The best way to avoid this type of injury is to look carefully at the bottom before putting your hands or feet down and shuffle your feet when walking in the shallows, rather than stepping up and out.

Cone shells are an example of a mollusk that has a spine and a venom sac. Cone shells eat other mollusks, worms, and small fish. They inject their prey with a toxin to stun them and then consume them. If a diver picks up a cone shell and is injured by the spine, they will also have the toxin introduced into the wound. This

FIGURE 8-19. SEA URCHINS WILL HURT YOU ONLY IF YOU BUMP INTO THEM.

FIGURE 8-20. STINGRAYS ARE NORMALLY DOCILE CREATURES.

can be life-threatening, but you can avoid this type of injury simply by not picking up such shells.

Animals That Sting and Scrape

Jellyfish are slimy, gelatin-like creatures that swim by *pulsing*, or contracting their bodies. They feed on small fish and other tiny creatures that float in the water. There are many different species of jellyfish, and they are found in most oceans.

Jellyfish are slow moving and do not attack divers. These creatures do cause injuries through a diver's accidental contact with their stinging cells, which are located on their tentacles. The tentacles can hang as much as 15 meters (50 feet) or more below the jellyfish. Most diving suits will protect you from the sting of a jellyfish. In addition, it is frequently possible to see these creatures from a distance and avoid them. Do not swim beneath them if you see them floating on the surface.

Marine creatures that can scrape you include corals and barnacles. These are slow growing animals that injure you only if you bump into them. Proper buoyancy control is your best avoidance technique.

Animals That Shock

There are a few species of electric fish, including an electric eel and electric ray, which immobilize their prey by emitting an electric shock. Electric eels are found in the Amazon basin in South America. You can find different species of electric rays throughout the world. Information about these creatures would be included in an orientation to a new area.

Verify What You Have Learned

Review the following questions about marine life:
14. True or False: Injuries from aquatic life are usually the result of an offensive action by the animal.
15. You should not _____ _____ even if you know what it is.
16. Sea urchins are an example of a _____.
17. Jellyfish are an example of a _____.

CONSERVATION

As a diver, you can have a profound effect on the underwater world. If you are a careful and conscientious diver, you can help ensure that the reefs where you dive today will be there for your children tomorrow. A careless or uncaring diver can destroy hundreds of years of coral growth in a single dive (figure 8-21).

FIGURE 8-21. A CARELESS DIVER CAN DESTROY HUNDREDS OF YEARS OF CORAL GROWTH IN A SINGLE DIVE.

FIGURE 8-22. AVOID TOUCHING CORAL OR OTHER MARINE CREATURES.

Most divers would not deliberately do anything to hurt the creatures in the underwater world. If you do not know or understand the delicate natures of certain fish or animals, it is easy to hurt them.

DIVER IMPACTS

As a diver, you have a choice to make either a negative or a positive impact on the underwater world. When you dive, you will see divers who constantly make an effort to leave only bubbles where they have been, and take only pictures. They enjoy the underwater world and leave no evidence that they have been there. Occasionally, you will see other divers who leave their mark on the underwater world, either consciously or not.

Negative Impacts

When you first dive on a coral reef, it can be difficult to imagine that the hard coral structures are actually thousands of delicate animals called *polyps*. If you are careless about your buoyancy control, you can break off pieces of coral or rub off its protective coating. It is easy to kill or injure coral through carelessness (figure 8-22).

Silt or sand landing on top of corals can also be extremely destructive (figure 8-23). The tiny polyps that live within the hard coral structure eat tiny microscopic plants and animals living in the water. If your buoyancy control is poor and you stir up large clouds of sand or silt, any sand or silt that lands on the corals can smother the polyps.

You can also damage animals that live in colder waters through accidental contact. For example, a rare form of red or purple hydrocoral grows at only a few dive sites in California. It is extremely beautiful, but also delicate and slow growing. It is easy to break and you must not handle it.

You can easily catch certain types of fish and other creatures that are slow moving, and this tempts some divers to handle and examine them, or to hold them while another diver photographs them. You must avoid this for several reasons. Most fish have a protective layer of slime that covers their body. When this slime is removed by human handling, it makes the fish vulnerable to harmful parasites. Also, handling a fish can damage its internal organs and kill it.

Positive Impacts

To have a positive effect on the environment, you must develop good personal diving skills and habits. Strive to perfect your buoyancy control so you always remain a few feet above the reef or bottom. Learn to dive

FIGURE 8-23. KEEP YOUR FINS OFF THE BOTTOM TO PREVENT SAND AND SILT FROM LANDING ON CORAL REEFS.

FIGURE 8-24. KEEP YOUR GAUGES AND OCTOPUS REGULATOR CLIPPED TO YOUR BUOYANCY COMPENSATOR.

in a slight head-down position to ensure that you keep your fins off the bottom. Make sure that your gauges and octopus regulator are clipped to your buoyancy compensator to keep them from dragging on the bottom (figure 8-24). If you have the opportunity to be photographed or videotaped while diving, analyze the video or photographs to see how you can improve your skills or reposition your gear to keep it closer to your body.

Develop an active conservation ethic and awareness of your environment. There are many active conservation groups around the world, working to ensure that your underwater world will not be destroyed. They do everything from counting fish to establishing moorings for dive boats so the boats will not have to use anchors, which destroy the bottom. Your instructor will have information on local conservation groups in your area.

Many dive shops, dive clubs, and other groups sponsor cleanup activities for water areas enjoyed by divers, boaters, and swimmers. Divers can have a tremendous positive effect when they participate in these cleanups because they can actually see the trash and remove it. Check with your local dive shop or dive club for cleanups in your area.

Many colleges, universities, dive clubs, dive shops, and other groups offer seminars you can attend to learn more about the underwater environment and its preservation. The more you can learn about conservation, the more prepared you will be to participate in helping preserve and improve our underwater world.

HUNTING

If you speak with any diver with more than 20 years of experience, they will probably tell you about the *good old days*, when game was plentiful and reefs were brimming with life. Sadly, the impact of divers, commercial as well as sport fishermen, and pollution, means many areas are not as healthy as they were in the past.

Divers must take responsibility for protecting the world's underwater resources for generations to come. If you hunt or take game under water, you must be familiar with the fishing regulations in your area. You must know which species you can legally take, the closed and open seasons, catch and size limits, legal methods of take, and any other pertinent information. Divers who violate fishing regulations give all divers a bad name, and they encourage governments to write further regulations that affect all diving.

Even if the fishing regulations in your area are generous, allowing substantial *bag limits* for a particular species on any given day, you must resist taking more game than you need for your personal consumption. Some bag limits exceed what a normal individual can use, but you certainly do not need to take everything you can get.

Most marine species are overused, and fishing regulations in most areas have not kept pace with the increasing demands placed on them by all groups. Some areas have serious competition between sport and

FIGURE 8-25. SHIPWRECKS WOULD BE EASILY DESTROYED IF EVERY DIVER TOOK A PIECE HOME.

FIGURE 8-26. CUT OPEN SIX-PACK RINGS TO AVOID THE POSSIBILITY OF A MARINE MAMMAL OR BIRD BECOMING TRAPPED IN THE RINGS.

commercial fisherman for the same species. However, the ultimate losers are the animals being caught.

COLLECTING

Many thousands of creatures with beautiful shells live under the sea, in tropical and in colder waters. Divers can observe these creatures in their natural habitats, so shell collecting is an activity enjoyed by many divers.

Some type of marine animal forms every shell seen under water. If you collect shells with living animals, you are removing that animal from the population and destroying its chances to reproduce. Conscientious divers only collect empty shells. Check that nothing is living inside the shell. It is usually possible to find a good specimen of the shell you want without resorting to collecting a live animal.

EXPLORING WRECKS

Most divers enjoy the thrill of exploring a sunken ship, whether a fishing boat that sank a few years ago, a warship sunk during World War II, or a mail steamship wrecked during the 1800s. Little can compete with the excitement of finding a new, unexplored wreck.

Many divers like to collect artifacts from shipwrecks to decorate their homes. Unfortunately, when you do this, you generally destroy part of the wreck to remove the item from it (figure 8-25). This takes away from the historical value and atmosphere of the wreck. If enough people remove artifacts, the wreck will be reduced to a pile of rubble on the sea floor.

Remember that wrecks can be the property of the original owners, or of the group salvaging it. In many areas, removing artifacts from shipwrecks is illegal and violators can lose all of their dive gear and face severe fines. Divers have received stiff fines for removing artifacts in marine parks or state-controlled waters.

CLEANING UP THE ENVIRONMENT

Many types of trash can be harmful to marine creatures, so you must not dump trash overboard when diving from a boat or carelessly discard it at the beach. Synthetic materials such as plastics can last for years in the marine environment and harm numerous animals.

If you buy soft drinks in six-packs with plastic rings holding the package together, you should cut these rings open before you discard them — even into trash receptacles (figure 8-26). This helps avoid the possibility of a marine mammal or bird becoming entangled in them if the plastic is lost. Recycle these rings whenever possible.

Plastic trash bags are especially harmful to sea turtles. These animals regularly feed on jellyfish as part of their diet, and a plastic bag floating in the ocean resembles a jellyfish closely enough that a sea turtle will eat it. Obviously, turtles cannot digest these bags. The bags block their digestive systems and kill the turtles.

You should dispose of trash properly and recycle it when possible. Looking at trash under water is not a fun part of diving.

Verify What You Have Learned

Review the following questions about conservation:

18. _____ or _____ can damage coral.

19. You should only collect shells that are

_____.

20. _____ mistake plastic trash bags as jellyfish.

FIGURE 8-27. BOAT DIVING REQUIRES SPECIAL PROCEDURES.

BOAT DIVING

Many of the best diving sites in the world are in remote locations and can be reached only by boat. To enjoy this experience, you must learn the proper procedures for diving from boats. Boat diving requires unique skills whether you dive from a small or large vessel.

It is important to become familiar with the procedures for diving from a charter boat. Go with an experienced diver or group to learn the correct techniques. You must know how to enter, exit, get your cylinder filled, keep your gear together, and all of the other procedures used for boat diving in your area (figure 8-27).

Commercial charter boats depart at a set time, so plan to arrive at least 30 minutes before its departure time. Sign in when you board the boat and stow your gear as directed by the crew. Tour the vessel and ask questions to familiarize yourself with its layout.

Diving from a small boat requires that you learn yet another set of procedures. Because of space limitations created by the size of the boat, you must learn how to manage your gear in as small an area as possible. For

example, you might need to assemble your scuba unit and don your diving suit on shore, board the boat, and ride out to the site.

Procedures for entering and exiting the water vary depending on the size and configuration of the vessel. On a small boat, care might be required to keep the boat balanced as you enter or exit it. In this situation, it is often helpful to don and remove your scuba equipment in the water rather than aboard the small boat. Some means to get back in the boat must also be available.

Additional safety procedures are also necessary for small boat diving. A written plan of your destination and your expected time of return must be left with someone on shore so they can summon help if you do not return within a reasonable time. This plan is called a *float plan*.

Good seamanship is important, and more than one person aboard any boat must be trained to operate it competently. Be sure to take a sanctioned course in small boat handling if you plan regular dives from small boats.

When you reach your dive site, you must set the anchor. After the anchor is set, it must be checked at the beginning of the dive to make sure it is secure. At the end, the anchor must be clear for lifting. For complete security, someone who can operate the boat should remain on board at all times.

Whether you dive from a large or small boat, you must remain near the vessel and upcurrent from it during your dive. A trail line with a float extended behind the boat is essential when even the possibility of a current exists.

Diving properly from boats requires training and diving with an experienced boat diver. This is particularly true for specialized activities from boats, such as drift diving. Learning about diving from someone more experienced helps to greatly reduce the risk of embarrassment, frustration, and unpleasant incidents.

POPULAR DIVING AREAS

After you complete your NAUI Scuba Diver certification course, you will be able to dive on your own under conditions similar to those in which you did your open water dives. If you are like most divers, you will want to travel to other areas and experience new and different dive sites. Following are descriptions of some different locales to give you an idea of the variety of diving you can find throughout the world.

California

California is one of the most popular diving areas in the world. With its mild year-round surface temperatures and good water conditions, diving is a favorite sport with many people in this part of the United States.

Most diving in California is concentrated among the giant kelp beds found offshore along the coast and nearby islands (figure 8-28). These kelp beds are home to numerous animals and fish, including sea lions and seals, many species of rockfish, lobsters, scallops, and thousands of other creatures. Diving in a kelp bed is like swimming through a forest, with light filtering down from the surface through the long kelp stalks.

Visibility in California can range from 3 meters (10 feet) along the beaches to over 30 meters (100 feet) at the islands. The average visibility is from 10 to 15 meters (30 to 50 feet). The water temperature ranges from a low of 10°C (50°F) in the winter to a high of 21°C (70°F) in the late summer and early fall. The average water temperature is 17°C (62° F).

FIGURE 8-28. KELP BEDS PROVIDE A BEAUTIFUL DIVING ENVIRONMENT.

Cozumel

Cozumel is located in the western Caribbean Sea close to the Yucatan peninsula in Mexico. The island is bordered by the world's second largest living coral reef system that extends south past Belize to the Bay Islands of Honduras. Drift diving, or swimming along with the current, is the way to enjoy the scenery of the Cozumel reef. Divers allow the current to move them along as their boat follows them by watching for their bubbles. The reefs are covered with colorful corals and sponges and are inhabited by a variety of tropical fish, as well as crabs, lobsters, eels, and grouper.

The air temperature ranges from 21°C (70°F) in the winter to 32°C (90°F) in the summer. The water temperature ranges from 25°C (78°F) in the winter to 31°C (88°F) in the summer. The visibility is in excess of 30 meters (100 feet).

Gulf Coast of Louisiana and Texas

The Louisiana and Texas coasts on the Gulf of Mexico offer diving at offshore oil platforms. These platforms are located far from shore, so diving is normally done from a boat.

The platforms are artificial reefs, attracting many different kinds of fish and other animals that live on the structure. You can see giant groupers weighing over 45 kilograms (100 pounds) at many of these sites.

Visibility at the platforms is good most of the year and ranges from 10 meters (30 feet) to 45 meters (150 feet). The water temperature in the summer varies from approximately 21°C (70°F) to 27°C (80°F).

Great Lakes

The Great Lakes of the central United States offer some of the finest freshwater diving in the world. There are numerous shipwrecks located in these waters, many of which are relatively intact because there is no salt to cause corrosion and no marine creatures that attack wood. Some of the wrecks in the Great Lakes are hundreds of years old, yet still in excellent condition.

Visibility in the Great Lakes can be very good, and can exceed 15 meters (50 feet) at some of the better dive spots. Most of the wrecks are covered with fine layers of silt that are easily stirred up, limiting visibility. These waters are quite cold, even during the summer months, and most divers wear dry suits. The lakes' great size allows ocean-like waves and storms to develop.

Turks and Caicos

The Turks & Caicos Islands are located in the British West Indies of the Caribbean Sea. The islands have coral walls, ledges, and drop-offs with plenty of underwater life(figure 8-29). Divers encounter reef fish, sea turtles, barracuda, eagle rays, and several species of sharks. Wrecked Spanish galleons and other ships are available to be explored.

The visibility ranges from 30 meters (100 feet) to 60 meters (200 feet) and the average water temperature is 27°C (80°F).

Truk, Federated States of Micronesia

Coral reefs surround Truk Lagoon, which is the permanent resting place of over 60 ships and 250 planes sunk during World War II. Truk is located in the South Pacific, with Palau to the west and the Fiji islands to the southeast. Some of the creatures found in Truk include angelfish, tangs, lionfish, triggerfish, and clownfish as well as rays, moray eels, tuna, and turtles.

FIGURE 8-29. TROPICAL LOCATIONS AFFORD OPPORTUNITIES TO DIVE CORAL WALLS, LEDGES, CHANNELS AND OVERHANGS TEEMING WITH EXOTIC MARINE LIFE

The average water temperature in Truk is 28°C to 29°C (82°F to 84°F) and the visibility can be up to 30 meters (100 feet).

Galapagos Islands

The Galapagos Islands are located 600 miles west of Ecuador in the Pacific Ocean. The islands are an Ecuadorian National Park and marine preserve. The islands are best known as the inspiration for Charles Darwin's theory of evolution. The islands are on the Equator, but the Humboldt Current, which originates in Antarctica, brings cool, nutrient-rich water north. The mixture of warm currents from Central America with the Humboldt Current has allowed the islands to produce an amazing array of sea life as well as birds and wildlife on the islands. The Galapagos islands are the home of sea lions, penguins, eagle rays, and schooling hammerhead sharks. Strong currents are a hazard in this area.

**Notes**

CHAPTER

9

Diving
Activities

LEARNING GOALS

In this chapter you will:

- Be introduced to some special interests you can develop in diving and how you can meet other divers with those interests.
- Learn about some of the courses you can take to continue your diving education.

By now, you have received (or nearly received) the knowledge, skills, and experience that will allow you to enjoy scuba diving on your own. Soon you will earn the NAUI certification card that will be your passport to the underwater world. It has taken study and physical effort to develop the needed ability. You can be proud of all you have accomplished. Now it is time to look ahead.

GETTING INVOLVED IN CLUBS

Get involved with other divers right away. Local dive clubs are an excellent source for diving companions, information about the local area, and introductions to many diving activities. Be sure to ask about joining a dive club in your area (figure 9-1).

FIGURE 9-1. DIVE CLUBS OFFER NEW DIVING COMPANIONS AND INFORMATION ABOUT DIVING ACTIVITIES.

FURTHERING YOUR EDUCATION

The best way to remain involved in diving after this course is to continue your diving education. By completing the NAUI Scuba Diver certification course, you will be prepared to dive in conditions similar to those in which you were trained. There are many other aspects of diving you will need to learn or further develop. You must consider your initial certification as a *license to learn* how to dive. Experience and additional training are needed for you to dive under other conditions.

The field of diving is always changing. Equipment is constantly being improved and new types developed. Discoveries even change our understanding of the effects of pressure on divers. Therefore, continuing education is important. You should subscribe to diving magazines, attend diving seminars and conferences, take refresher courses every year or two, and obtain the highest level of certification possible. All will help to keep your knowledge current.

SPECIALTY COURSES

To further your diving education, you can learn diving specialties by taking a NAUI-sanctioned Specialty Course. A few of the many specialty courses available are Night Diver, Rescue Diver, Cavern Diver, Nitrox Diver or Underwater Photographer (figure 9-2). While experience is a good teacher, it frequently gives you the test before the lesson. This results in frustration and wasted time. It can also be unsafe. To get the most from a diving specialty, and to get it quickly in today's fast-paced world, complete a NAUI Specialty Course. This way, you will quickly achieve success and be able to take advantage of your NAUI instructor's years of experience in your area of interest.

THE ADVANCED SCUBA DIVER COURSE

The Advanced Scuba Diver course introduces you to a variety of diving activities. It is designed for newly certified divers who desire additional training and an

FIGURE 9-2. NAUI SPECIALTY DIVING COURSES ARE A GOOD WAY TO LEARN NEW ACTIVITIES THAT WILL EXPAND YOUR DIVING EXPERIENCES.

FIGURE 9-3. THE NAUI MASTER SCUBA DIVER COURSE WILL TEACH YOU MANY ADVANCED SKILLS.

orientation to a variety of diving sites and conditions. The types of dives include navigation, deep, and night or limited visibility diving as well as instructor-specified dives. The instructor-specified dives can include light salvage, underwater mapping, shore diving, or boat diving as well as many other activities.

THE MASTER SCUBA DIVER COURSE

After you have completed the NAUI Advanced Scuba Diver course and several specialty courses, you should take the NAUI Master Scuba Diver course. You need not be an expert diver to take this course, but you should have the desire to learn skills that are more advanced (figure 9-3). This course provides you with eight additional supervised dives where you learn new, useful skills. It also adds to your knowledge and introduces you to various specialty areas. Underwater navigation, limited-visibility or night diving, search and recovery, light salvage techniques, and deep-diving procedures are included in the course.

Every diver should complete a NAUI Master Scuba

Diver course. At this level, you will have the knowledge, skills, and ability to enjoy diving in a variety of conditions and locations.

TRAINING ASSISTANT SPECIALTY COURSE

You can also gain certification as a NAUI Training Assistant. A NAUI Training Assistant helps other divers during training activities supervised by a NAUI instructor. Helping other divers can include acting as an escort on an underwater tour or assisting a tired diver. To enter the NAUI Training Assistant course, you must be certified as a NAUI Advanced Scuba Diver and as a NAUI Scuba Rescue Diver.

LEADERSHIP COURSES

Perhaps you will want to get involved in a leadership role in diving. Once you have completed the Master

FIGURE 9-4. NAUI LEADERS TEACH DIVING IN LOCATIONS ALL OVER THE WORLD.

Scuba Diver and Scuba Rescue Diver courses, you can strive for the NAUI Assistant Instructor or Divemaster ratings. For this, you will need experience verified by a required number of logged dives. Ask your instructor about leadership training opportunities.

It is rewarding to help others realize the dream of becoming a diver or having an underwater adventure. NAUI has the finest leadership programs and training available. If you find that diving becomes more than a hobby to you, remember that through NAUI there are many opportunities to work as a professional. By becoming a NAUI Assistant Instructor, Divemaster, or Instructor, you can profit from your diving ability, training, and experience (figure 9-4). Your instructor is an example of this, and will be glad to provide you with information about NAUI Worldwide leadership training programs.

DEVELOPING SPECIAL INTERESTS

Donning scuba equipment and exploring the world beneath the surface of the water is exciting. You will quickly find that diving is simply a means that allows you to do something in the underwater world rather than being an end in itself. Soon, you will want to inspect old wrecks, take pictures, take game, collect things, study aquatic ecosystems, or dive in unusual places (figure 9-5). Such challenges make diving exciting and rewarding. Remember that specialty areas can

FIGURE 9-5. IT IS MORE FUN TO DEVELOP A SPECIAL INTEREST AREA IN DIVING. ONE EXAMPLE IS MARINE IDENTIFICATION.

be learned much more quickly and easily through training than by trial and error.

One reason you should get involved with local divers is to learn about the special diving interests in your area and to be introduced to them. When you have an underwater objective, your enthusiasm for diving multiplies many times over, and you will have some of the best times of your life developing and refining your interest area.

Little compares with the feeling of accomplishing a goal in the underwater world, whether it be taking a perfect photograph of a rare fish, finding an ancient wreck, or exploring a site where no diver has been before. Imagine the excitement and satisfaction you can experience. Realize that relatively few people learn how to

Diving Activities

dive and will ever feel the exhilaration you experience because of your success in inner space. Learn about the special activities of diving and get involved.

☑ BEING A RESPONSIBLE DIVER

When you are certified as a NAUI diver, you will continue to learn through your diving experiences. During these experiences, you should remember that you have certain responsibilities to yourself, your buddy, and others. The following is a partial list of what is expected of you as a NAUI diver:

- Keep yourself mentally and physically fit for diving.
- Continue your diving education.
- Use complete, correct, and well-maintained equipment.
- Know your dive site, and avoid or abort diving in hazardous conditions.
- Be prepared to handle emergencies.
- Always dive with a buddy, and remain together while diving.
- Avoid running low on air, control your buoyancy at all times, and ascend properly.
- Keep conservation in mind regarding the environment.
- Demonstrate proper etiquette toward boaters, fishermen, and the public.

It is now time to look ahead to fun, adventure, and all the excitement you envisioned when you started this course. That strange, wonderful world of inner space is finally accessible and waiting for you to enter. Enjoy yourself, and fulfill your responsibilities as a NAUI diver. Your instructor looks forward to working with you again soon in your next NAUI course.

APPENDIX A
ANSWERS TO REVIEW QUESTIONS

CHAPTER 1
Health and Fitness

1. You must be sound in mind and body to dive.
2. They are not feeling well.
3. False.
4. Dive regularly.
5. Medication only masks the symptoms of your illness, it does not cure the illness. The illness will affect your physiology underwater and could be hazardous.

CHAPTER 2
Basic Equipment

1. Comfort and fit.
2. A, purge valve.
3. Length of the tube, inside diameter of the tube, sharp bends.

Cylinders

4. A "J" valve has a reserve lever and a "K" valve does not.
5. Aluminum, steel.
6. Visual inspection each year, hydrostatic test every 5 years.

Regulators, Alternate Air Sources, and Instrumentation

7. Ease of breathing.
8. Dust cap.
9. Convenience, low price, integrated system.
10. Completely independent air supply.

11. Capillary.
12. Submersible pressure gauge.

Instrumentation

13. Computer.
14. Able to withstand pressure, elapsed time.
15. Rinsing after each diving day, having them serviced once per year.

Buoyancy Compensators

16. Jacket style, back flotation, and horse collars.
17. Overinflation valve, oral inflator.
18. To remove salt crystals and to prevent damage to the inside of the BC.

Weight Belts

19. Quick release.
20. Compensates for the compression of a wetsuit at depth.
21. They are more comfortable, less likely to cause damage if dropped.

Diving Suits

22. Skin suit.
23. Wetsuit.
24. Dry suit.
25. False.

Accessory Equipment

26. To cut line underwater.
27. Dive near the flag, only display the flag when divers are in the water.
28. You might be required to provide proof of experience, documentation of experience for leadership training.
29. Slate, goodie bag, underwater light, marker buoy, spare parts kit, checklists.

CHAPTER 3

Using Mask, Snorkel, and Fins

1. Backward.
2. Use your buddy or wall for support, sit down.
3. Blast, displacement.
4. Displacement.

Assembling Scuba Gear

5. So the inlet to the first stage of the regulator lines up with the outlet from the cylinder valve.
6. Counterclockwise.
7. Undo any clips on the front of the BC and the waistband; lift your unit as a buddy team; make sure you have your regulator, octopus, and gauges out of the way when you fasten your waistband and clips; let your buddy know when you have the waistband fastened and can support the weight of the cylinder yourself.
8. After you don your scuba unit.

Entries and Exits

9. Buoyancy compensator, air supply, regulator, octopus, weight belt.
10. BC should be partially inflated to provide buoyancy, hold your mask firmly in place to avoid flooding it or having it come off, breathe from your regulator during the entry, make sure that the entry area below you is clear and sufficiently deep for the type of entry you are using.
11. Get yourself into the water with minimal effort and effect on you and your equipment.
12. A. Distance to the water is several feet.
    B. Low, unstable platform or small boat.
    C. Able to sit at the edge of the water.

Mask Skills

13. Orient your mask so that the inside of the mask is facing you and your snorkel is on the left side, place the mask strap on the back of your head and position the mask over your eyes and nose,

pull the mask away from your forehead and make sure that all of your hair or your hood is out of the mask, inhale a breath of air, put the heel of your hand to the top of the mask frame and push in, start exhaling through your nose as you tip your head back.
14. Toward the bottom.

Regulator Skills

15. Blow tiny bubbles.
16. Blast, purge.
17. Hold the mouthpiece loosely in your mouth.

Buoyancy

18. Exchange your snorkel for your regulator, note the exact time that your head leaves the surface, deflate your BC, equalize your ears before you start your descent, exhale and begin your feet-first descent.
19. Maintain eye contact with your buddy, equalize your air spaces often, control buoyancy, control rate of descent.
20. Signal buddy, agree to ascend, look up, reach up, swim up, control buoyancy, ascend no faster than 9 meters (30 feet) per minute.
21. Amount of weight you wear, amount of air in your BC, amount of air in your lungs, objects you are carrying, type of diving suit you are wearing, amount of air in your cylinder.
22. Vent the air.

Safety Skills

23. Two.
24. You and your buddy should agree on which regulator will be used before the dive.
25. Practice before the dive and again at the very beginning of the dive while on the surface.
26. When no source of air is available and you are deeper than 40 feet.

Buddy System

27. Discuss the dive before you get in the water and agree on the location, purpose, activity, and general course you will follow underwater; maintain your same position relative to each other for your entire dive; establish your direction of travel underwater and then follow that heading until you or your buddy suggest a change with a clear signal.

28. Get yourself vertical in the water and do a slow 360° turn looking for your buddy or their bubbles, rise about three meters (10 feet) in the water and do another 360° turn looking for your buddy or their bubbles, ascend slowly to the surface after a minute if you do not see your buddy, surface, note your position relative to two points on the shore, and wait for your buddy, when your buddy surfaces, get back together and continue your dive, signal for help if your buddy does not surface.

Communication

29. Hand signals, slate, rapping, or touch.
30. Visual signals or audible signals.
31. Answer it with a distinct hand signal.
32. Signals must be discussed and agreed upon before the dive.

Handling Scuba Equipment in the Water

33. You want to be positively buoyant at the surface and negatively buoyant at the bottom.
34. Keeping the hose inside your arms.
35. Hold the belt by the free end, keep your body between the belt and the bottom.

Navigation

36. Ripple marks, sun and shadows, surge, landmarks.
37. Align the compass with your body, keep the compass level, sight across the compass.
38. A heading 180° from your original heading (the opposite direction from which you started).

CHAPTER 4

Density and Its Effects

1. 20.9%, nitrogen.
2. False.
3. False.
4. Streamlining.
5. Larger, closer.
6. False.

Buoyancy

7. Weight of your body, the weight of your gear (diving suit, weight belt, and scuba unit), body size, the thickness of your diving suit, and the volume of your gear.
8. Change amount of weight worn, change amount of air in BC, change amount of air in lungs.
9. Decrease.
10. Decrease.

Pressure

11. 10.3 meters (34 feet), 10 meters (33 feet).
12. 5 times.
13. 3 atm.

Air Quantity in Balloon

Pressure	Volume	Density
Doubles	Halves	Doubles
Triples	One third	Triples
Halves	Doubles	Halves
Quadruples	One fourth	Quadruples

Air Consumption

14. Depth, physical activity, physical size, mental state, warmth of diving suit.
15. Submersible pressure gauge.

Squeezes and Blocks

16. Ears, sinuses, lungs, intestines, teeth.
17. Difficult or impossible to equalize pressure in your sinuses.
18. Exhale through your nose into your mask.
19. Squeeze.
20. Vertigo, ruptured ear drum, hearing loss.
21. Swollen or congested sinuses.
22. Mask squeeze.
23. Block or reverse block.

Lungs and Breathing

24. Holding your breath, not breathing properly.
25. Normal.
26. Carbon dioxide.
27. Slowly, deeply.
28. Keep the mouthpiece in your mouth.

Indirect Effects of Pressure

29. Have cylinders filled with compressed air only.
30. Have cylinders filled at a reputable air station.
31. Dive within your depth and time limits, ascend slowly.
32. Dive at shallow depths.
33. Ascend a few feet to relieve the symptoms.

Thermal Effects of Diving

34. Conducting heat away from your body, compressed air to your body temperature.
35. The air cools.
36. Surface tension.
37. Prevent dehydration.
38. True.

CHAPTER 5

Ingassing and Outgassing

1. Ingasses, equilibrium.
2. Relieve pressure by ascending too fast.

3. Six meters (20 feet).
4. In excess of normal nitrogen that remains in your body after a dive.

Dive Table Rules

5. 9 meters (30 feet).
6. 10 minutes, 1 hour.
7. 18 meters (60 feet)/30 minutes
   15 meters (50 feet)/20 minutes
   9 meters (30 feet)/40 minutes.
8. 12 meters (40 feet)/40 minutes.

Table 1

9. H.
10. I.
11. D.

Table 2

12. E.
13. B.
14. F.

Table 3

15. 31 minutes.
16. 18 minutes.
17. False.
18. 30 minutes.
19. 73 minutes.
20. 37 minutes.
21. 42 minutes.

Dive Planning Worksheet

22. See Figure A-1.
23. See Figure A-2.

Dive Computers

24. Ascend.
25. 30 meters (100 feet).
26. Initialization sequence.

27. Scrolling.
28. Decompression sickness.
29. Flashing, beeping.

Sample Problems

1. See Figure A-3.
2. See Figure A-4.
3. See Figure A-5.
4. See Figure A-6.
5. See Figure A-7.

CHAPTER 6

Long-Range Planning

1. a. Plan the objective.
   b. Select your location.
   c. Determine the date and time.
   d. Make travel arrangements.
   e. Determine equipment needs.
   f. Determine if you need a refresher.
2. Months.
3. Two weeks.

Short-Range Planning

4. Air fills for your scuba cylinders, extra batteries for your dive light or camera, sunscreen, seasickness medication, fishing license, light sticks for night diving, defog for your mask, spare parts.
5. They can summon help if you do not return at the scheduled time.
6. Weather trends, water conditions, tides, long range weather forecast.

Preparing to Dive

7. Mask, fins, booties, diving suit, knife.
8. Regulator, buoyancy compensator.
9. Twelve hours.

Conducting Your Dive

10. Site survey, emergency plan, activity.
11. Whether it is safe to dive at the site.
12. When to change course, when to begin the return leg, and when to surface.
13. Five minutes.
14. Working.
15. Depth, time, remaining air supply.

Diving Your Plan

16. Confusion.
17. Challenge, rewarding.

Contingency Planning

18. Alternate site, alternate activity.
19. Alternate exit point.

Recording Your Dive

20. Dive number, date, air temperature, water temperature, visibility, starting air supply, ending air supply, average depth, deepest depth.
21. Keep track of your total hours of bottom time.
22. Diving suit and the amount of weight you were wearing, whether you liked the site, what you saw.

CHAPTER 7

Diving Situations

1. Rewarm yourself by ending your dive and getting out of the water, getting into warm, dry clothing as soon as possible, drinking warm drinks, taking a warm (not hot) bath, if not excessively chilled.
2. Get out of your exposure suit and get wet to start cooling down, drink cool water to rehydrate your body, stay out of the sun and rest.
3. Stretch and massage cramped muscle, proceed slowly with different kick after recovery.
4. Determine where you are caught and try to get

clear by reversing direction or sinking, remove scuba unit, cutting yourself free as a last resort.

5. Hold onto a solid object or hug yourself until the dizziness passes.

6. Disconnect inflator hose, and vent BC or suit.

7. Stay out of the cabin or any enclosed space on the boat, get into fresh air, settle yourself in a stable spot on the boat, look at the horizon.

8. Keep mouthpiece in place and swallow several times in rapid succession.

9. Stop all activity, rest, and breathe deeply.

Assisting Other Divers

10. Help to keep problems from occurring, help your buddy overcome any problems that do occur.

11. Surface.

12. Establishing buoyancy, resting and breathing, providing assistance.

Rescues

13. Unconscious and possibly not breathing.

14. First aid, cardiopulmonary resuscitation (CPR), diving rescue, life saving.

15. Establish buoyancy for yourself.

16. Get them to the surface.

17. Keeping the victim's airway dry, maintaining the breathing cycle.

18. Get them to shore quickly where CPR can be administered and medical assistance obtained.

Emergencies and First Aid

19. Training, equipment, contact information, determination to take action.

20. Update training periodically, practice frequently.

21. First aid kit, oxygen kit, blanket, supply of clean freshwater.

22. Divers Alert Network (DAN).

CHAPTER 8

Physical Characteristics of a Site

1. NAUI leader (NAUI Instructor or NAUI Divemaster), experienced diver.

2. Cave diving, cavern diving, penetration wreck diving, ice diving.

3. Artificial reef, oil rig, breakwater, jetty, shipwreck.

4. Submarine canyons with sheer drop-offs, lakes, rivers, caves, coral and rock reefs.

5. Mud, silt, clay, sand, pebbles, rocks, coral.

6. Shoreline.

Water Conditions

7. Thin zone of radical change in temperature between two distinct layers of water.

8. Locale, seasons, weather, water movement, bottom composition.

9. Disorientation and dizziness.

Water Movement

10. Wind, tides, currents.

11. Across the current.

12. Into or against.

13. Gravitational pull, sun, moon.

Marine Life

14. False.

15. Touch something.

16. Sticker.

17. Stinger.

Conservation

18. Touching, breaking.

19. Contain no animals.

20. Sea turtles.

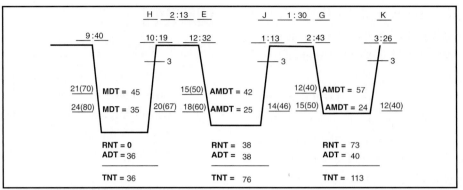

FIGURE A-1 PLANNING WORKSHEET PROBLEM 1

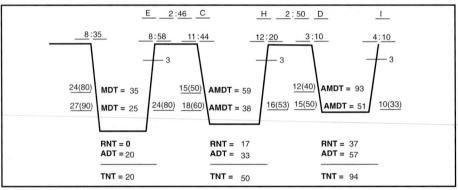

FIGURE A-2 PLANNING WORKSHEET PROBLEM 2

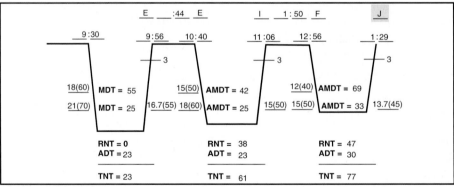

FIGURE A-3 SAMPLE PROBLEM 1

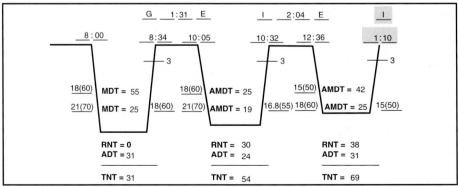

FIGURE A-4 SAMPLE PROBLEM 2

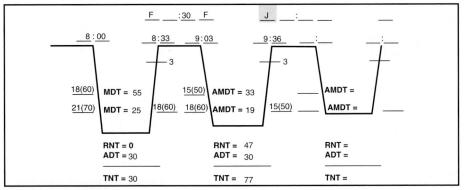

FIGURE A-5 SAMPLE PROBLEM 3

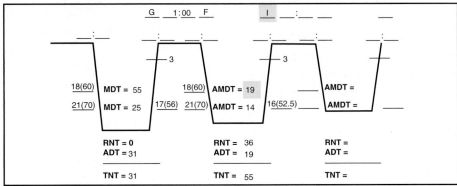

FIGURE A-6 SAMPLE PROBLEM 4

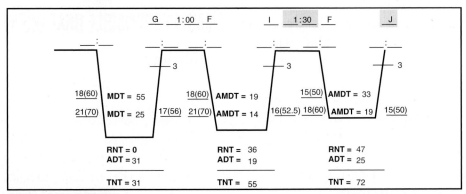

FIGURE A-7 SAMPLE PROBLEM 5

APPENDIX B
BEING A RESPONSIBLE DIVER

As a responsible diver, you must follow certain guidelines for *etiquette* (good manners), boat diving, and diving in general.

DIVER ETIQUETTE

As a NAUI diver, you should observe the following guidelines for proper etiquette:

- Manage your equipment and vehicles as compactly as possible so that you do not block sidewalks, driveways, or public accesses. Maintain a tidy equipment area to avoid clutter at the dive site.
- Take care with spearguns. Loaded spearguns are forbidden on land and on boats, and any spearing should not be done in crowded beach areas.
- Ask before using or crossing private property, whether to gain access to a dive site or for recreation after a dive.
- Do not change clothes in public. Be discreet, and use vehicles, changing robes, or tents. Think of others who are passing the site or using the beaches.
- Create a good impression of divers. Talk pleasantly to interested non-divers who are curious about your sport. Be careful of your language and behavior, particularly regarding the use of alcohol or other drugs around dive activities.
- Do not violate the rights of others to enjoy the environment, run businesses, or have a pleasant town to live in.
- Obey all laws, whether they are fish and game regulations or designated parking and access areas. Cooperate with local police.
- Do not litter beaches or otherwise destroy property. Beach environments are often fragile ecological systems that require your careful use if they are to survive.
- Patronize local merchants. Divers can have a positive economic impact on an area, from restaurants to dive stores to motels. Good economic rapport with a community means continuing good communication and access for divers.
- Begin your dives early in the day for optimum diving conditions, less crowded beaches, more parking, and more freedom of choice regarding dive sites. Do not exceed your diving capabilities in selecting your site. Ask local residents or divers about possible sites, and rely on their knowledge of water and bottom conditions.
- Make sure that your fishing license is current, and obey local fishing regulations. Take only as much game as you can use. Collect as little as possible, clean fish only in designated areas, and dispose of any waste properly.
- Be helpful to other users of our aquatic environment. It makes you, as a diver, better than the faceless crowd, and it gains respect for your sport. Also, it removes many hassles of diving and makes you a happier, calmer, and safer diver.

NAUI RESPONSIBLE BOAT DIVING PRACTICES

The NAUI Responsible Boat Diving Practices include the following:

- Select a licensed boat that is fully equipped with all required safety gear, including oxygen and other diver support and safety equipment.
- Ask to receive boat diving techniques training as part of your Advanced or Master Scuba Diver course.
- Rely on the captain's knowledge of the most suitable dive sites. Plan your dive using the specific site information provided by the crew or divemaster.
- Sign up only for trip destinations consistent with your ability and dive plan.
- Arrive at the boat at least one-half hour before departure. Stow your well-marked gear in its assigned location, and respect the boat facilities, such as no wetsuits in the bunk cabin or not dropping weights or cylinders on the deck.

- Between dives, keep your gear in your bag to avoid loss or breakage, and always assist your buddy with their cylinder. Do not sit on the deck to don your scuba unit, or you might get hit in the head by another diver's cylinder.
- Use your equipment properly to dive easily and safely. Do not overweight yourself. Only use your buoyancy compensator to fine-tune your buoyancy during the dive or to compensate for a heavy game bag at the end.
- Do not take a loaded speargun on a boat or boarding ramp. Bring a container for your game. Help keep the deck clean and clear.
- Use the boat exit points that are identified by the crew. Move away from the boat exit once you are in the water, and either snorkel clearly on the surface or begin your descent down the anchor line. Do not use scuba to skim just beneath the surface. Doing so, you cannot be seen by passing boats or other divers.
- Put your fins on last, while you are waiting near the exit. Do not walk around the deck wearing fins.
- Use a compass and submersible pressure gauge. Plan your dive so that you end with a reserve of air and are able to return to the boat while still under water, if need be.
- Be aware of changes in current conditions during the dive. Use natural clues such as seaweed. Look for trail lines extended behind the boat on the surface, and do not hesitate to pull yourself hand-over-hand back to the boat using this line, if need be.
- Use common sense, training, and experience. Ask questions if you are unsure. Allow a margin of reserve, and do not push your endurance limits. Watch for other divers who are waving their arms on the surface. This signals a diver who is in distress. Divers who maintain personal control and are comfortable in the water have safe, enjoyable experiences under water.

NAUI'S RESPONSIBLE DIVER PRACTICES

As a responsible NAUI diver I understand that I should:
- Be trained and certified for scuba diving.
- Maintain good physical and mental conditioning for diving and only dive when feeling well. Never use alcohol or other inappropriate intoxicants before diving.
- Always breathe continually and avoid "skip-breathing" or breath-holding while submerged on scuba.
- Use complete, well maintained diving equipment and check it before each dive. Never loan my equipment to non-certified divers.
- Always evaluate environmental conditions before each dive and allow a margin of safety to be prepared for emergencies.
- Understand my personal limitations as well as the limitations of my training and strive to stay within them.
- Set moderate limits for depth and time under water. Save sufficient breathing gas to use as a contingency at the end of the dive and to complete a precautionary decompression stop.
- Use the buddy system when diving and be prepared to assist my buddy and others if needed. Periodically review and practice rescue and assist skills previously learned in my NAUI course.
- Use surface support, such as a boat or dive float and diver down flag whenever required or feasible.
- Comply with local rules and ordinances.
- Be respectful of others rights and strive to represent the diving community in a positive role.
- Accept responsibility for my safety when diving and preparing to dive.
- Seek professional training and assistance to learn new diving techniques, use unfamiliar equipment or when planning to dive in unfamiliar locations.
- Plan each dive and utilize dive tables or a dive computer to track my decompression status.
- Delay flying or ascending to altitude after diving consistent with current recommendations.
- Respect game and collecting regulations and the fragility of the aquatic environment. Practice good buoyancy control and avoid unnecessarily making contact with corals or other aquatic plants and animals. Help others to understand the need to protect and preserve aquatic resources.

APPENDIX C
CHECKLISTS

Checklists are an excellent way to make sure you do not forget anything when planning a dive or dive trip and packing for a dive. Use the checklists in this appendix as a base for creating your own personal checklists for dive planning, equipment, and first aid.

DIVE PLANNING CHECKLIST

Use the following dive planning checklists as guidelines for long-term planning, short-term planning, and on-site planning.

Long-Term Planning

- ❑ Determine the objective of the dive
- ❑ Select your dive buddy
- ❑ Select your location
- ❑ Select an alternate location or activity
- ❑ Research the dive sites
- ❑ Obtain emergency contact information
- ❑ Identify nearest chamber
- ❑ Determine the date and time of your trip
- ❑ Make your travel arrangements
- ❑ Determine your equipment needs
- ❑ Check your equipment
- ❑ Have your equipment serviced, if necessary
- ❑ Determine whether you need to take a NAUI Refresher Experience
- ❑ Locate your certification card

Short-Term Planning

- ❑ Inventory your gear
- ❑ Replace dried or cracked fin straps and mask straps and lost or frayed O-rings
- ❑ Buy items needed for your trip
  - ❑ Air fills
  - ❑ Batteries
  - ❑ Sunscreen
  - ❑ Seasickness medication
  - ❑ Fishing license
  - ❑ Light sticks
  - ❑ Defog
- ❑ Check the weather forecast, water conditions, tides, and long-range forecast
- ❑ Prepare a copy of your plans to leave with someone at home

Preparing to Dive

- ❑ Gather all your equipment and personal articles in one place
- ❑ Pack your dive gear in reverse order of its use
- ❑ Pack your personal gear in a separate bag
- ❑ Get a good night's rest
- ❑ Leave a copy of your dive plan with someone before you depart

On-Site Planning

- ❑ Site Survey
  - ❑ Evaluate the conditions at the site
  - ❑ Determine the leader of the dive
- ❑ Emergency
  - ❑ Determine your out-of-air plan
  - ❑ Determine your lost buddy plan
  - ❑ Determine how to summon help in case of an accident
  - ❑ Find the nearest phone
- ❑ Activity
  - ❑ Agree on your activity and objective
  - ❑ Review your hand signals
  - ❑ Decide on your entry and exit points and your dive pattern
  - ❑ Set your limits for depth, time, and remaining air supply
- ❑ Buoyancy
  - ❑ Check your buddy's weight system for its quick release
  - ❑ Check your buddy's BC to be sure you know how to power inflate, orally inflate, and deflate the BC
  - ❑ Locate the releases on your buddy's BC

❏ Air
    ❏ Check your buddy's cylinder valve to be sure it is fully open and back 1/4 turn
    ❏ Check that the cylinder is secure in the tank strap
    ❏ Check that your buddy's cylinder is full
    ❏ Check your buddy's primary and backup regulators for proper operation

❏ Gear and Go
    ❏ Check that your buddy does not have any entangled gear and that their alternate air source and console are secured
    ❏ Check that your buddy has mask, fins, and snorkel ready to don
    ❏ Check that you have any necessary accessory equipment
    ❏ Proceed to your entry point
    ❏ Enjoy your dive

DIVING EQUIPMENT CHECKLIST

Use the following list as a guideline for the gear you need to pack for a dive trip.

Primary Dive Gear

❏ Mask
❏ Snorkel with keeper
❏ Fins
❏ Booties
❏ Diving suit
❏ Hood
❏ Gloves
❏ Weight belt
❏ Buoyancy compensator
❏ Cylinder
❏ Regulator set-up
    ❏ Primary regulator
    ❏ Octopus regulator or alternate air source
    ❏ Depth gauge, submersible pressure gauge, compass
❏ Timing device
❏ Dive computer
❏ Dive knife
❏ Gear bag
❏ Dive tables

Additional Dive Gear

❏ Float, flag, and float anchor
❏ Dive light
❏ Slate and pencil
❏ Thermometer
❏ Marker buoy
❏ Game bag

Spare Equipment

❏ Cylinders
❏ Weights
❏ Mask strap
❏ Fin straps

- ❏ O-rings
- ❏ Snorkel keeper
- ❏ Tools

Emergency Items

- ❏ First-aid kit
- ❏ Telephone numbers for local emergency services, nearest chamber, and DAN
- ❏ Oxygen kit

Personal Items

- ❏ Certification card
- ❏ NAUI logbook
- ❏ Fishing license
- ❏ Swimsuit
- ❏ Towel
- ❏ Hat or visor
- ❏ Sunscreen lotion
- ❏ Sunglasses
- ❏ Lunch or snacks
- ❏ Drinks
- ❏ Jacket
- ❏ Extra clothing
- ❏ Tickets
- ❏ Money and credit cards
- ❏ Seasickness medication
- ❏ Toiletries

FIRST AID KIT CHECKLIST

You should have a first aid kit with you whenever you dive. The following items are basic. You can supplement them according to your personal needs, level of first aid training, and distance from medical assistance.

General

- ❏ Sterile compress pads
- ❏ Assorted sterile gauze pads
- ❏ Assorted adhesive bandages
- ❏ Triangular bandage
- ❏ Roll of 5 centimeter (2 inch) gauze bandage
- ❏ Adhesive tape, 2.5 centimeter (1 inch)
- ❏ Cotton swabs
- ❏ Aspirin or other analgesic
- ❏ Assorted safety pins/needles
- ❏ Scissors
- ❏ Tweezers or splinter remover
- ❏ Antiseptic soap
- ❏ Antiseptic cream or spray
- ❏ Medicated stick
- ❏ Isopropyl alcohol (70% solution)
- ❏ White vinegar
- ❏ Sunscreen lotion
- ❏ Change for telelphone
- ❏ Emergency telephone numbers

Optional

- ❏ Hydrogen peroxide
- ❏ Gauze scrub pads
- ❏ Baking soda
- ❏ First-aid book
- ❏ Sports drinks
- ❏ Waterproof matches
- ❏ Drinking water and paper cups
- ❏ Blanket
- ❏ Seasick pills

Notes

Glossary

A

Absolute Pressure: The total surrounding pressure and the result when atmospheric pressure is added to gauge or water pressure.

Actual Dive Time: The total time spent under water from the beginning of descent until breaking the surface at the end of the dive. The precautionary decompression stop need not be included.

Adjusted Maximum Dive Time: The Maximum Dive Time for a specific depth minus the Residual Nitrogen Time for a specific letter group and depth.

Alternate Air Source: An additional second stage regulator that provides air to a diver's buddy in an emergency. A true alternate air source is a completely independent unit consisting of a cylinder and regulator. See also Octopus Regulator.

ADT: Actual Dive Time.

Air Embolism: The blockage of blood flow in the body by bubbles in the blood.

Ambient Pressure: The total surrounding pressure. See absolute pressure.

AMDT: Adjusted Maximum Dive Time.

Alveoli: The air sacs in the lungs where gas exchange occurs.

Atmospheric Pressure: The pressure exerted by the atmosphere.

B

Back Flotation System: A buoyancy control device whose entire bladder is behind the diver and does not wrap around the diver in any way.

Backpack: A piece of equipment designed to hold a scuba cylinder on a diver's back, usually integral with the buoyancy compensator.

Backup Scuba: A redundant second stage or total scuba unit for use in out of air situations.

BC: Buoyancy Compensator.

Bends: Another name for one type of decompression sickness.

Bezel: A movable ring on a compass or watch inscribed with index marks. On a watch, the ring can be rotated only counterclockwise and is used to measure elapsed time.

Buoyancy: An upward force on an object placed in water that is equal to the weight of the water displaced. Loosely, buoyancy is applied to the net state of an object, such as "positive buoyancy" for an object that floats.

Buoyancy Compensator: A piece of equipment that can provide increased volume by adding air to a bladder, thus providing lift.

Buoyancy Jacket: A buoyancy control device shaped and worn like a vest.

Boyle's Law: Statement of a physical principle – The inverse relationship between pressure and volume of a gas.

Buddy System: The practice of never diving alone. You always have someone to assist you, if necessary, and with whom to share experiences.

C

C-Card: Certification card.

Carbon Monoxide Toxicity: A risk or condition that results from breathing air contaminated with carbon monoxide.

Cardio-pulmonary Resuscitation: The first-aid procedure that sustains ventilation and pulse until a person's heart and breathing resume on their own or until other medical procedures can be initiated.

Ceiling: The minimum depth (usually displayed by a computer) to which a diver can ascend without enhanced risk of decompression sickness.

Certification Card: A card awarded by NAUI as evidence of completing specific diver training.

Clearing: The movement of air from the lungs to other air spaces, such as the ear and the sinuses to equalize pressure.

Compass: A piece of equipment that aids in underwater navigation by indicating the direction of magnetic north from your position.

Condensation: The water that forms on a surface because of the cooling of air containing water vapor.

Console: A device designed to hold assorted gauges and instruments around or in line with the submersible pressure gauge.

Coral: A marine animal without a backbone that usually lives together with other animals of the same species and forms a colony. Many corals produce a hard external skeleton.

CPR: Cardiopulmonary resuscitation.

Current: The flow or movement of water in a specific direction. Wind, gravity, temperature, the Earth's rotation, and other factors cause currents.

Cylinder Valve: A mechanism used to control the flow of air in and out of a scuba cylinder. The cylinder valve includes the attachment point for a scuba regulator.

D

Decompression Stop: The specified depth and time a diver stops and waits during ascent to allow for nitrogen elimination before surfacing.

Decompression Sickness: The adverse physiological symptoms or condition caused by the formation of bubbles of nitrogen within the body of a diver. When these bubbles act on various parts of

the body, such as the nerves, they have a negative impact and cause a variety of signs and symptoms that signal the diver is suffering from decompression sickness.

Defog Solution: A substance rubbed or sprayed on the lens of the mask to keep it free of condensation. Saliva is often used as a defog solution.

Dehydration: A lack of adequate body fluids.

Density: The mass per unit of volume.

Depth Gauge: An instrument or device that indicates depth.

Dive Computer: An electronic device that senses pressure, measures time, continuously calculates the amount of nitrogen in several theoretical body compartments, and displays the information to help divers avoid decompression sickness.

Dive Schedule: An abbreviated statement of the depth and duration of a dive expressed as depth/time. For example, 21 meters (70 feet) for 40 minutes or 21/40 (70/40).

Dive Time Calculator: A rotary calculator containing the NAUI Dive Tables in a format that eliminates the mathematical calculations associated with the dive tables.

Drag: The resistance encountered when moving through the water because of the water's density.

Drift Diving: A dive made using a current as the primary means of propulsion.

Dry Suit: A protective suit that excludes water and prevents it from coming into contact with covered portions of the body.

E

Ear Drum: The membrane that separates the middle and outer ears.

Entry Scuba Experience Program: A NAUI program to introduce non-divers to scuba diving. This program does not award certification.

Equalization: The method of preventing and correcting squeezes. Also see Clearing.

ESE Program: Entry Scuba Experience program.

Eustachian Tube: The tube that connects the middle ear with the throat, through which divers can equalize their ears.

F

Fins: A piece of equipment that attaches a blade to the foot to increase the surface area of the foot to increase propulsion thrust.

Foam Neoprene: A rubber-based material saturated with tiny gas bubbles to provide insulation. This material is used to manufacture diving suits.

G

Gauge Pressure: The pressure indicated by a gauge calibrated to ignore atmospheric pressure.

Goggles: A piece of equipment that only covers the eyes to prevent water from irritating them. Goggles are not an acceptable substitute for a mask.

H

Heat Exhaustion: A condition resulting from overheating that is characterized by a pale, clammy appearance and a feeling of weakness.

Heat Stroke: A condition resulting from overheating that is characterized by hot, dry, and flushed skin. This is a life-threatening emergency.

Hose Protector: A piece of heavy plastic or rubber that fits over the end of a hose to relieve the stress caused by the weight of the equipment.

Hydrostatic Test: A test required to ensure the safety of scuba cylinders. This test is done using water as the medium to provide pressure to check the expansion and recovery of the scuba cylinder walls.

Hyperventilation: Breathing much more deeply and rapidly than required. This lowers the carbon dioxide level in the blood, which decreases the stimulus to breathe.

I

Index Marks: The points on a compass bezel that provide a place to lay the needle to stay on a desired course.

Integrated Weight System: A system in which weight is combined with the backpack and buoyancy compensator.

L

Letter Group Designation: A letter used to identify set amounts of residual nitrogen in a diver's body after a dive.

Longshore Current: A current that runs parallel to a coastline.

Low-Pressure Inflator: A device that allows air from the scuba cylinder to be added to the buoyancy compensator.

Lubber Line: The reference line on a compass. The stationary line that shows the direction of travel.

Lungs: The organs of the body that allow oxygen to transfer from inhaled air to the blood. One of the body's air spaces.

M

Mask: A piece of equipment that holds a pocket of air around the eyes to improve underwater vision. The nose is always included in any mask to allow pressure inside it to be equalized.

Maximum Dive Time: The length of time that can be spent at a given depth without being required to stop during ascent to reduce the likelihood of decompression sickness.

MDT: Maximum Dive Time.

Mediastinal Emphysema: The condition that exists when air from a lung overexpansion injury escapes into the chest area near the heart.

Middle Ear: The space in the ear containing the auditory bones. It opens into the throat through the Eustachian tube.

Multilevel Dive: A dive involving periods of time at different depths.

N

NAUI: National Association of Underwater Instructors. Also called NAUI Worldwide.

Negative Buoyancy: The state that exists when an object sinks. Actually a contradiction in terms. Buoyancy is positive by definition.

Neutral Buoyancy: The state that exists when an object neither floats nor sinks.

Nitrogen: The gas that forms 78% of the atmosphere. It is metabolically inert but is the gas that causes decompression sickness and nitrogen narcosis.

Nitrogen Narcosis: The name given to the disorienting effect nitrogen has on the brain at increased pressure.

O

Octopus Regulator: An extra second stage attached to the regulator for use in out of air situations.

One Atmosphere: The force of the atmosphere at sea level on the earth taken as a constant, equal to 14.7 pounds per square inch, or approximately 1 bar.

Overexpansion Injury: An injury caused by the expansion of air rupturing enclosed body spaces.

Overpressure Valve: An device built into buoyancy compensators, which allows the escape of excess air without damage to the buoyancy compensator.

Oxygen: The gas that is necessary to sustain life. Oxygen makes up approximately 20.9% of the air.

P

Pneumothorax: The condition that exists when air from an overexpansion injury escapes into a pleural cavity.

Positive Buoyancy: The state that exists when an object floats or rises in water. Actually a redundancy, as buoyancy is always a positive (upward) force.

Precautionary Decompression Stop: A period of three to five minutes spent at a depth of 5 meters (15 feet) as a safety precaution even though the Maximum Dive Time has not been exceeded.

Pressure: The application of force. In diving used for the force of the weight of the air and water above a diver measured in bar or pounds per square inch.

Pressure Gauge: A piece of equipment that allows one to measure the pressure of air in a scuba cylinder.

Pressure Relief Disk: A thin piece of metal placed in cylinder valves, that ruptures to prevent pressure from reaching dangerous levels. Also called a burst disk. It is a one-time use device that must be replaced if it bursts.

PSI: Pounds per square inch.

Q

Quick Release Buckle: A buckle designed to be operated with one hand so it can be opened quickly in an emergency.

R

Rapture of the Deep: An older, quaint term for nitrogen narcosis.

Reference Line: The lubber line on a compass. The stationary line that shows the direction of travel.

Regulator: The piece of equipment that reduces high-pressure air in the scuba cylinder to ambient pressure on demand.

Relative Humidity: The amount of water held in the air compared to what the air can hold at that temperature.

Repetitive Dive: Any dive made before complete outgassing from a previous dive. On the NAUI Dive Tables, this is 24 hours.

Required Decompression Stop: An amount of time specified by dive tables, a calculator, or a computer that must be spent at a specific depth whenever the Maximum Dive Time is exceeded.

Residual Nitrogen: The dissolved nitrogen remaining in the body because of a previous dive or dives.

Reverse Block: The opposite of a squeeze. The situation that exists when the internal pressure of an air space is greater than the external pressure and blocks its own escape route by deforming body tissues.

Rip Current: A current that results when water pushed up on the beach by waves rushes back to the sea through a narrow channel.

RNT: Residual Nitrogen Time.

S

SAC Rate: Surface Air Consumption Rate.

Safety Stop: See Precautionary Decompression Stop.

Scrolling: A sequential display on a dive computer between dives to provide the Maximum Dive Times for various depths, on the next dive, or other lists of data.

Scuba: Self-contained underwater breathing apparatus.

Scuba Diver Course: The first course in NAUI's complete diver education program. This course leads to certification.

Scuba Cylinder: The piece of equipment containing the high pressure air to be breathed while underwater.

Service Pressure: The working pressure of the scuba cylinder. It is stamped on the shoulder of the cylinder.

Sinus: An air cavity in the skull lined with mucus membranes. Sinuses can cause problems with equalizing if they are blocked because of swelling, as with colds or allergies.

SIT: Surface Interval Time.

Skip Breathing: The hazardous practice of taking a breath and holding it as long as possible before exhaling while scuba diving. This practice is done to supposedly extend bottom time.

Snorkel: A tubular piece of equipment that allows a person to breathe while keeping their face in the water.

SPG: Submersible Pressure Gauge.

Squeeze: The condition that results when the pressure outside an enclosed air space is greater than the internal pressure.

Standing Current: A water flow that is constant and steady.

Submersible Pressure Gauge: A piece of equipment that provides a display of tank pressure during a dive.

Surface Air Consumption Rate: The amount of air consumed at the surface in a set period.

Surface Interval Time: The time spent on the surface between dives.

Skin Diving: A type of diving that is done by holding your breath. Also known as free diving or breath-hold diving.

T

Test Date: A date stamped on a scuba cylinder indicating the date of the last hydrostatic test.

Thermocline: The dividing line between water of different temperatures.

Tide: The change in water level of the ocean caused by the gravitational attraction between the Earth, Moon, and Sun.

Tidal Current: A water flow that accompanies changes in the tide, usually a result of water flowing into or away from an area such as an inlet or bay.

Timing Device: A device used to record the length of a dive. For example, a watch or bottom timer.

Total Nitrogen Time: The sum of Residual Nitrogen Time and Actual Dive Time following a repetitive dive.

Trail Line: A floating rope used while boat diving. It is extended from the stern of the boat with an attached float to aid divers returning to the boat.

Transitory Current: A current that lasts only for a short time and, unlike a tidal current, does not occur with any predictability.

V

Valsalva Maneuver: The term popularly used to describe the attempted exhalation against a closed nose and mouth to open the Eustachian tubes and equalizes the ears.

Vertigo: A loss of the sense of balance. Severe dizziness.

Visual Inspection: A periodic inspection of a scuba cylinder that checks for corrosion and to ensure the integrity of the cylinder. It is also known as a Visual Cylinder Inspection (VCI) or Visual Inspection Program (VIP).

W

Wetsuit: A diving suit that allows a small amount of water to enter the covered area. This water is trapped inside the suit and warmed by the body, thus providing a certain amount of protection from the cold, in addition to the insulation afforded by the suit itself.

Index

C

T